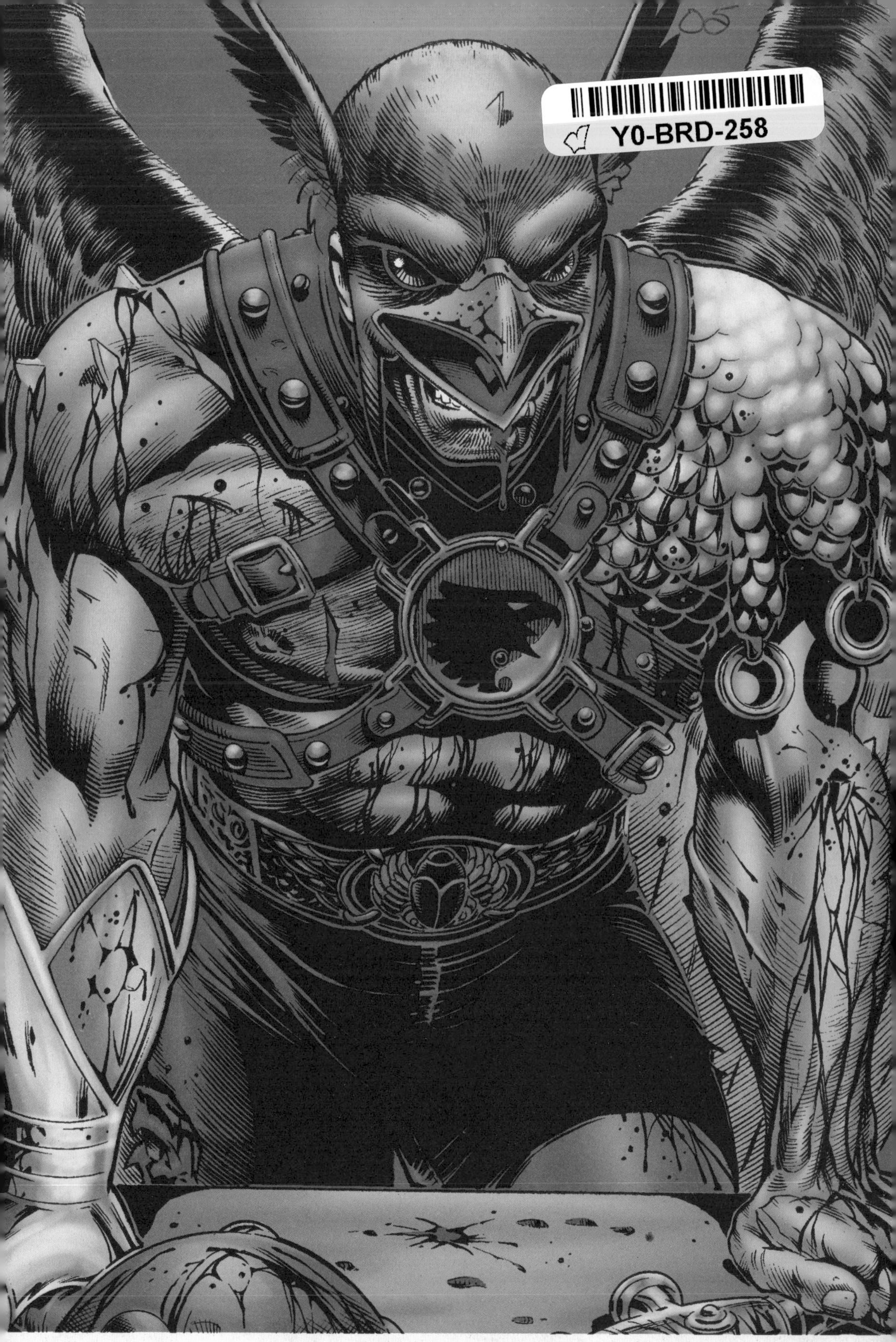



# JSA BLACK REIGN

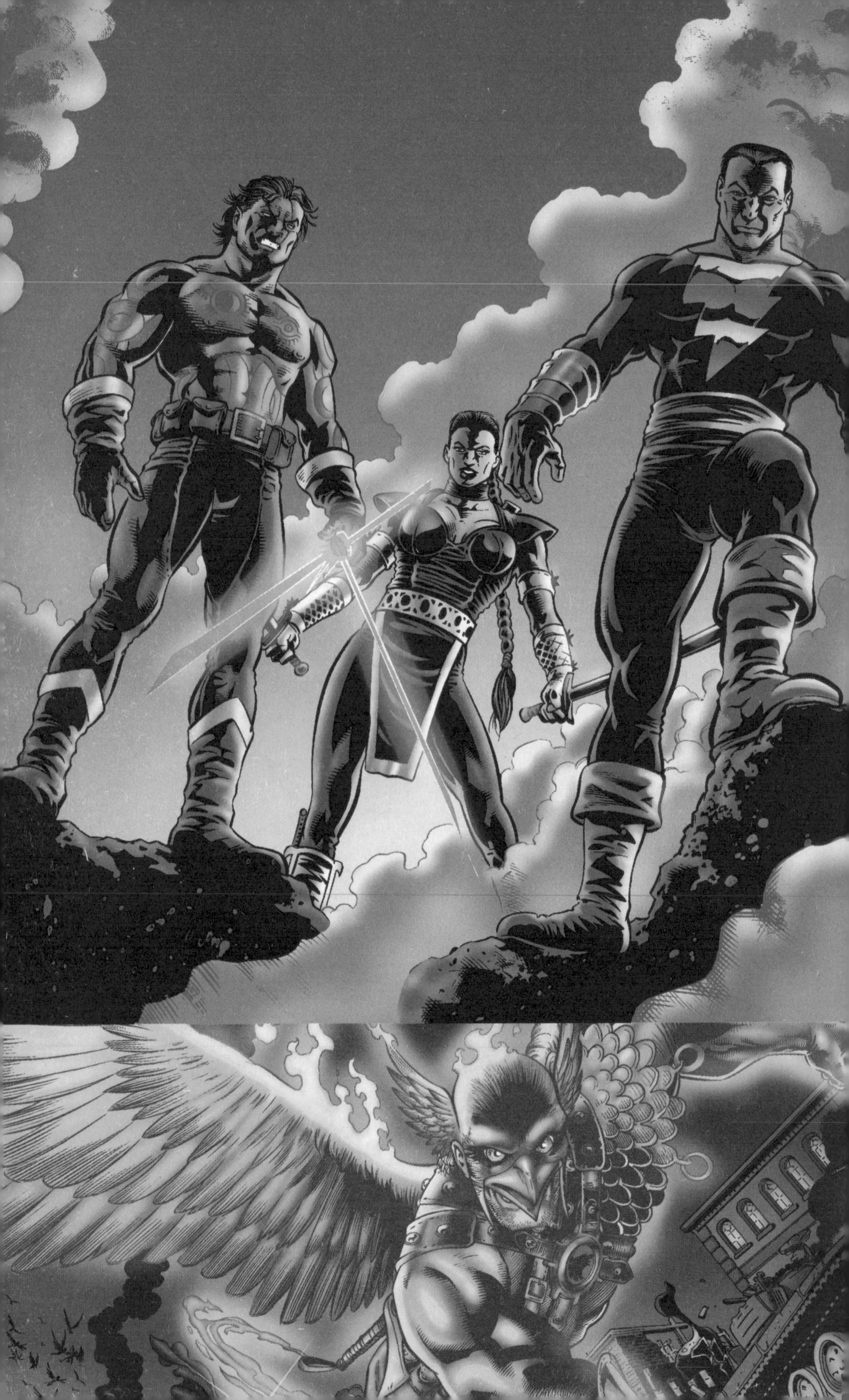

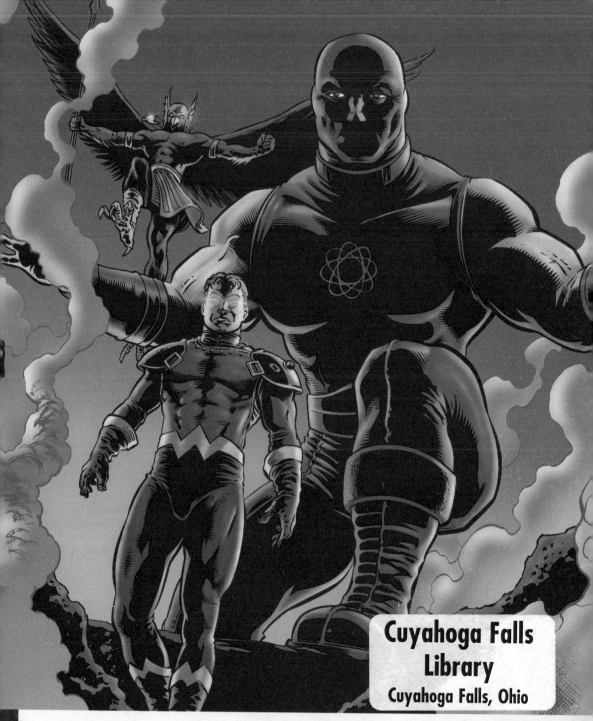

# JSA BLACK REIGN

GEOFF JOHNS WRITER   RAGS MORALES   DON KRAMER   PENCILLERS   MICHAEL BAIR

KEITH CHAMPAGNE INKERS   JOHN KALISZ COLORIST   KEN LOPEZ LETTERER

JOHN WATSON ORIGINAL COVERS

Dan DiDio VP-Executive Editor   Peter Tomasi Editor-original series   Stephen Wacker Associate Editor-original series   Robert Greenberger Senior Editor-collected edition   Robbin Brosterman Senior Art Director   Paul Levitz President & Publisher   Georg Brewer VP-Design & Retail Product Development   Richard Bruning Senior VP-Creative Director   Patrick Caldon Senior VP-Finance & Operations   Chris Caramalis VP-Finance   Terri Cunningham VP-Managing Editor   Stephanie Fierman   Senior VP-Sales & Marketing   Alison Gill VP-Manufacturing   Rich Johnson VP-Book Trade Sales   Hank Kanalz VP-General Manager, WildStorm   Lillian Laserson Senior VP & General Counsel   Jim Lee Editorial Director-WildStorm   Paula Lowitt Senior VP-Business & Legal Affairs   David McKillips VP-Advertising & Custom Publishing   John Nee VP-Business Development   Gregory Noveck Senior VP-Creative Affairs   Cheryl Rubin Senior VP-Brand Management   Bob Wayne VP-Sales

JSA: BLACK REIGN Published by DC Comics. Cover, introduction and compilation copyright © 2005 DC Comics. All Rights Reserved. Originally published in single magazine form in JSA 56-58, HAWKMAN 23-25. Copyright © 2003, 2004 DC Comics. All Rights Reserved. All characters, their distinctive likenesses and related elements featured in this publication are trademarks of DC Comics. The stories, characters and incidents featured in this publication are entirely fictional. DC Comics does not read or accept unsolicited submissions of ideas, stories or artwork. DC Comics, 1700 Broadway, New York, NY 10019. A Warner Bros. Entertainment Company. Printed in Canada. First Printing. ISBN: 1-4012-0480-5. Cover illustration by John Watson.

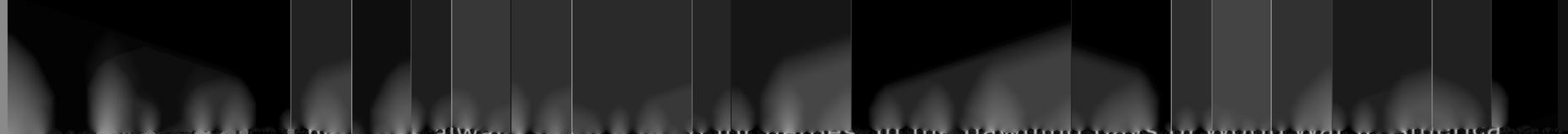

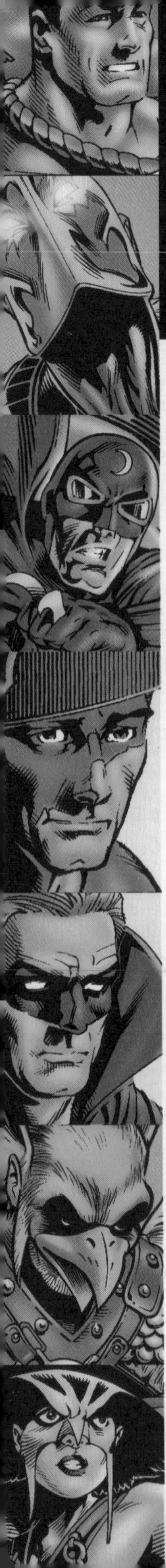

There has always been a need for heroes. In the dawning days of World War II, America produced a generation of heroes the likes of which had never before been seen. The mightiest of them banded together to protect the innocent as the Justice Society of America. For a decade they fought the good fight, retiring from the public spotlight when their day had passed.

But now the need for heroes has never been greater. So the JSA lives once more, led by the survivors of the original team who are training a new generation of crime-fighters. Under their elders' guidance, these younger heroes not only learn how to harness their power but also come to understand who paved their way and the tremendous legacy that they have inherited.

Since its re-formation, the JSA has rediscovered old friends, fought familiar enemies, and buried some of their comrades. The team has also reestablished its roots in New York City, with their headquarters doubling as meeting place and museum open to the public.

As we begin, the JSA is..

## CAPTAIN MARVEL

Entrusted by the wizard Shazam with the combined magical might of Solomon, Hercules, Atlas, Zeus, Achilles, and Mercury, teenager Billy Batson needs only speak his mentor's name to be transformed into Captain Marvel, the World's Mightiest Mortal. Batson currently shares the power of Shazam with several other champions, joining a long line of warriors who have acted as Shazam's avatars over the millennia.

## DR. FATE

Nabu, a Lord of Order, was exiled to Earth in 3,500 B.C. Once here, he took the guise of an Egyptian sorcerer and served as an advisor to Prince Khufu. Later, his essence and powers were entombed in a golden helmet and amulet. In 1940, Kent Nelson assumed the golden armaments and became the first Dr. Fate. Several others have worn the mantle since then, and its current possessor is Hector Hall, the son of Hawkman. He searches to find his wife, Lyta, also known as Fury, who was taken from this plane of existence.

## DR. MID-NITE

A medical prodigy, Pieter Anton Cross refused to work within the system. Treating patients on his own, he came into contact with a dangerous drug that altered his body chemistry, letting him see light in the infrared spectrum. Although he was blinded in an explosion intended to kill him, he continues to protect the weak in the assumed identity of Dr. Mid-Nite.

## THE FLASH

The first in a long line of super-speedsters, Jay Garrick is capable of running at velocities near the speed of light. A scientist, Garrick has also served as mentor to other speedsters and heroes over several generations.

## GREEN LANTERN

Engineer Alan Scott found a lantern carved from a meteorite known as the Starheart. Fulfilling a prophecy to grant power, Scott tapped into the emerald energy and fought injustice as the Green Lantern. He has gone through many changes but is currently a living embodiment of the Starheart.

## HAWKMAN and HAWKGIRL

Thousands of years ago, in ancient Egypt, Prince Khufu and his Princess Chay-Ara discovered an alien spacecraft from the planet Thanagar. The ship was powered by a mysterious anti-gravity element, which they called Nth metal. The unearthly energies of the Nth metal, enhanced by the strength of their love, transformed the souls of the Prince and Princess. For centuries, they were reincarnated, life after life, destined to meet one another and rekindle their love... until today. Today, he is Carter Hall, archaeologist and adventurer. She is Kendra Saunders, trained to inherit the mantle of Hawkgirl. But Kendra has no recollection of her past lives or her past love with Carter, nor any interest whatsoever in renewing that love.

# HOURMAN

Rick Tyler struggled for a while before accepting his role as the son of the original Hourman. It hasn't been an easy road — he endured addiction to the Miraclo drug that increases his strength and endurance, and nearly died from a strange disease. Now, after mastering the drug, he uses a special hourglass to see one hour into the future.

# MR. TERRIFIC

Haunted by the death of his wife, Olympic gold medal-winning decathlete Michael Holt was ready to take his own life. Instead, inspired by the Spectre's story of the original Mr. Terrific, he rededicated himself to ensuring fair play among the street youth using his wealth and technical skills.

# POWER GIRL

She thought herself a princess of ancient Atlantis or a survivor of the doomed planet Krypton, but Karen Starr is now less certain of her origins than of her commitment to justice. Her enhanced strength and powers of flight and invulnerability are matched only by her self-confidence, which borders on arrogance.

# STARGIRL

When Courtney Whitmore first discovered the cosmic converter belt once worn by the JSA's original Star-Spangled Kid, she saw it as an opportunity to cut class and kick some butt. Now, she is beginning to learn about the awesome legacy she has become a part of, wielding the powerful cosmic rod of the previous Starman.

# WILDCAT

A former heavyweight boxing champ, Ted Grant, a.k.a. Wildcat, prowls the mean streets defending the helpless. One of the world's foremost hand-to-hand combatants, he has trained many of today's best fighters — including Black Canary, Catwoman, and the Batman.

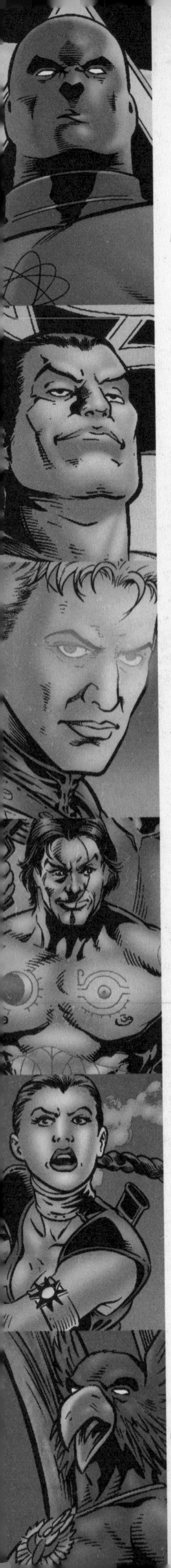

AND, AT THE TIME OF THIS STORY, THEIR OPPONENTS

## ATOM SMASHER

Al Rothstein never wanted anything more than to become a member of the Justice Society of America. Although his grandfather was the super-villain known as Cyclotron, Al is trying to live up to the legacy of a hero — his godfather, the original Atom. Al inherited his superhuman strength and the ability to increase his mass from his grandfather's atomic-powered physiology.

## BLACK ADAM

Teth-Adam was the first to wield the mystical powers bestowed by the wizard Shazam. As Mighty Adam, he battled evil during Egypt's 15th Dynasty until the power ultimately corrupted him. Shazam imprisoned Adam in a scarab that was lost for centuries. A few years ago, two archaeologists, C.C. and Mary Batson, unearthed the scarab. Teth-Adam's powers and soul took root in the body of his descendant, Theo Adam, a thief and murderer. Now he struggles for redemption.

## BRAINWAVE

Henry King, Jr., the son of the longtime villain Brainwave, was born with the same telepathic mutant ability as his father. Attempting to avoid his father's path, Henry Jr. joined Infinity, Inc. and enjoyed a romance with Jade. When Henry Sr. died, his telepathic abilities were transferred to his son, making the second Brainwave one of the Earth's most powerful telepaths. Such power, though, mentally unhinged him and he went from hero to menace. He not only can read minds but also create realistic illusions that can prove deadly.

## ECLIPSO

The first Spirit of God's wrath, Eclipso found himself an outcast. A god of revenge, he was then trapped in a black diamond for years until accidentally freed by scientist Bruce Gordon. Eclipso sought dominion over humanity but met defeat time and again. After Gordon and Eclipso were no longer mystically tethered, Eclipso grew more savage, hungering for a chance to crush lives until the Spectre once more imprisoned him in the black diamond.

## NEMESIS

Soseh Mykros and her sister Elena were the genetically engineered daughters of Dr. Anatol Mykros, a member of the Council, a group bent on world domination. After being trained as an assassin, Soseh rejected her father's influence, adopted the identity of Nemesis, which brought her into conflict with the Council and her own sister. The JSA aided her in stopping the Council's goals, with Soseh forced to slay Elena. Later, Black Adam killed Dr. Mykros, ending the threat and gaining Nemesis as an ally.

## NORTHWIND

The hybrid child of a human father and a mother from the Feitherian race of bird-people, Norda was raised in their hidden society in northern Greenland. The godson of Hawkman, the teen Norda left his home to join Infinity, Inc. but eventually returned to help his people. Recently, Norda has evolved into a giant bird-like creature, losing the ability to speak. He was recruited by Black Adam to help accomplish goals the JSA rejected.

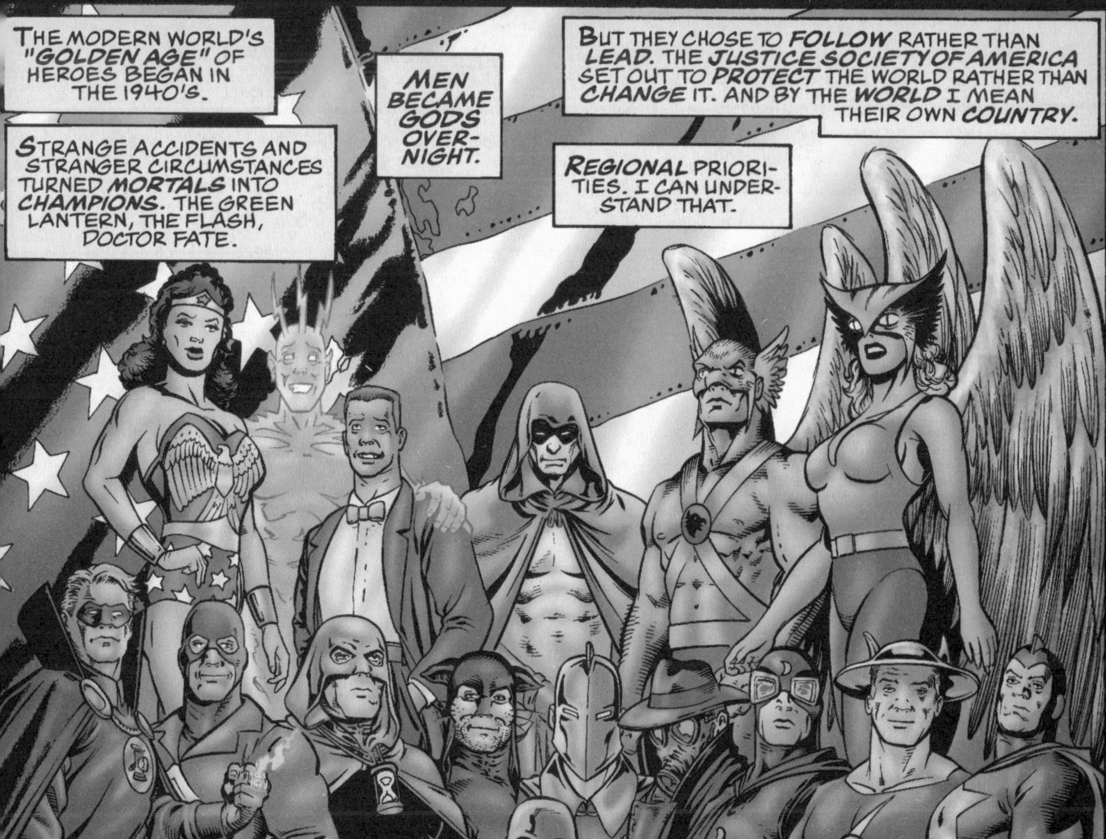
THE MODERN WORLD'S "GOLDEN AGE" OF HEROES BEGAN IN THE 1940'S.
STRANGE ACCIDENTS AND STRANGER CIRCUMSTANCES TURNED MORTALS INTO CHAMPIONS. THE GREEN LANTERN, THE FLASH, DOCTOR FATE.
MEN BECAME GODS OVER-NIGHT.
BUT THEY CHOSE TO FOLLOW RATHER THAN LEAD. THE JUSTICE SOCIETY OF AMERICA SET OUT TO PROTECT THE WORLD RATHER THAN CHANGE IT. AND BY THE WORLD I MEAN THEIR OWN COUNTRY.
REGIONAL PRIORI-TIES. I CAN UNDER-STAND THAT.
TODAY, THE JSA CONTINUES. THE SONS AND DAUGHTERS AND INHERITORS OF THE MANTLES HAVE JOINED THE REMAINING ORIGINAL MEMBERS.
BUT STILL REACTING-- INTERVENTION INSTEAD OF PREVENTION.
I HAVE OPERATED WITH THEM FOR SOME TIME NOW... I HAVE LEARNED THEIR HISTORY... BUT I STILL ASK--HOW DEDICATED ARE THEY TO A BETTER WORLD?
MEN BECAME GODS OVERNIGHT--
--IT IS TIME THEY STARTED ACTING LIKE IT.

# BLACK REIGN

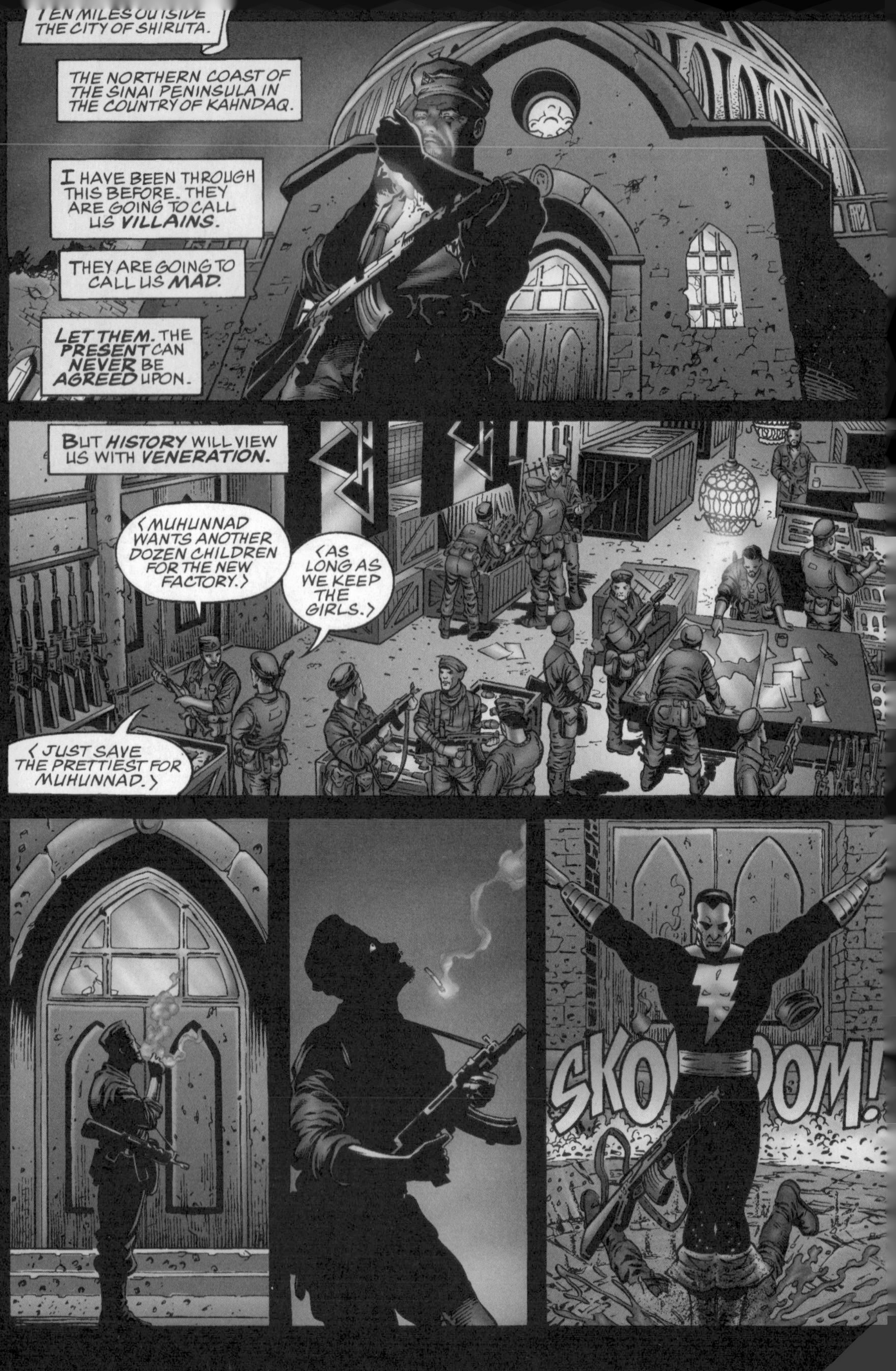

TEN MILES OUTSIDE THE CITY OF SHIRUTA.
THE NORTHERN COAST OF THE SINAI PENINSULA IN THE COUNTRY OF KAHNDAQ.
I HAVE BEEN THROUGH THIS BEFORE. THEY ARE GOING TO CALL US VILLAINS.
THEY ARE GOING TO CALL US MAD.
LET THEM. THE PRESENT CAN NEVER BE AGREED UPON.
BUT HISTORY WILL VIEW US WITH VENERATION.
‹MUHUNNAD WANTS ANOTHER DOZEN CHILDREN FOR THE NEW FACTORY.›
‹AS LONG AS WE KEEP THE GIRLS.›
‹JUST SAVE THE PRETTIEST FOR MUHUNNAD.›
SKO OOM!

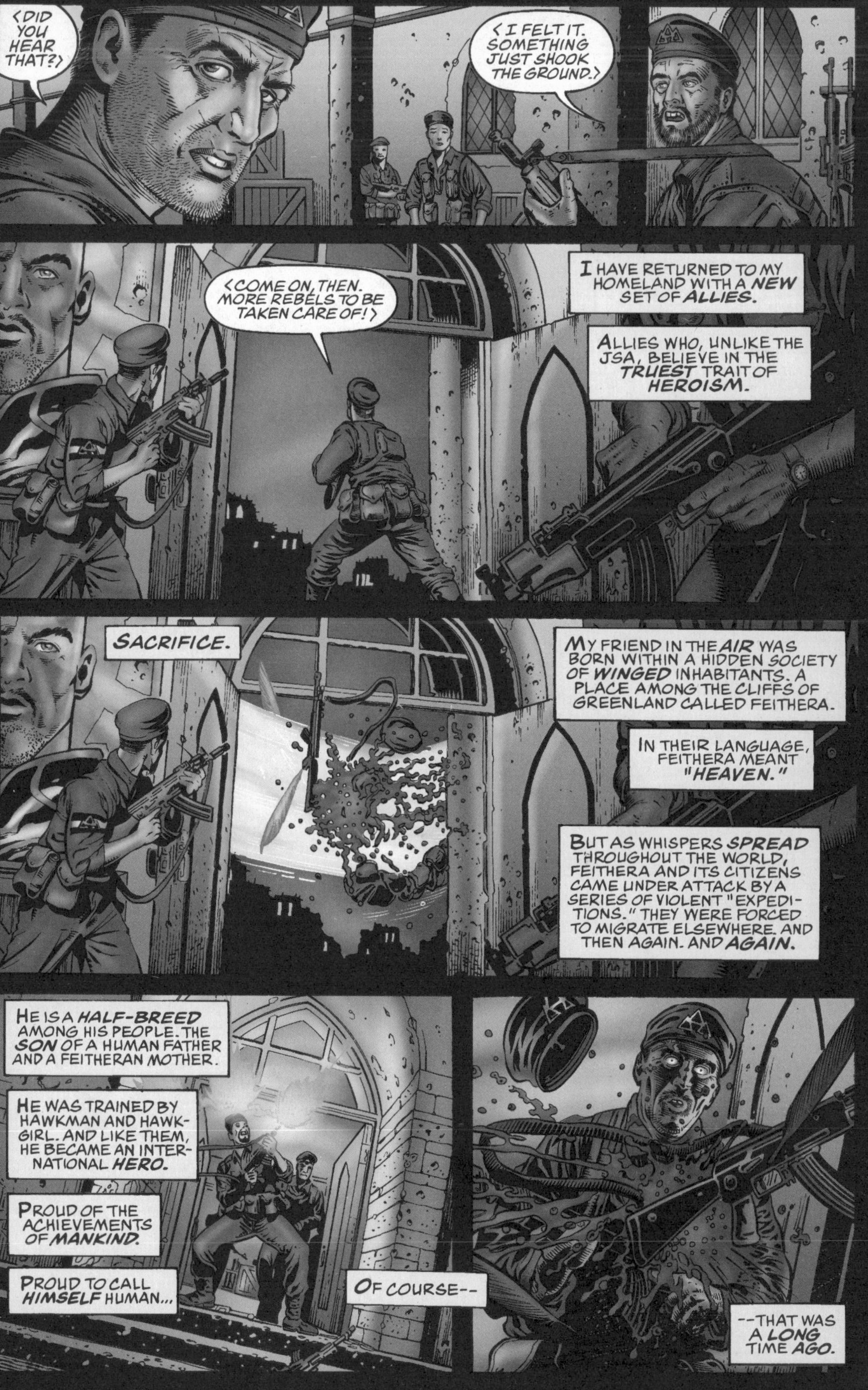
<DID YOU HEAR THAT?>
<I FELT IT. SOMETHING JUST SHOOK THE GROUND.>
<COME ON, THEN. MORE REBELS TO BE TAKEN CARE OF!>
I HAVE RETURNED TO MY HOMELAND WITH A NEW SET OF ALLIES.
ALLIES WHO, UNLIKE THE JSA, BELIEVE IN THE TRUEST TRAIT OF HEROISM.
SACRIFICE.
MY FRIEND IN THE AIR WAS BORN WITHIN A HIDDEN SOCIETY OF WINGED INHABITANTS. A PLACE AMONG THE CLIFFS OF GREENLAND CALLED FEITHERA.
IN THEIR LANGUAGE, FEITHERA MEANT "HEAVEN."
BUT AS WHISPERS SPREAD THROUGHOUT THE WORLD, FEITHERA AND ITS CITIZENS CAME UNDER ATTACK BY A SERIES OF VIOLENT "EXPEDITIONS." THEY WERE FORCED TO MIGRATE ELSEWHERE. AND THEN AGAIN. AND AGAIN.
HE IS A HALF-BREED AMONG HIS PEOPLE. THE SON OF A HUMAN FATHER AND A FEITHERAN MOTHER.
HE WAS TRAINED BY HAWKMAN AND HAWKGIRL. AND LIKE THEM, HE BECAME AN INTERNATIONAL HERO.
PROUD OF THE ACHIEVEMENTS OF MANKIND.
PROUD TO CALL HIMSELF HUMAN...
OF COURSE--
--THAT WAS A LONG TIME AGO.

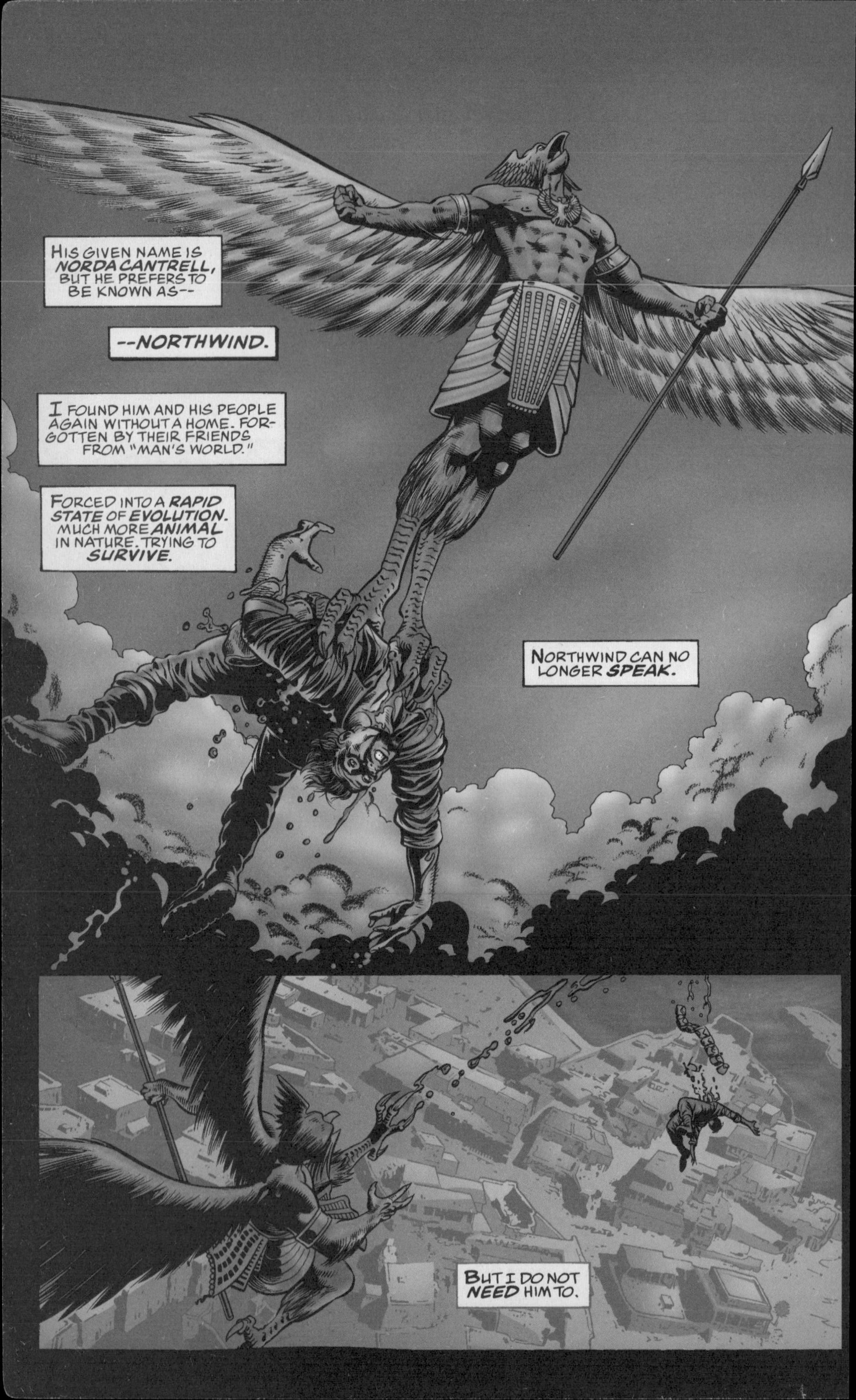
HIS GIVEN NAME IS NORDA CANTRELL, BUT HE PREFERS TO BE KNOWN AS--
--NORTHWIND.
I FOUND HIM AND HIS PEOPLE AGAIN WITHOUT A HOME. FORGOTTEN BY THEIR FRIENDS FROM "MAN'S WORLD."
FORCED INTO A RAPID STATE OF EVOLUTION. MUCH MORE ANIMAL IN NATURE. TRYING TO SURVIVE.
NORTHWIND CAN NO LONGER SPEAK.
BUT I DO NOT NEED HIM TO.

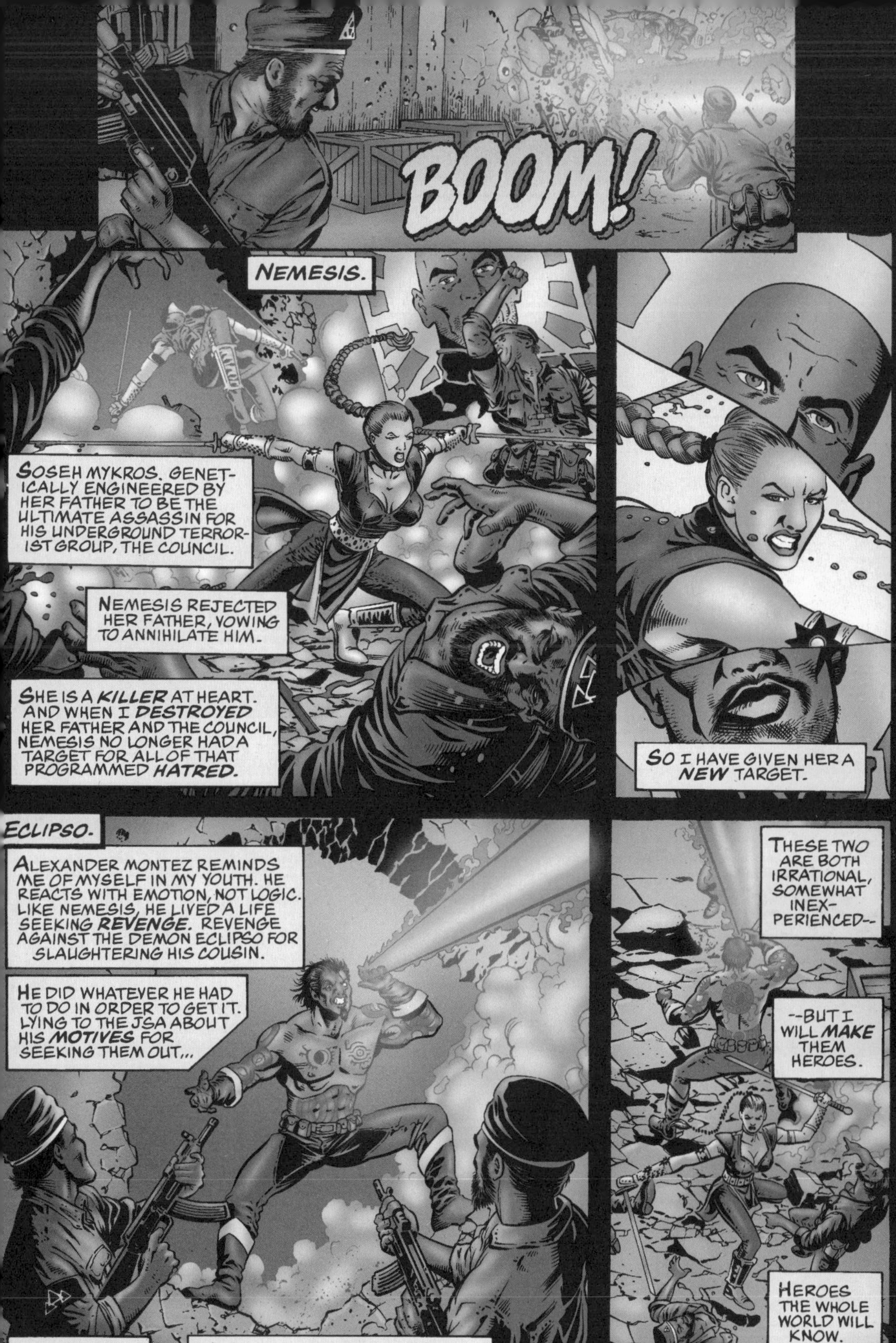
BOOM!
NEMESIS.
SOSEH MYKROS. GENETICALLY ENGINEERED BY HER FATHER TO BE THE ULTIMATE ASSASSIN FOR HIS UNDERGROUND TERRORIST GROUP, THE COUNCIL.
NEMESIS REJECTED HER FATHER, VOWING TO ANNIHILATE HIM.
SHE IS A KILLER AT HEART. AND WHEN I DESTROYED HER FATHER AND THE COUNCIL, NEMESIS NO LONGER HAD A TARGET FOR ALL OF THAT PROGRAMMED HATRED.
SO I HAVE GIVEN HER A NEW TARGET.
ECLIPSO.
ALEXANDER MONTEZ REMINDS ME OF MYSELF IN MY YOUTH. HE REACTS WITH EMOTION, NOT LOGIC. LIKE NEMESIS, HE LIVED A LIFE SEEKING REVENGE. REVENGE AGAINST THE DEMON ECLIPSO FOR SLAUGHTERING HIS COUSIN.
HE DID WHATEVER HE HAD TO DO IN ORDER TO GET IT. LYING TO THE JSA ABOUT HIS MOTIVES FOR SEEKING THEM OUT...
...LYING TO GET HIS HANDS ON THE BLACK DIAMOND...
WITH THOSE BINDING TATTOOS AND THE GEM THAT CONTAINS THE DEMON WITHIN, ALEXANDER NOW CONTROLS ECLIPSO'S SPIRIT AND POWER.
THESE TWO ARE BOTH IRRATIONAL, SOMEWHAT INEXPERIENCED--
--BUT I WILL MAKE THEM HEROES.
HEROES THE WHOLE WORLD WILL KNOW.

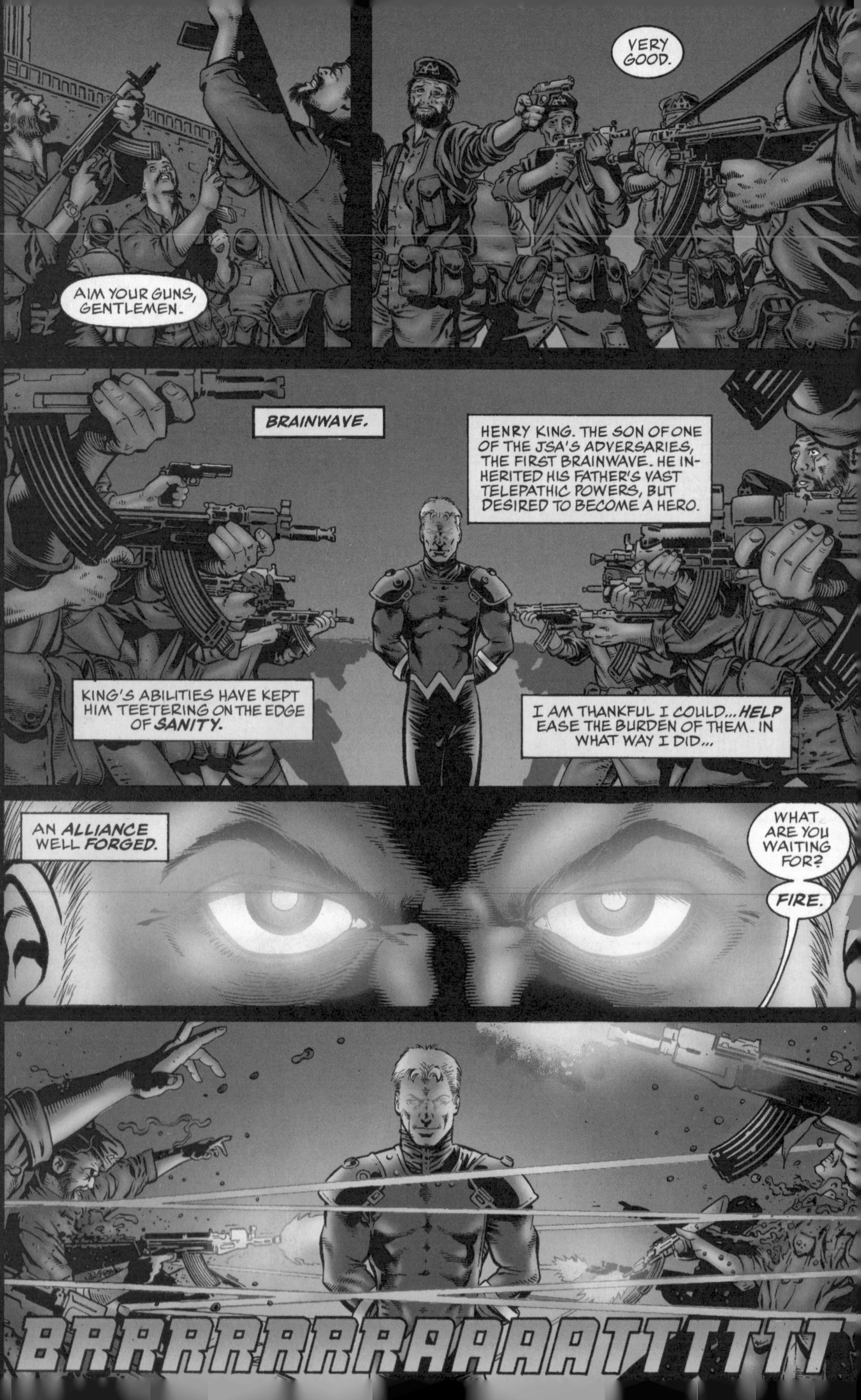
AIM YOUR GUNS, GENTLEMEN.
VERY GOOD.
BRAINWAVE.
HENRY KING. THE SON OF ONE OF THE JSA'S ADVERSARIES, THE FIRST BRAINWAVE. HE INHERITED HIS FATHER'S VAST TELEPATHIC POWERS, BUT DESIRED TO BECOME A HERO.
KING'S ABILITIES HAVE KEPT HIM TEETERING ON THE EDGE OF SANITY.
I AM THANKFUL I COULD... HELP EASE THE BURDEN OF THEM. IN WHAT WAY I DID...
AN ALLIANCE WELL FORGED.
WHAT ARE YOU WAITING FOR?
FIRE.
BRRRRRRRRAAAAATTTTTT

I FIND IT FASCINATING. INSPIRING IN ALL TRUTH.

THE LAST THOUGHTS OF THE DYING. LIKE A SOUND FADING INTO THE DISTANCE. ANGUISH, GUILT, FEAR. A HINT OF LOVE...

BUT NOT A SINGLE SHRED OF ANGER. NOT ONE BAD THOUGHT.

EVEN AS HIS HEART STOPS AND HIS BLOOD STILLS, THIS ONE WORRIES ABOUT THE SAFETY OF HIS FAMILY. HE WORRIES THAT NOW ASIM MUHUNNAD WILL TAKE HIS CHILDREN AS HE HAS OTHERS.

THE HUMAN MIND.

PUREST IN THE BEGINNING--

--AND THE END.

THEY DIDN'T POSE MUCH OF A CHALLENGE.

THEY RELY ON THEIR WEAPONS AND PEASANTS WHO DO NOT FIGHT BACK--

YOU HAVE A TRACE OF GUILT PLAGUING YOUR MIND, NEMESIS. I HEAR IT NAGGING YOU.

I CAN STILL REACH INTO THEIR COOLING BRAINS AND PULL OUT MEMORIES OF EVERY HEINOUS ACT THESE SOLDIERS PERFORMED. I CAN PROJECT IT BACK INTO YOUR HEAD.

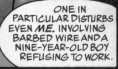

ONE IN PARTICULAR DISTURBS EVEN ME. INVOLVING BARBED WIRE AND A NINE-YEAR-OLD BOY REFUSING TO WORK.

SEE THIS AND I VERY MUCH DOUBT THAT ANY FEELINGS OF GUILT WILL RETURN.

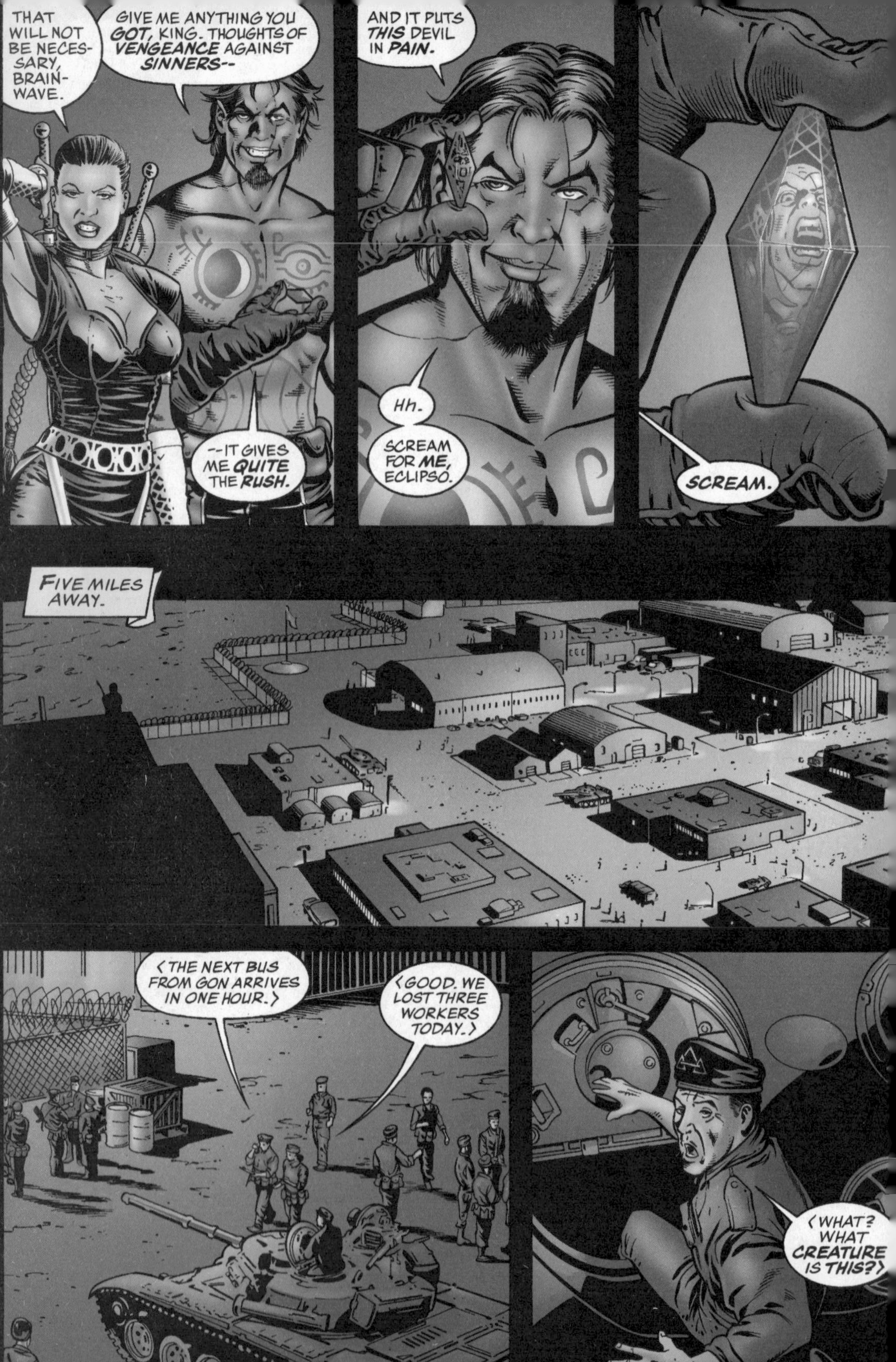
THAT WILL NOT BE NECES-SARY, BRAIN-WAVE.
GIVE ME ANYTHING YOU GOT, KING. THOUGHTS OF VENGEANCE AGAINST SINNERS--
--IT GIVES ME QUITE THE RUSH.
AND IT PUTS THIS DEVIL IN PAIN.
Hh.
SCREAM FOR ME, ECLIPSO.
SCREAM.
FIVE MILES AWAY.
<THE NEXT BUS FROM GON ARRIVES IN ONE HOUR.>
<GOOD. WE LOST THREE WORKERS TODAY.>
<WHAT? WHAT CREATURE IS THIS?>

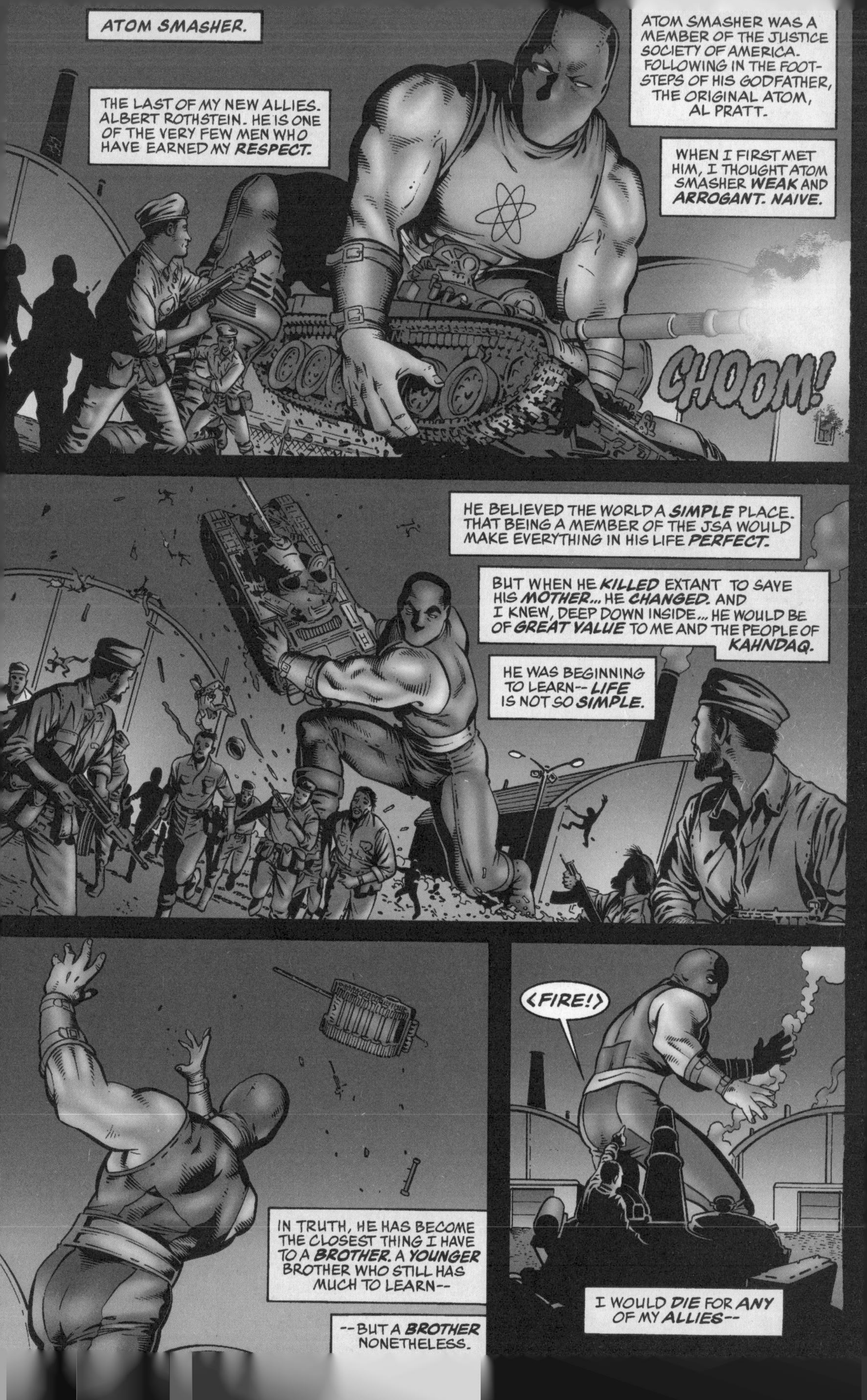

ATOM SMASHER.
THE LAST OF MY NEW ALLIES. ALBERT ROTHSTEIN. HE IS ONE OF THE VERY FEW MEN WHO HAVE EARNED MY RESPECT.
ATOM SMASHER WAS A MEMBER OF THE JUSTICE SOCIETY OF AMERICA. FOLLOWING IN THE FOOTSTEPS OF HIS GODFATHER, THE ORIGINAL ATOM, AL PRATT.
WHEN I FIRST MET HIM, I THOUGHT ATOM SMASHER WEAK AND ARROGANT. NAIVE.
CHOOM!
HE BELIEVED THE WORLD A SIMPLE PLACE. THAT BEING A MEMBER OF THE JSA WOULD MAKE EVERYTHING IN HIS LIFE PERFECT.
BUT WHEN HE KILLED EXTANT TO SAVE HIS MOTHER... HE CHANGED. AND I KNEW, DEEP DOWN INSIDE... HE WOULD BE OF GREAT VALUE TO ME AND THE PEOPLE OF KAHNDAQ.
HE WAS BEGINNING TO LEARN-- LIFE IS NOT SO SIMPLE.
IN TRUTH, HE HAS BECOME THE CLOSEST THING I HAVE TO A BROTHER. A YOUNGER BROTHER WHO STILL HAS MUCH TO LEARN--
--BUT A BROTHER NONETHELESS.
<FIRE!>
I WOULD DIE FOR ANY OF MY ALLIES--

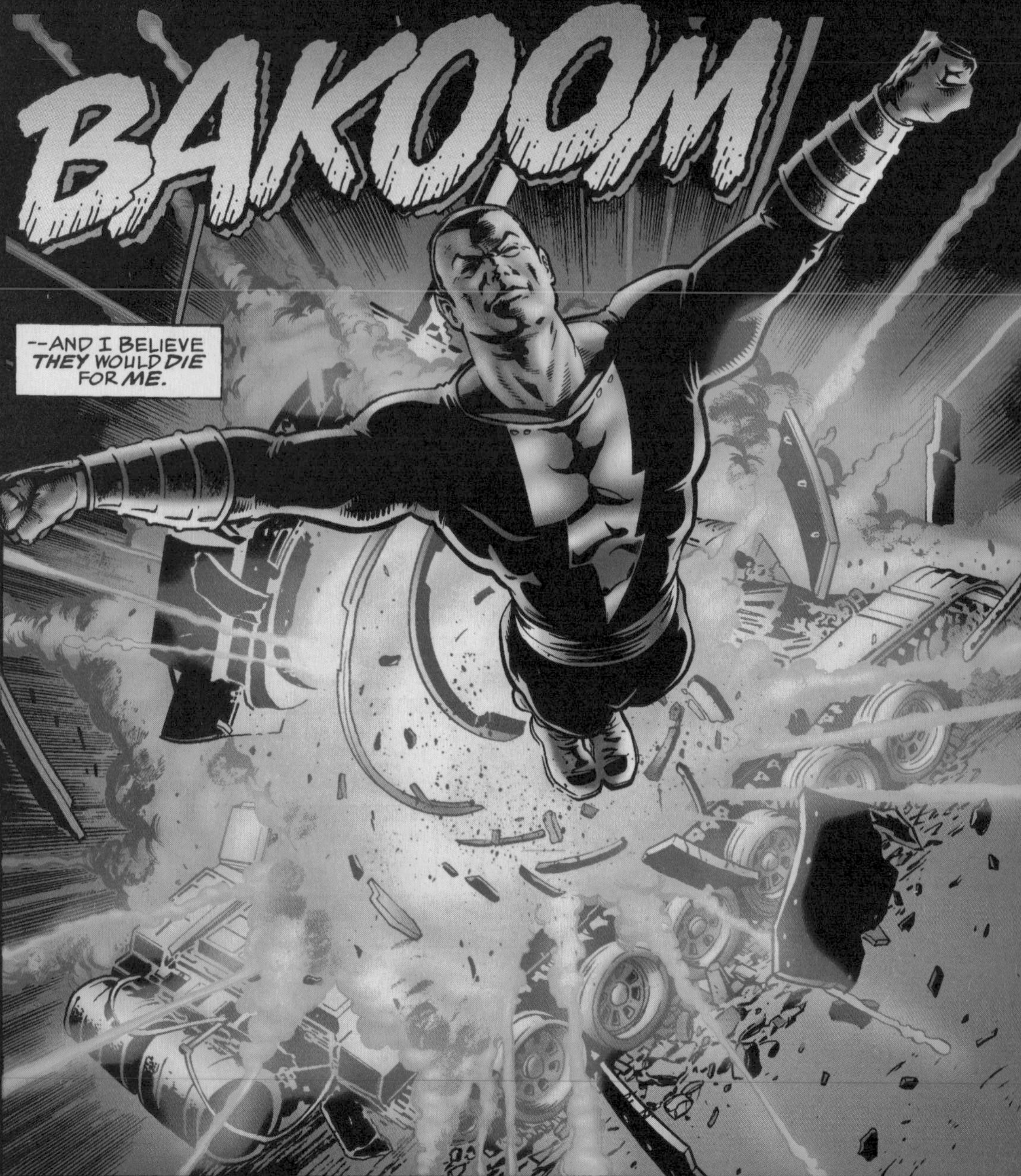
BAKOOM
--AND I BELIEVE THEY WOULD DIE FOR ME.

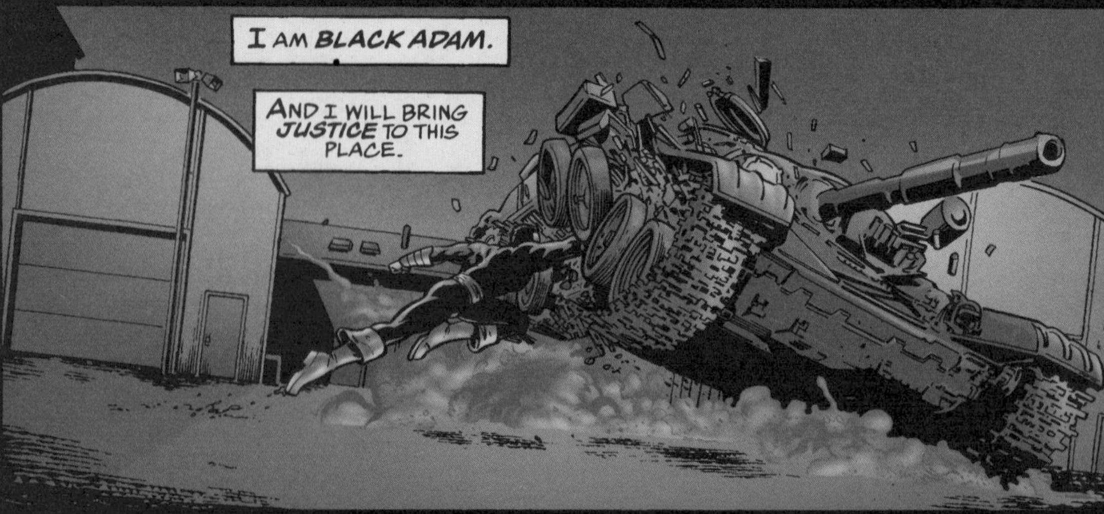
I AM BLACK ADAM.
AND I WILL BRING JUSTICE TO THIS PLACE.

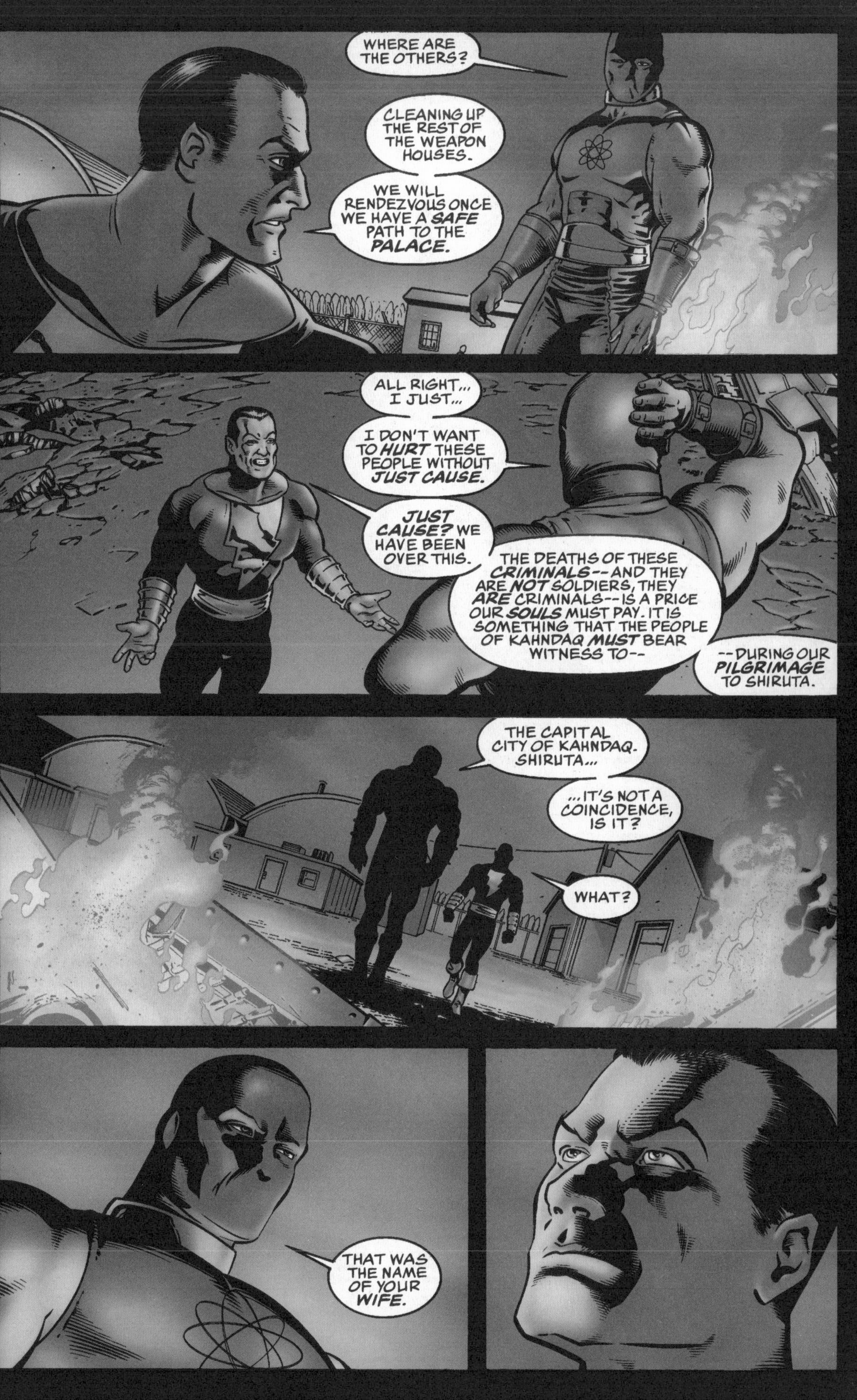
WHERE ARE THE OTHERS?
CLEANING UP THE REST OF THE WEAPON HOUSES.
WE WILL RENDEZVOUS ONCE WE HAVE A SAFE PATH TO THE PALACE.
ALL RIGHT... I JUST...
I DON'T WANT TO HURT THESE PEOPLE WITHOUT JUST CAUSE.
JUST CAUSE? WE HAVE BEEN OVER THIS.
THE DEATHS OF THESE CRIMINALS-- AND THEY ARE NOT SOLDIERS, THEY ARE CRIMINALS--IS A PRICE OUR SOULS MUST PAY. IT IS SOMETHING THAT THE PEOPLE OF KAHNDAQ MUST BEAR WITNESS TO--
--DURING OUR PILGRIMAGE TO SHIRUTA.
THE CAPITAL CITY OF KAHNDAQ. SHIRUTA...
...IT'S NOT A COINCIDENCE, IS IT?
WHAT?
THAT WAS THE NAME OF YOUR WIFE.

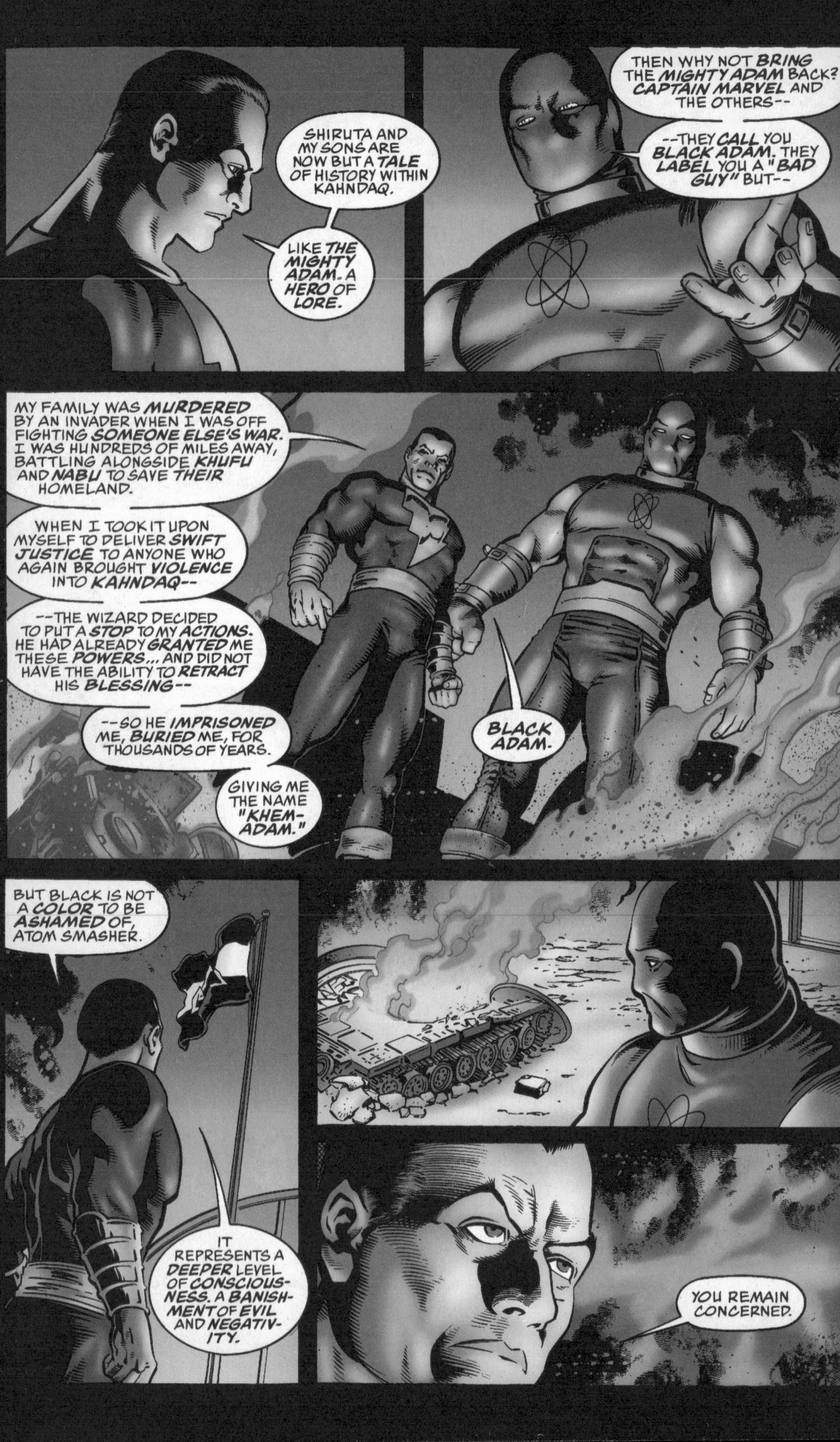
SHIRUTA AND MY SONS ARE NOW BUT A TALE OF HISTORY WITHIN KAHNDAQ.
LIKE THE MIGHTY ADAM- A HERO OF LORE.
THEN WHY NOT BRING THE MIGHTY ADAM BACK? CAPTAIN MARVEL AND THE OTHERS--
--THEY CALL YOU BLACK ADAM. THEY LABEL YOU A "BAD GUY" BUT--
MY FAMILY WAS MURDERED BY AN INVADER WHEN I WAS OFF FIGHTING SOMEONE ELSE'S WAR. I WAS HUNDREDS OF MILES AWAY, BATTLING ALONGSIDE KHUFU AND NABU TO SAVE THEIR HOMELAND.
WHEN I TOOK IT UPON MYSELF TO DELIVER SWIFT JUSTICE TO ANYONE WHO AGAIN BROUGHT VIOLENCE INTO KAHNDAQ--
--THE WIZARD DECIDED TO PUT A STOP TO MY ACTIONS. HE HAD ALREADY GRANTED ME THESE POWERS... AND DID NOT HAVE THE ABILITY TO RETRACT HIS BLESSING--
--SO HE IMPRISONED ME, BURIED ME, FOR THOUSANDS OF YEARS.
GIVING ME THE NAME "KHEM-ADAM."
BLACK ADAM.
BUT BLACK IS NOT A COLOR TO BE ASHAMED OF, ATOM SMASHER.
IT REPRESENTS A DEEPER LEVEL OF CONSCIOUSNESS. A BANISHMENT OF EVIL AND NEGATIVITY.
YOU REMAIN CONCERNED.

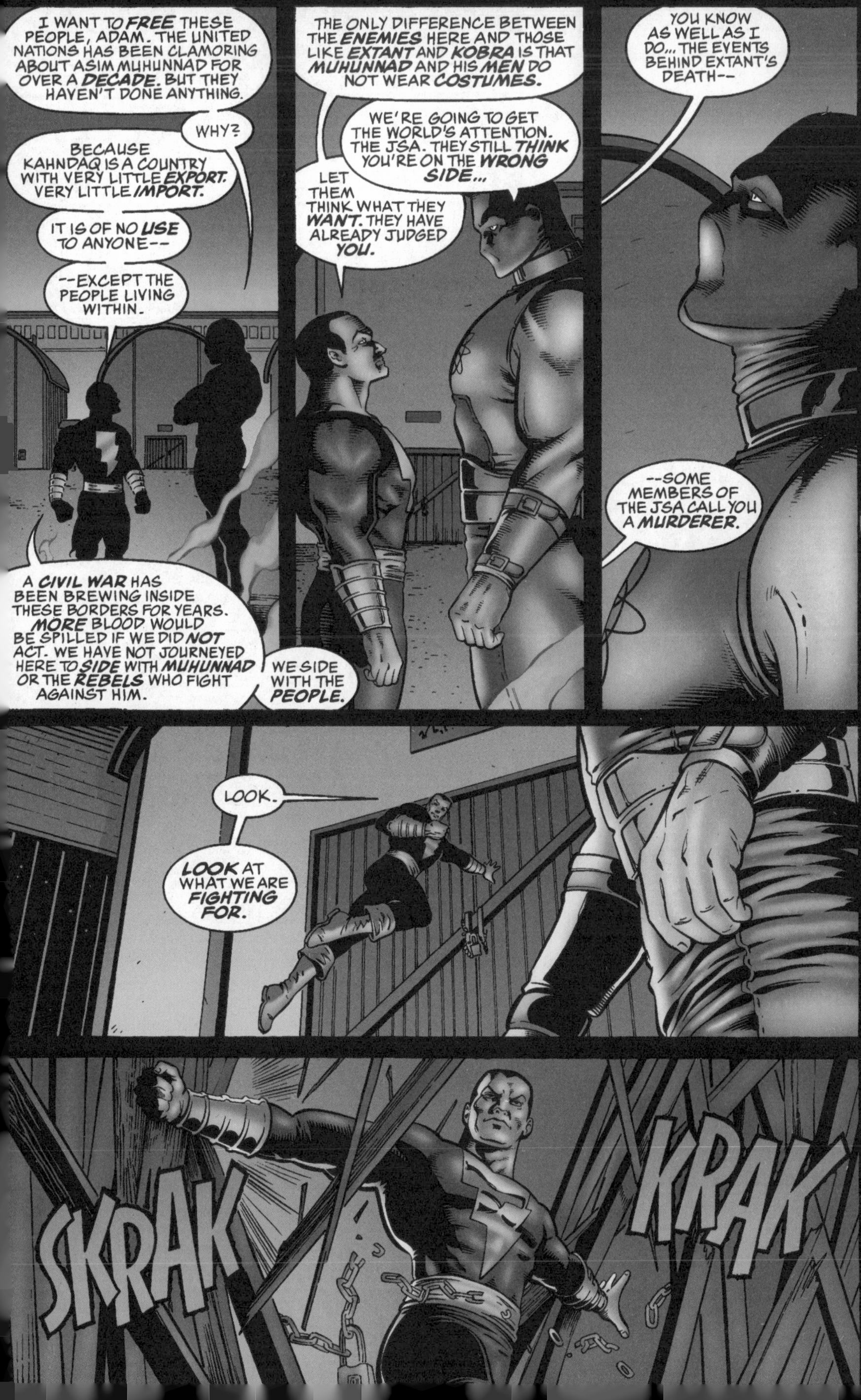

I WANT TO FREE THESE PEOPLE, ADAM. THE UNITED NATIONS HAS BEEN CLAMORING ABOUT ASIM MUHUNNAD FOR OVER A DECADE. BUT THEY HAVEN'T DONE ANYTHING.
WHY?
BECAUSE KAHNDAQ IS A COUNTRY WITH VERY LITTLE EXPORT. VERY LITTLE IMPORT.
IT IS OF NO USE TO ANYONE--
--EXCEPT THE PEOPLE LIVING WITHIN.
A CIVIL WAR HAS BEEN BREWING INSIDE THESE BORDERS FOR YEARS. MORE BLOOD WOULD BE SPILLED IF WE DID NOT ACT. WE HAVE NOT JOURNEYED HERE TO SIDE WITH MUHUNNAD OR THE REBELS WHO FIGHT AGAINST HIM.
WE SIDE WITH THE PEOPLE.
THE ONLY DIFFERENCE BETWEEN THE ENEMIES HERE AND THOSE LIKE EXTANT AND KOBRA IS THAT MUHUNNAD AND HIS MEN DO NOT WEAR COSTUMES.
WE'RE GOING TO GET THE WORLD'S ATTENTION. THE JSA. THEY STILL THINK YOU'RE ON THE WRONG SIDE...
LET THEM THINK WHAT THEY WANT. THEY HAVE ALREADY JUDGED YOU.
YOU KNOW AS WELL AS I DO... THE EVENTS BEHIND EXTANT'S DEATH--
--SOME MEMBERS OF THE JSA CALL YOU A MURDERER.
LOOK.
LOOK AT WHAT WE ARE FIGHTING FOR.
SKRAK
KRAK

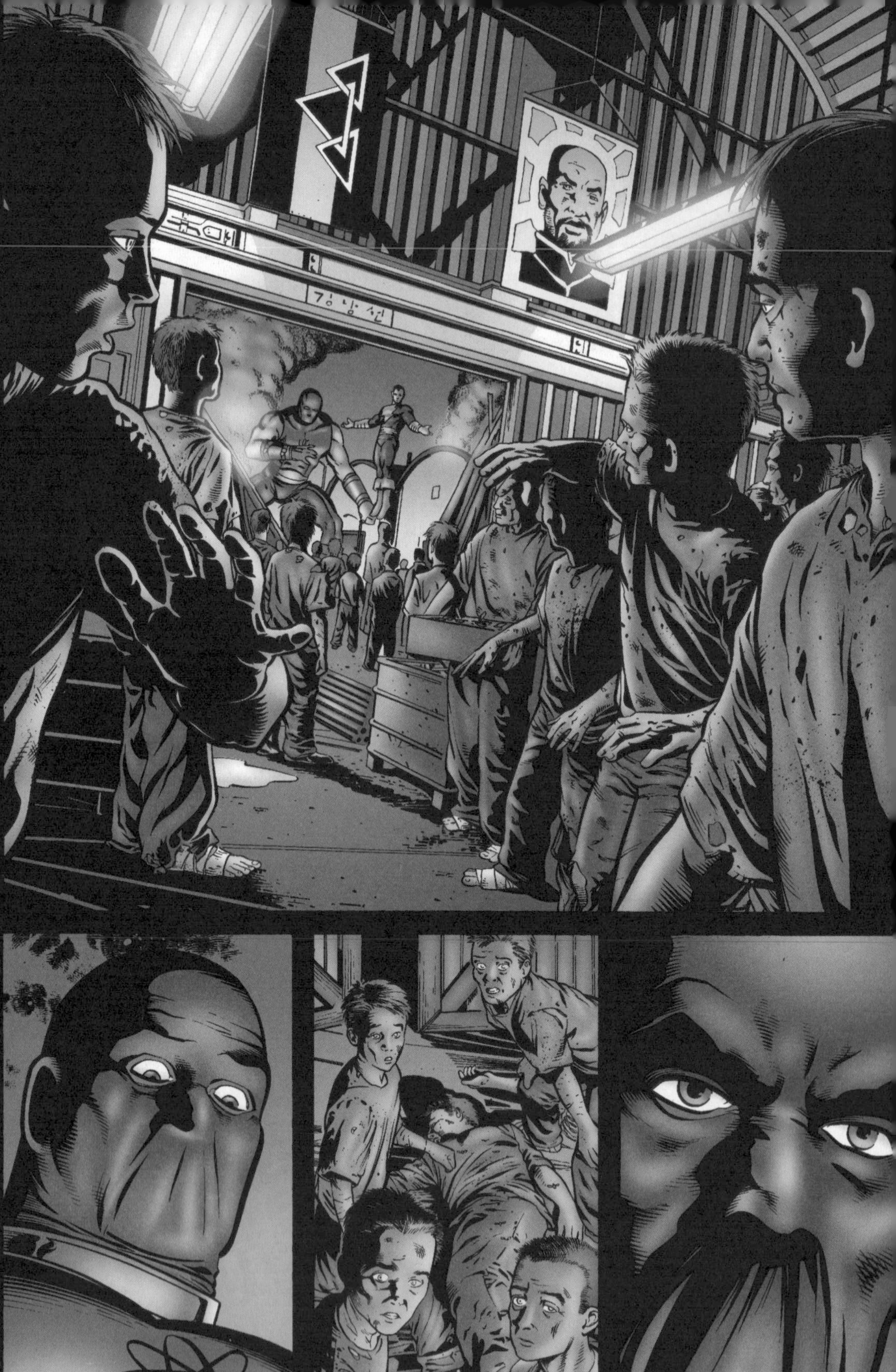

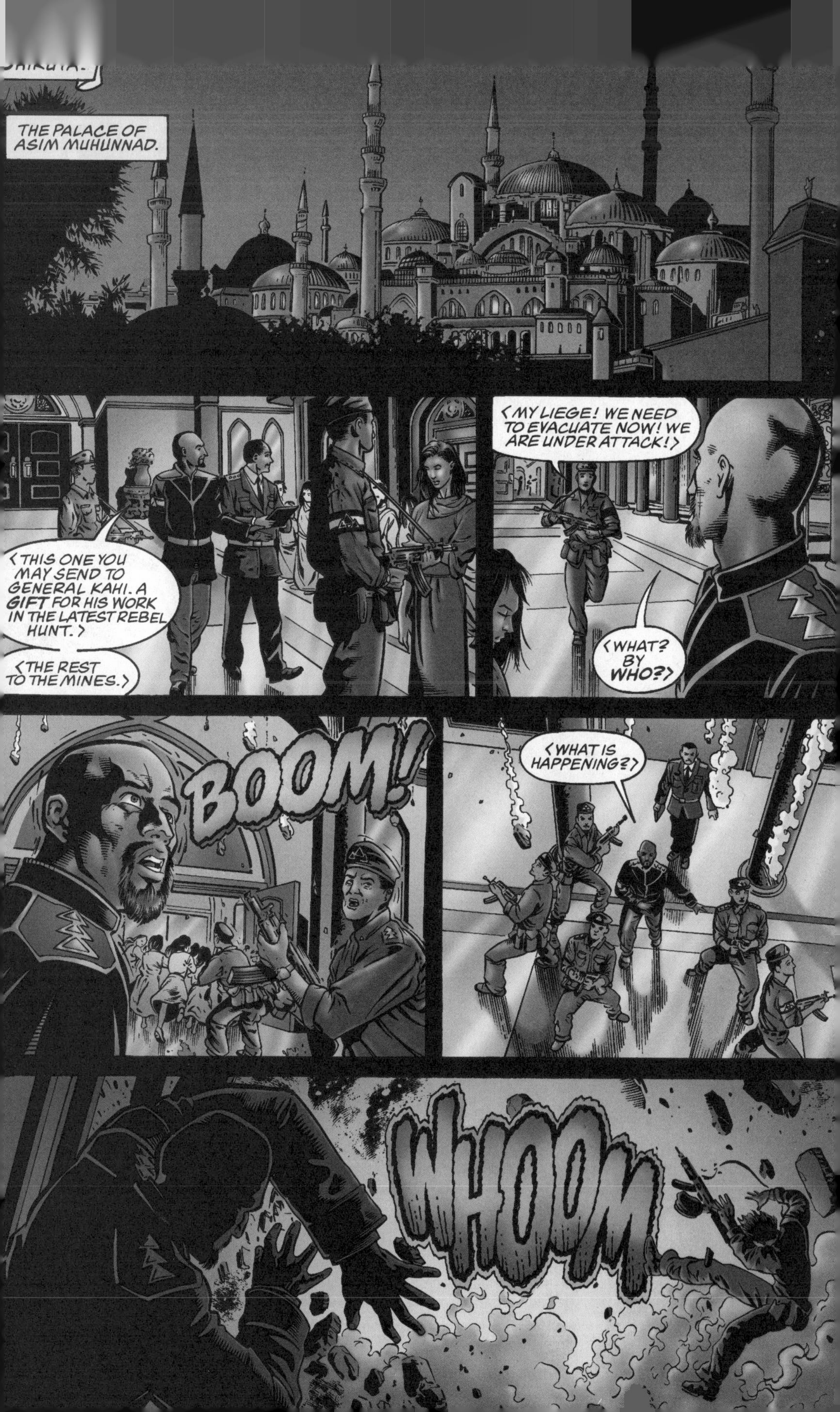

THE PALACE OF ASIM MUHUNNAD.
<THIS ONE YOU MAY SEND TO GENERAL KAHI. A GIFT FOR HIS WORK IN THE LATEST REBEL HUNT.>
<THE REST TO THE MINES.>
<MY LIEGE! WE NEED TO EVACUATE NOW! WE ARE UNDER ATTACK!>
<WHAT? BY WHO?>
BOOM!
<WHAT IS HAPPENING?>
WHOOM

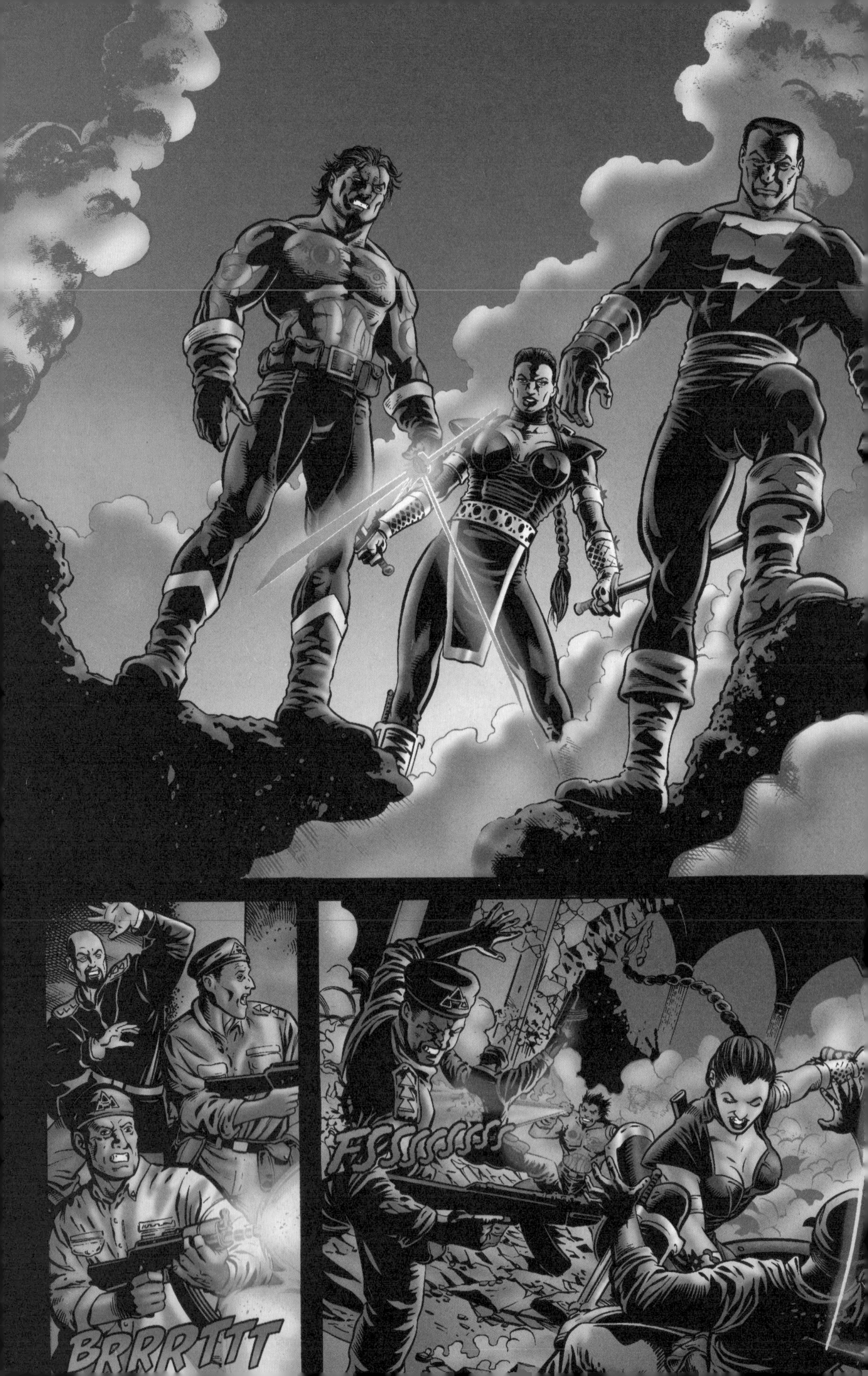
BRRRTTT
FSSSSSSSS

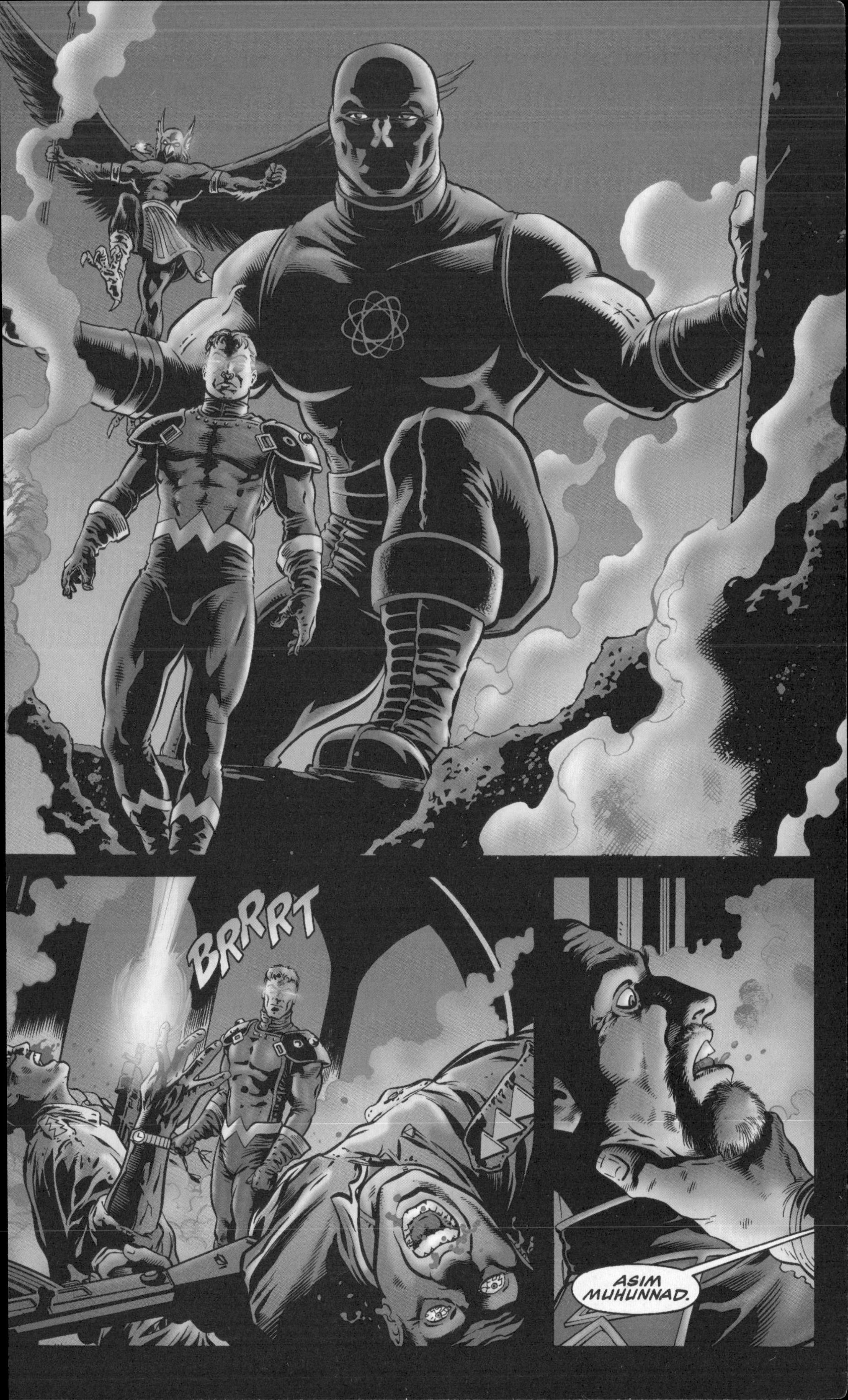
BRRRT
ASIM MUHUNNAD.

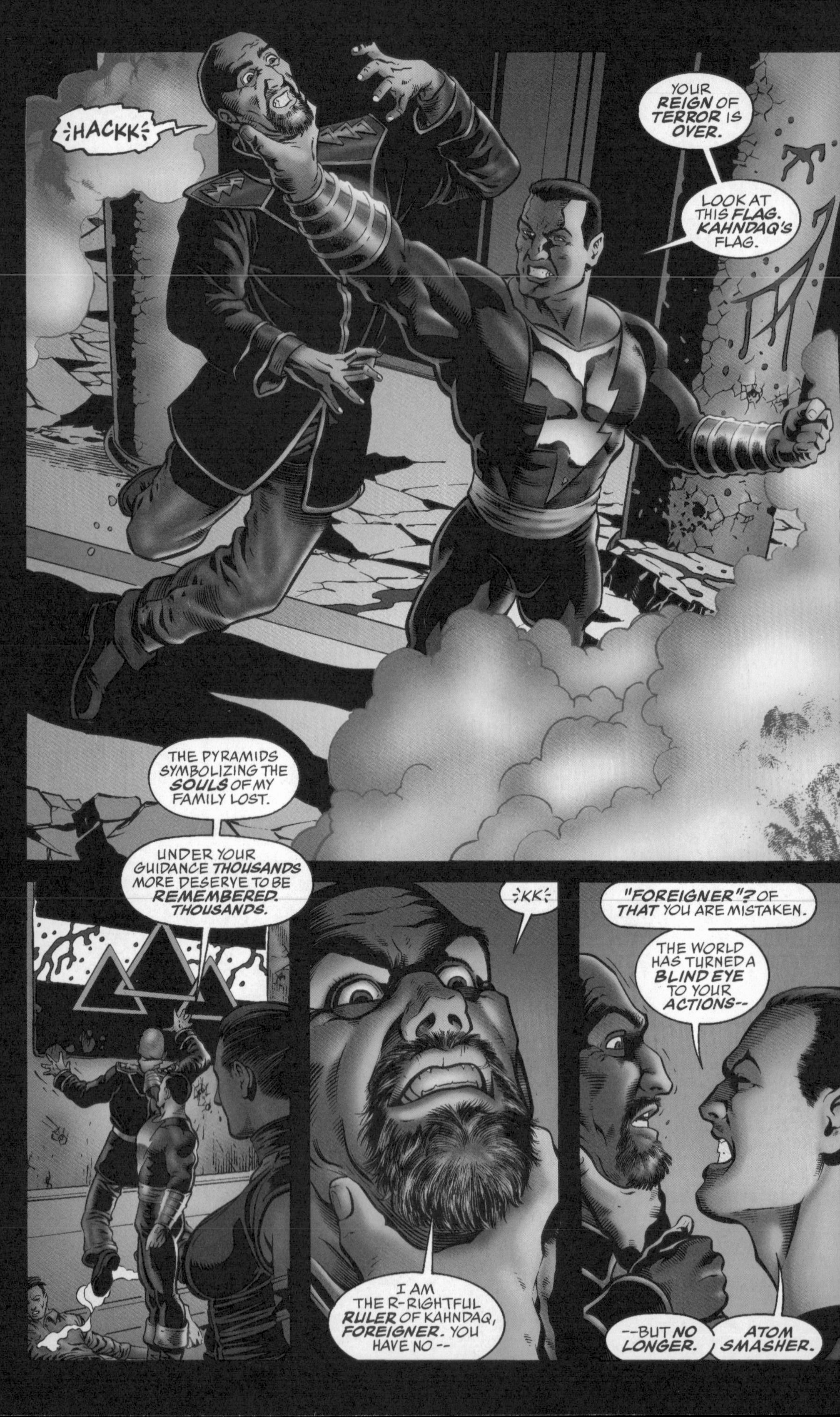

HACKK
YOUR REIGN OF TERROR IS OVER.
LOOK AT THIS FLAG. KAHNDAQ'S FLAG.
THE PYRAMIDS SYMBOLIZING THE SOULS OF MY FAMILY LOST.
UNDER YOUR GUIDANCE THOUSANDS MORE DESERVE TO BE REMEMBERED. THOUSANDS.
KK
I AM THE R-RIGHTFUL RULER OF KAHNDAQ, FOREIGNER. YOU HAVE NO --
"FOREIGNER"? OF THAT YOU ARE MISTAKEN.
THE WORLD HAS TURNED A BLIND EYE TO YOUR ACTIONS--
--BUT NO LONGER.
ATOM SMASHER.

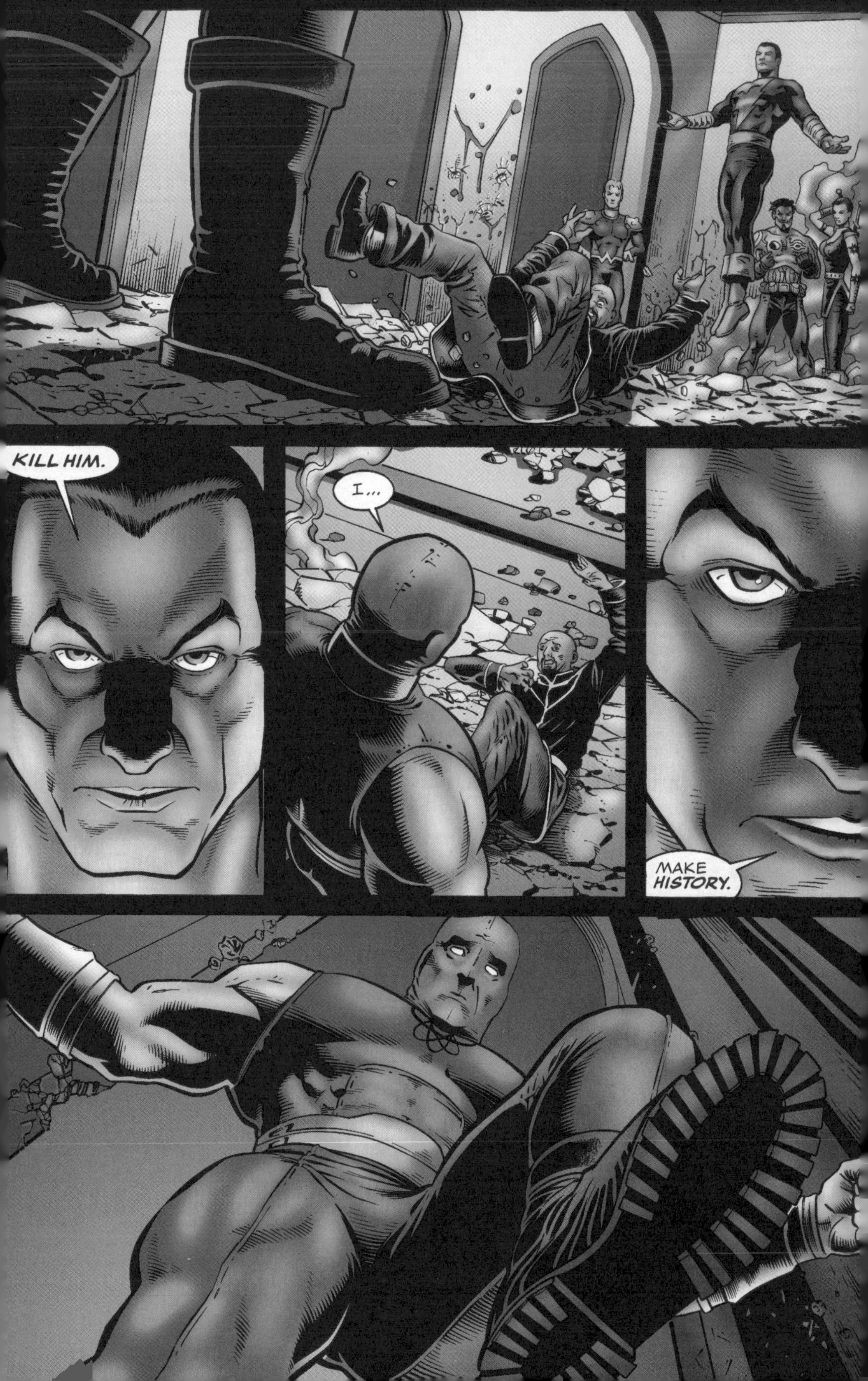
KILL HIM.
I...
MAKE HISTORY.

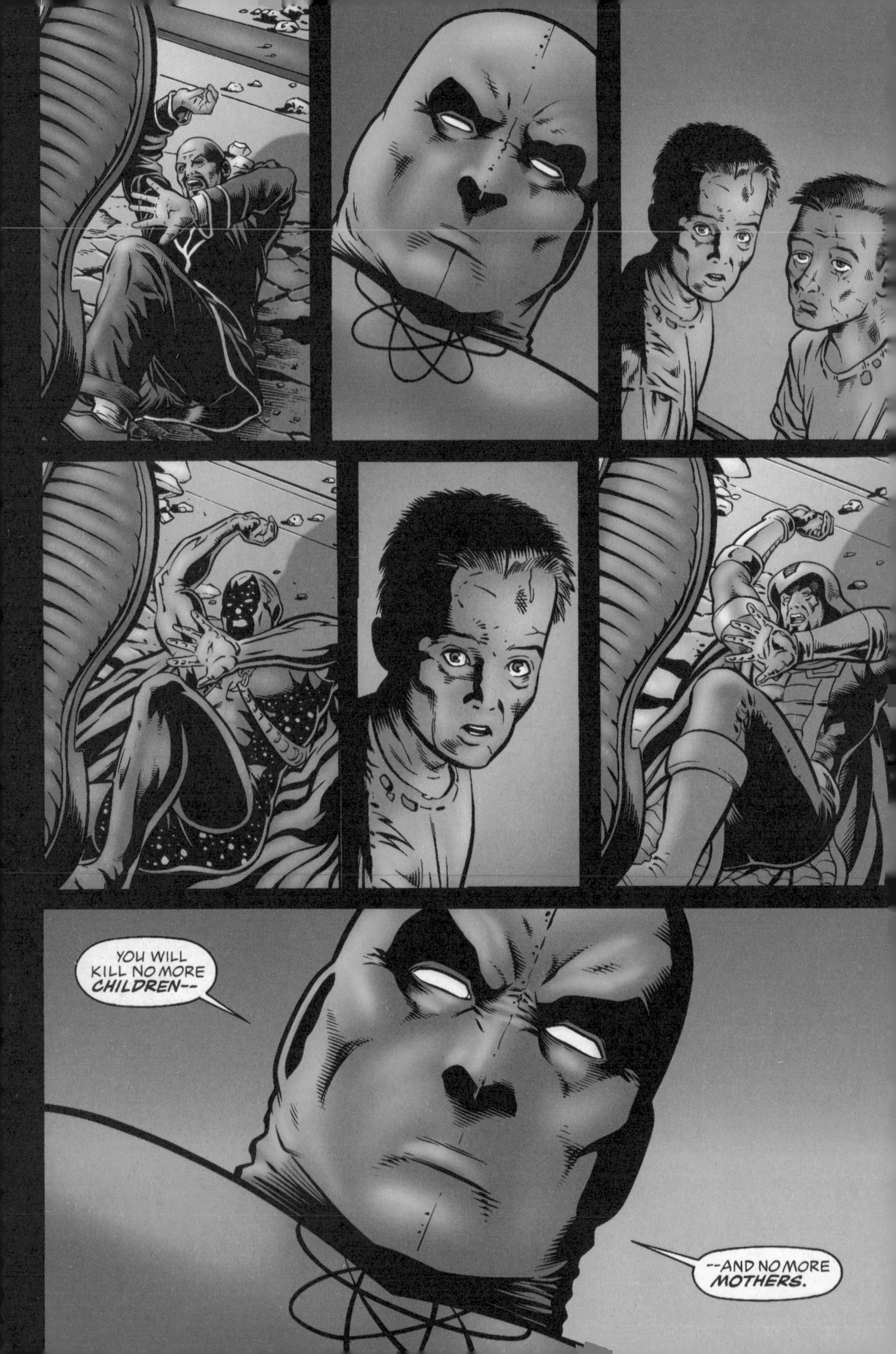
YOU WILL KILL NO MORE CHILDREN--
--AND NO MORE MOTHERS.

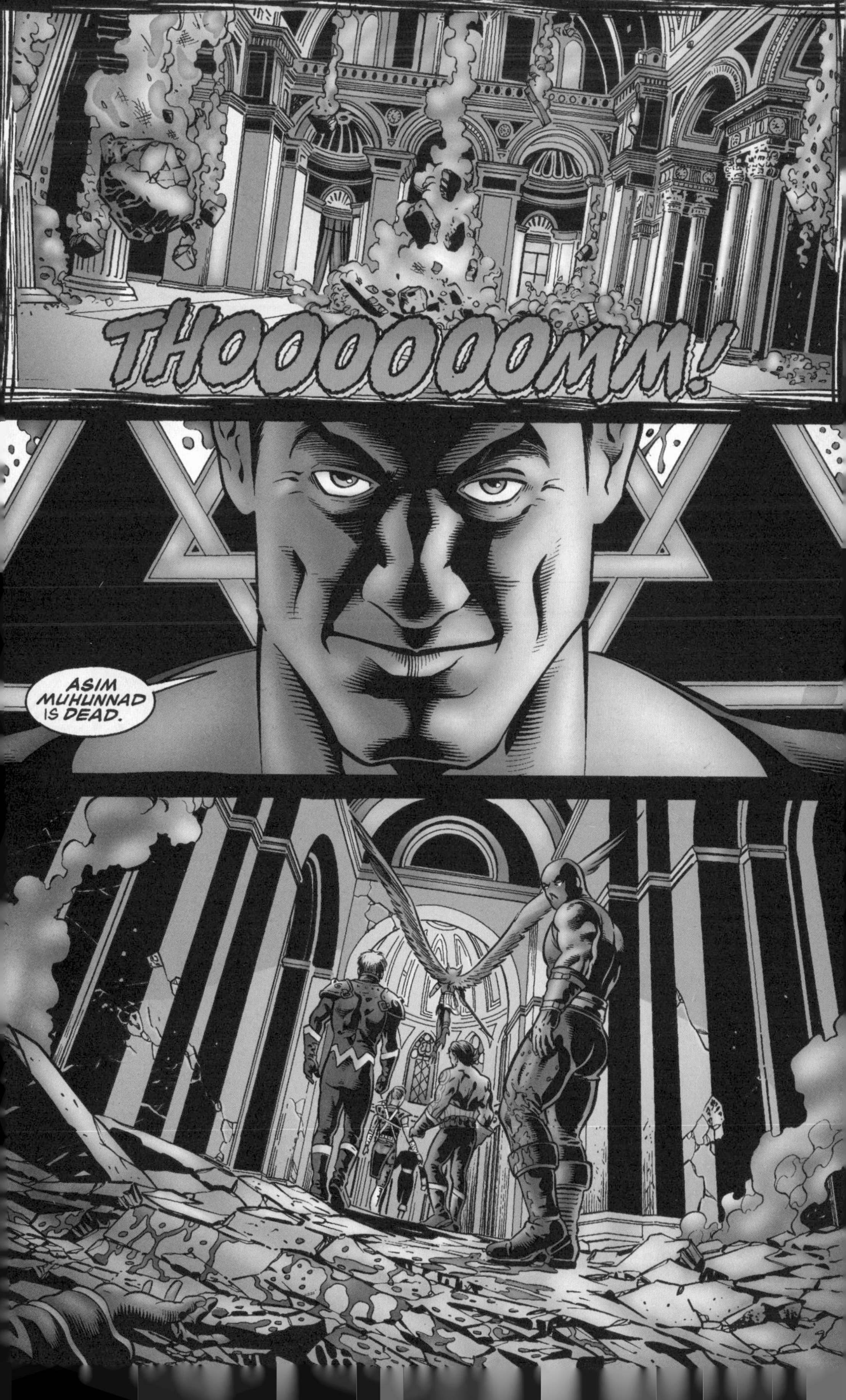
THOOOOOOMM!
ASIM MUHUNNAD IS DEAD.

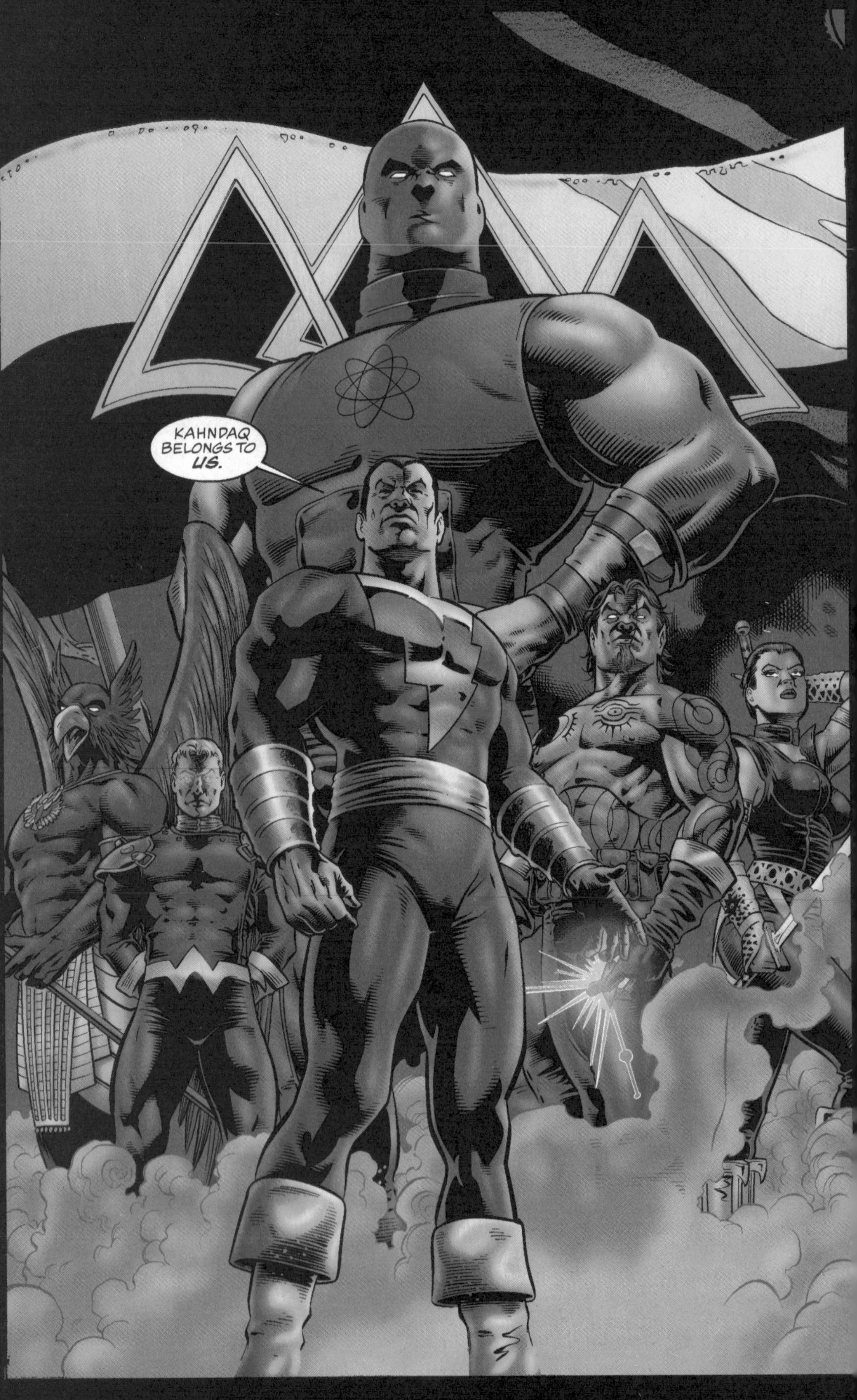
KAHNDAQ BELONGS TO US.

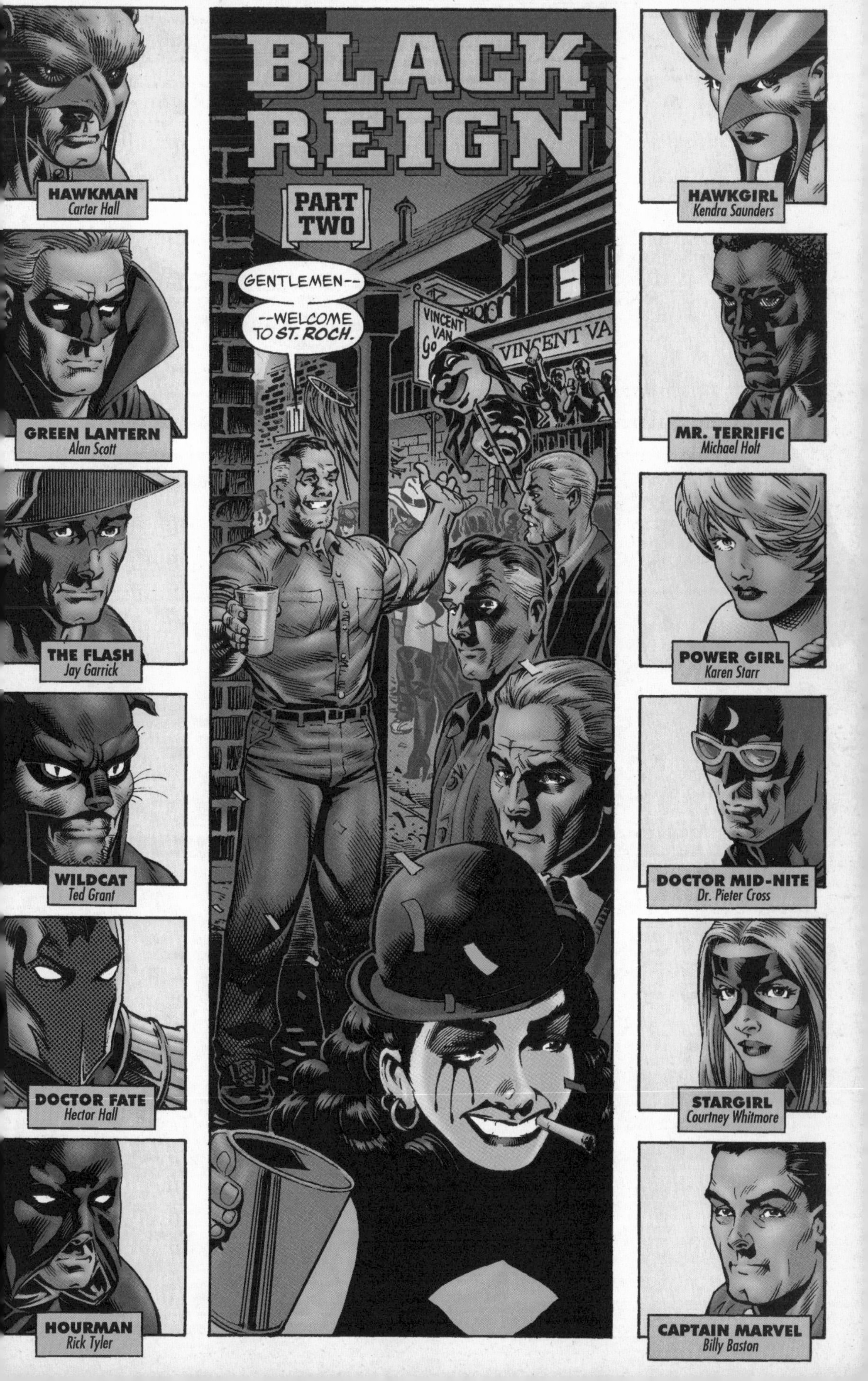
HAWKMAN
Carter Hall
GREEN LANTERN
Alan Scott
THE FLASH
Jay Garrick
WILDCAT
Ted Grant
DOCTOR FATE
Hector Hall
HOURMAN
Rick Tyler
BLACK REIGN
PART TWO
GENTLEMEN--
--WELCOME TO ST. ROCH.
VINCENT VAN Go
VINCENT VA
HAWKGIRL
Kendra Saunders
MR. TERRIFIC
Michael Holt
POWER GIRL
Karen Starr
DOCTOR MID-NITE
Dr. Pieter Cross
STARGIRL
Courtney Whitmore
CAPTAIN MARVEL
Billy Baston

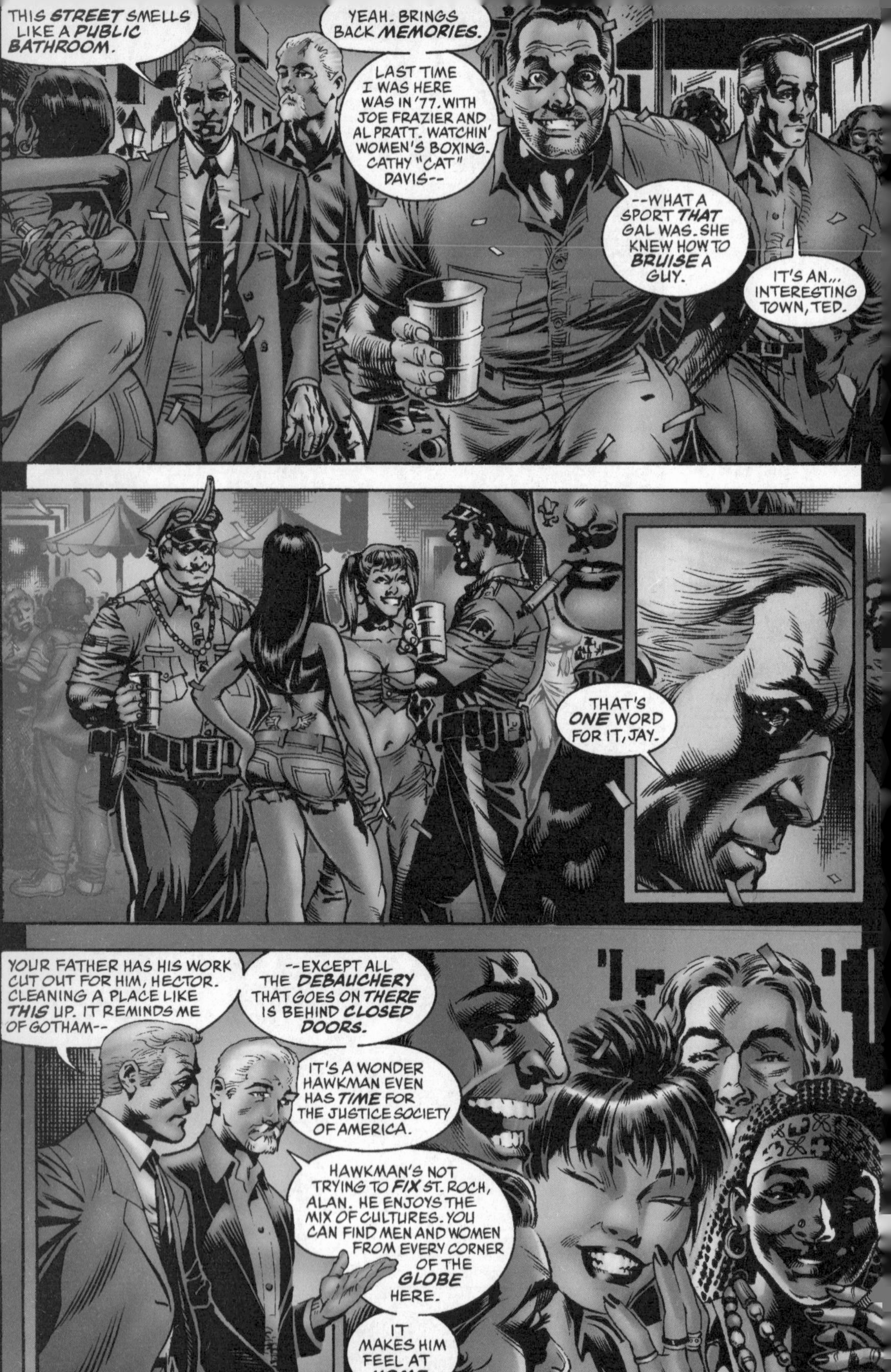
THIS STREET SMELLS LIKE A PUBLIC BATHROOM.
YEAH. BRINGS BACK MEMORIES.
LAST TIME I WAS HERE WAS IN '77. WITH JOE FRAZIER AND AL PRATT. WATCHIN' WOMEN'S BOXING. CATHY "CAT" DAVIS--
--WHAT A SPORT THAT GAL WAS. SHE KNEW HOW TO BRUISE A GUY.
IT'S AN... INTERESTING TOWN, TED.
THAT'S ONE WORD FOR IT, JAY.
YOUR FATHER HAS HIS WORK CUT OUT FOR HIM, HECTOR. CLEANING A PLACE LIKE THIS UP. IT REMINDS ME OF GOTHAM--
--EXCEPT ALL THE DEBAUCHERY THAT GOES ON THERE IS BEHIND CLOSED DOORS.
IT'S A WONDER HAWKMAN EVEN HAS TIME FOR THE JUSTICE SOCIETY OF AMERICA.
HAWKMAN'S NOT TRYING TO FIX ST. ROCH, ALAN. HE ENJOYS THE MIX OF CULTURES. YOU CAN FIND MEN AND WOMEN FROM EVERY CORNER OF THE GLOBE HERE.
IT MAKES HIM FEEL AT HOME.

REGARDLESS, IT WAS NICE OF CARTER TO INVITE US DOWN HERE FOR THE WEEKEND--

ACTUALLY, JAY, IT WAS KENDRA'S IDEA. MY FATHER'S BEEN A LITTLE DISTANT LATELY. SPENDING ALL HIS TIME *HUNTING*--

--NEGLECTING EVERYTHING ELSE.

KENDRA HAD TO USE THE LURE OF LONGTIME *FRIENDS* AND HIS FAVORITE *RESTAURANT* TO GET HIM TO AGREE TO *SIT DOWN*. SHE'S GOING TO SURPRISE HIM. HAVE A LITTLE *BIRTHDAY* CELEBRATION.

I DIDN'T KNOW IT *WAS* HIS BIRTHDAY.

IT'S NOT REALLY, JAY. KENDRA JUST FIGURES-- HE WAS BORN ON THIS DAY *SOMETIME*, SOMEWHERE--

--WHAT?

NO, I DON'T--

--ENOUGH, NABU. I TOLD YOU--

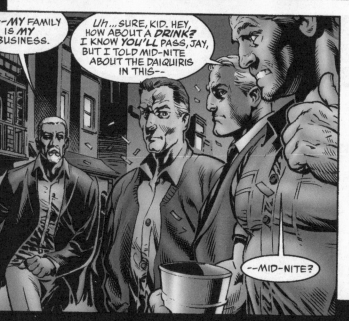

--MY FAMILY IS *MY* BUSINESS.

UH... SURE, KID. HEY, HOW ABOUT A *DRINK?* I KNOW *YOU'LL* PASS, JAY, BUT I TOLD MID-NITE ABOUT THE DAIQUIRIS IN THIS--

--MID-NITE?

DOC?

THOUGHT HE WAS RIGHT BE-HIND US.

I'M PLEASED TO HEAR YOU'RE PLAYING IT SAFE, REBECCA--

--BUT TWENTY DOLLARS TO LET SOMEONE INVADE YOU? HARM YOU? LET ME GIVE YOU SOME ADVICE.

YOU ONLY HAVE ONE BODY TO LIVE IN. YOU'RE ON THE PATH TO DESTROYING IT WITH THIS "PROFESSION." YOU NEED TO STOP.

IT'S NOT LIKE I REALLY HAVE A CHOICE.

YOU DO HAVE A CHOICE.

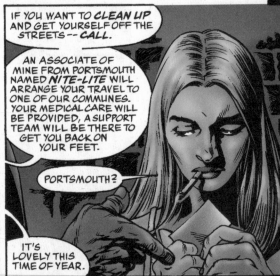

IF YOU WANT TO CLEAN UP AND GET YOURSELF OFF THE STREETS -- CALL.

AN ASSOCIATE OF MINE FROM PORTSMOUTH NAMED NITE-LITE WILL ARRANGE YOUR TRAVEL TO ONE OF OUR COMMUNES. YOUR MEDICAL CARE WILL BE PROVIDED, A SUPPORT TEAM WILL BE THERE TO GET YOU BACK ON YOUR FEET.

PORTSMOUTH?

IT'S LOVELY THIS TIME OF YEAR.

YOU JUST MET ME AND YOU WANT TO HELP? I DON'T UNDERSTAND... WHAT DO YOU WANT?

ONLY TO GIVE YOU AN OPTION.

BUT... I DON'T THINK I CAN LEAVE.

WHY NOT?

BECAUSE SHE'S WORKING FOR ME.

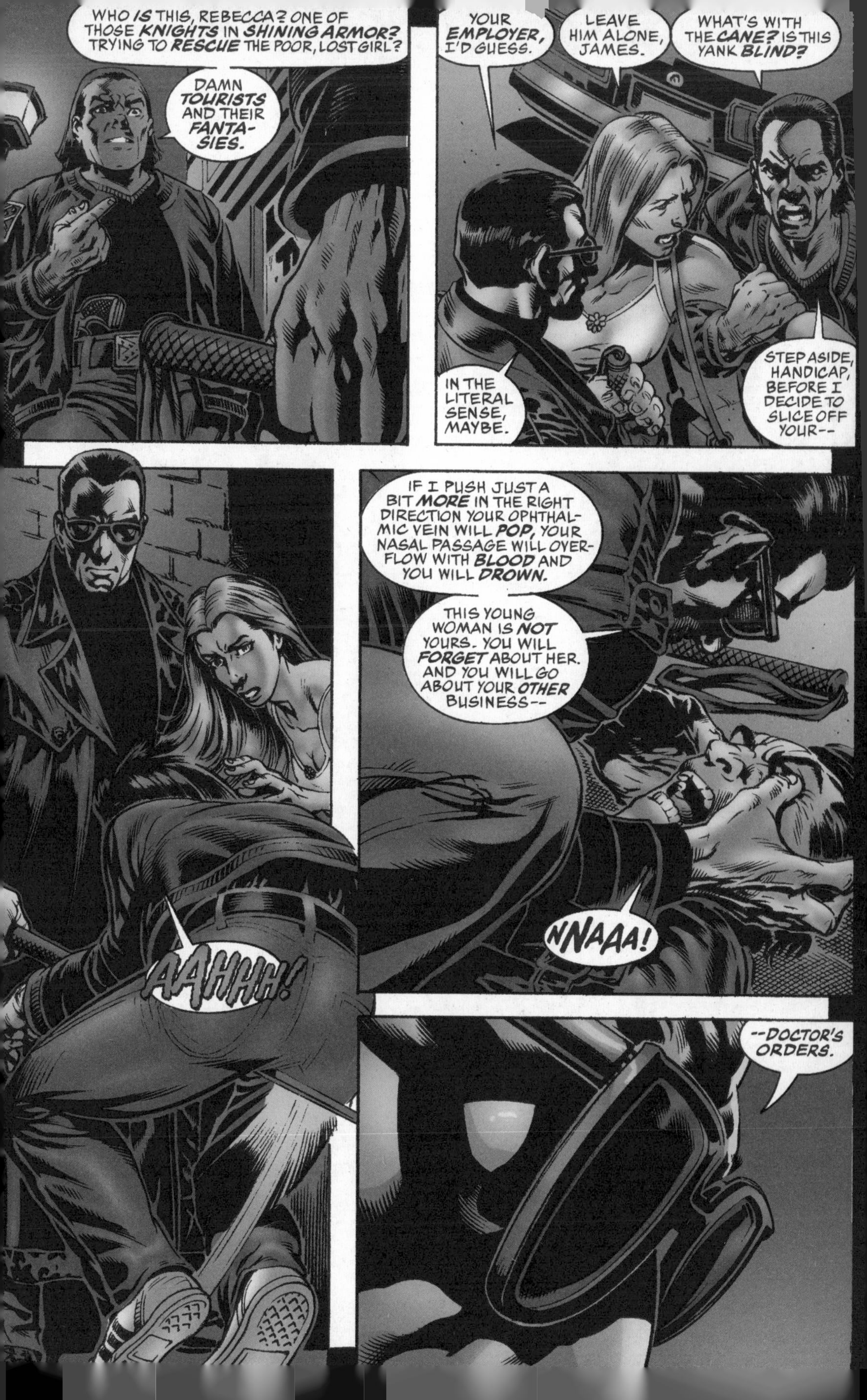
WHO IS THIS, REBECCA? ONE OF THOSE KNIGHTS IN SHINING ARMOR? TRYING TO RESCUE THE POOR, LOST GIRL?
DAMN TOURISTS AND THEIR FANTASIES.
YOUR EMPLOYER, I'D GUESS.
LEAVE HIM ALONE, JAMES.
WHAT'S WITH THE CANE? IS THIS YANK BLIND?
IN THE LITERAL SENSE, MAYBE.
STEP ASIDE, HANDICAP, BEFORE I DECIDE TO SLICE OFF YOUR--
AAHHH!
IF I PUSH JUST A BIT MORE IN THE RIGHT DIRECTION YOUR OPHTHALMIC VEIN WILL POP, YOUR NASAL PASSAGE WILL OVERFLOW WITH BLOOD AND YOU WILL DROWN.
THIS YOUNG WOMAN IS NOT YOURS. YOU WILL FORGET ABOUT HER. AND YOU WILL GO ABOUT YOUR OTHER BUSINESS--
NNAAA!
--DOCTOR'S ORDERS.

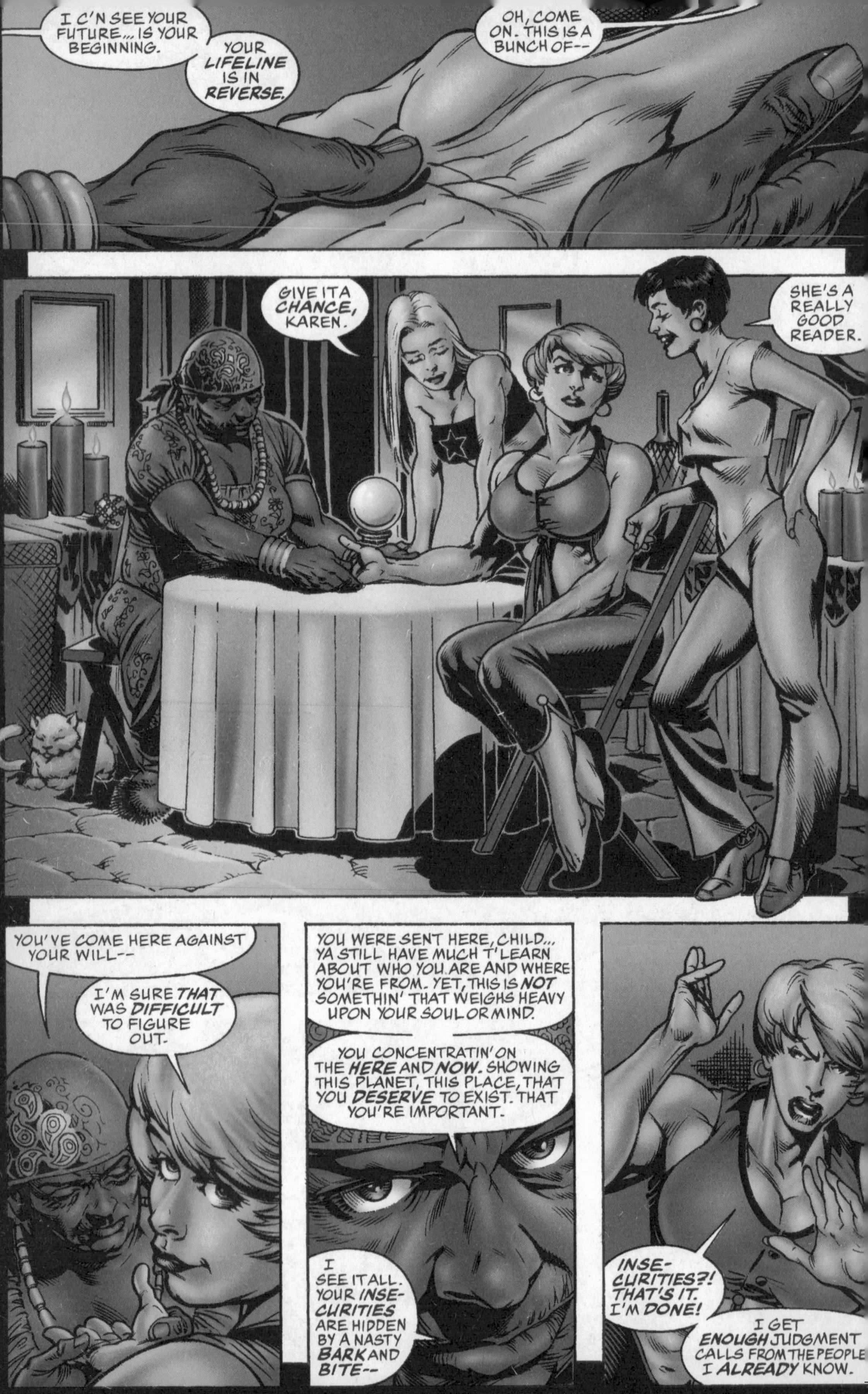

I C'N SEE YOUR FUTURE... IS YOUR BEGINNING.
YOUR LIFELINE IS IN REVERSE.
OH, COME ON. THIS IS A BUNCH OF--
GIVE IT A CHANCE, KAREN.
SHE'S A REALLY GOOD READER.
YOU'VE COME HERE AGAINST YOUR WILL--
I'M SURE THAT WAS DIFFICULT TO FIGURE OUT.
YOU WERE SENT HERE, CHILD... YA STILL HAVE MUCH T'LEARN ABOUT WHO YOU ARE AND WHERE YOU'RE FROM. YET, THIS IS NOT SOMETHIN' THAT WEIGHS HEAVY UPON YOUR SOUL OR MIND.
YOU CONCENTRATIN' ON THE HERE AND NOW. SHOWING THIS PLANET, THIS PLACE, THAT YOU DESERVE TO EXIST. THAT YOU'RE IMPORTANT.
I SEE IT ALL. YOUR INSECURITIES ARE HIDDEN BY A NASTY BARK AND BITE--
INSECURITIES?! THAT'S IT. I'M DONE!
I GET ENOUGH JUDGMENT CALLS FROM THE PEOPLE I ALREADY KNOW.

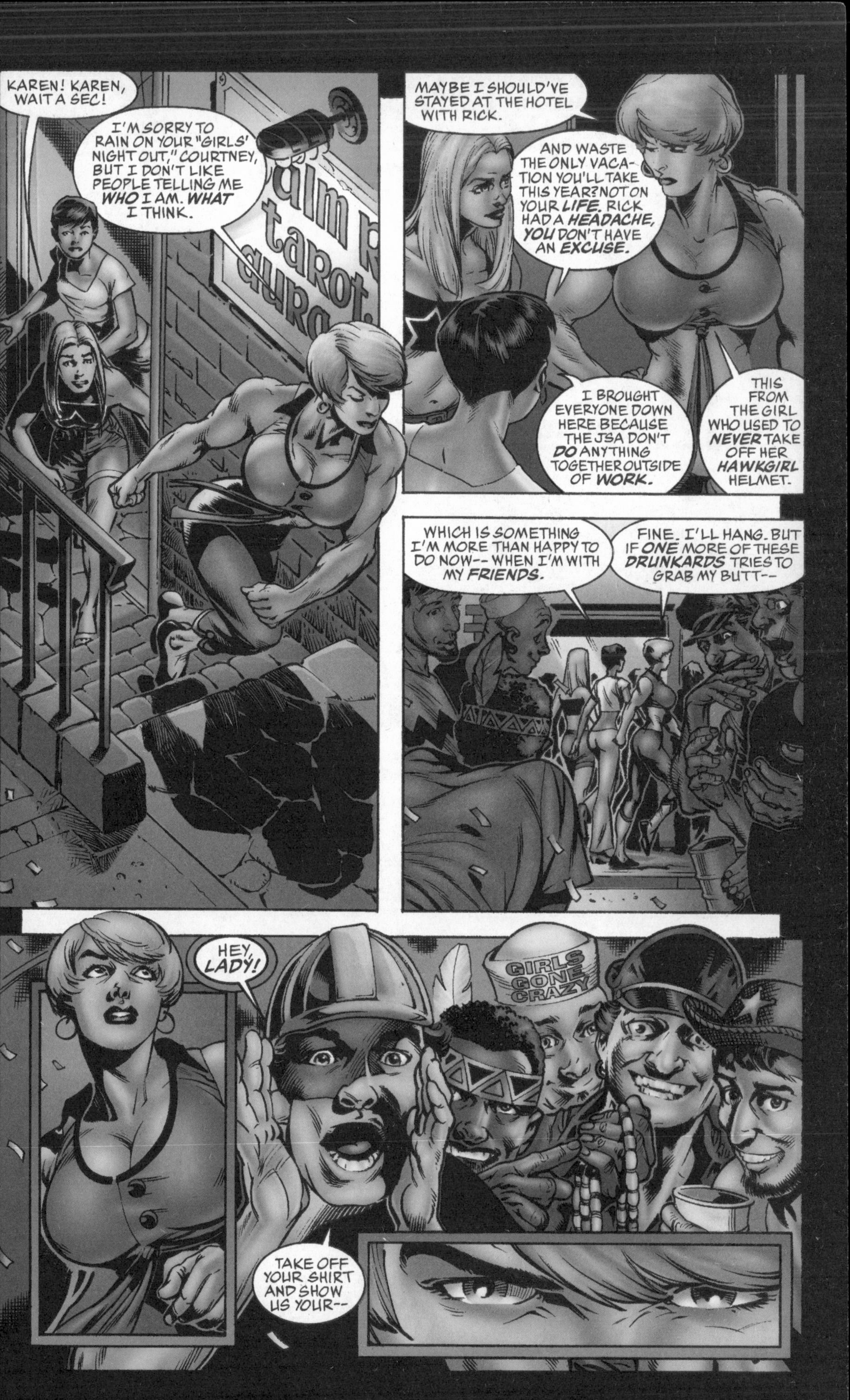
KAREN! KAREN, WAIT A SEC!
I'M SORRY TO RAIN ON YOUR "GIRLS' NIGHT OUT," COURTNEY, BUT I DON'T LIKE PEOPLE TELLING ME WHO I AM. WHAT I THINK.
MAYBE I SHOULD'VE STAYED AT THE HOTEL WITH RICK.
AND WASTE THE ONLY VACATION YOU'LL TAKE THIS YEAR? NOT ON YOUR LIFE. RICK HAD A HEADACHE, YOU DON'T HAVE AN EXCUSE.
I BROUGHT EVERYONE DOWN HERE BECAUSE THE JSA DON'T DO ANYTHING TOGETHER OUTSIDE OF WORK.
THIS FROM THE GIRL WHO USED TO NEVER TAKE OFF HER HAWKGIRL HELMET.
WHICH IS SOMETHING I'M MORE THAN HAPPY TO DO NOW-- WHEN I'M WITH MY FRIENDS.
FINE. I'LL HANG. BUT IF ONE MORE OF THESE DRUNKARDS TRIES TO GRAB MY BUTT--
HEY, LADY!
GIRLS GONE CRAZY
TAKE OFF YOUR SHIRT AND SHOW US YOUR--

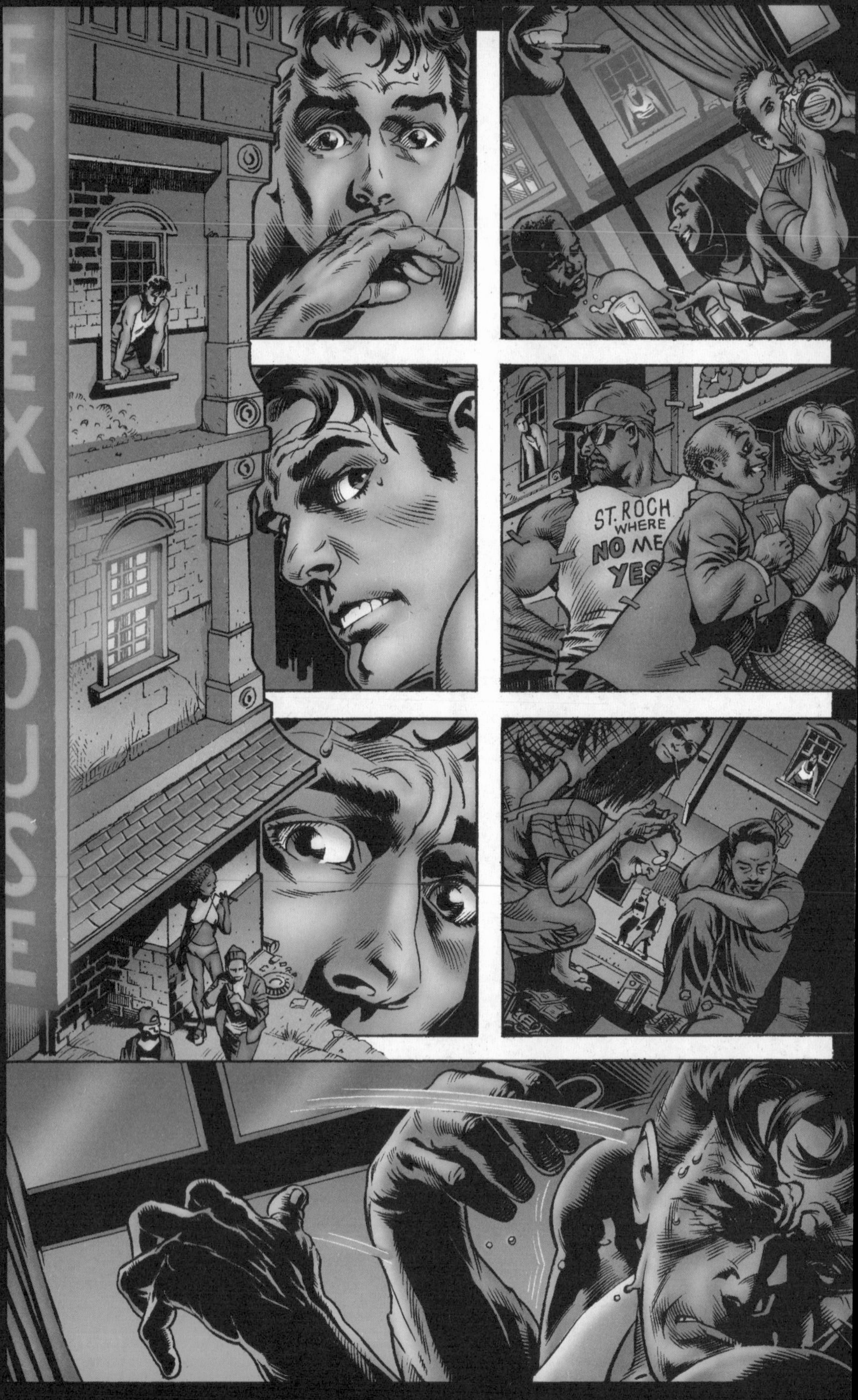
ESSEX HOUSE
ST. ROCH
WHERE
NO ME
YES

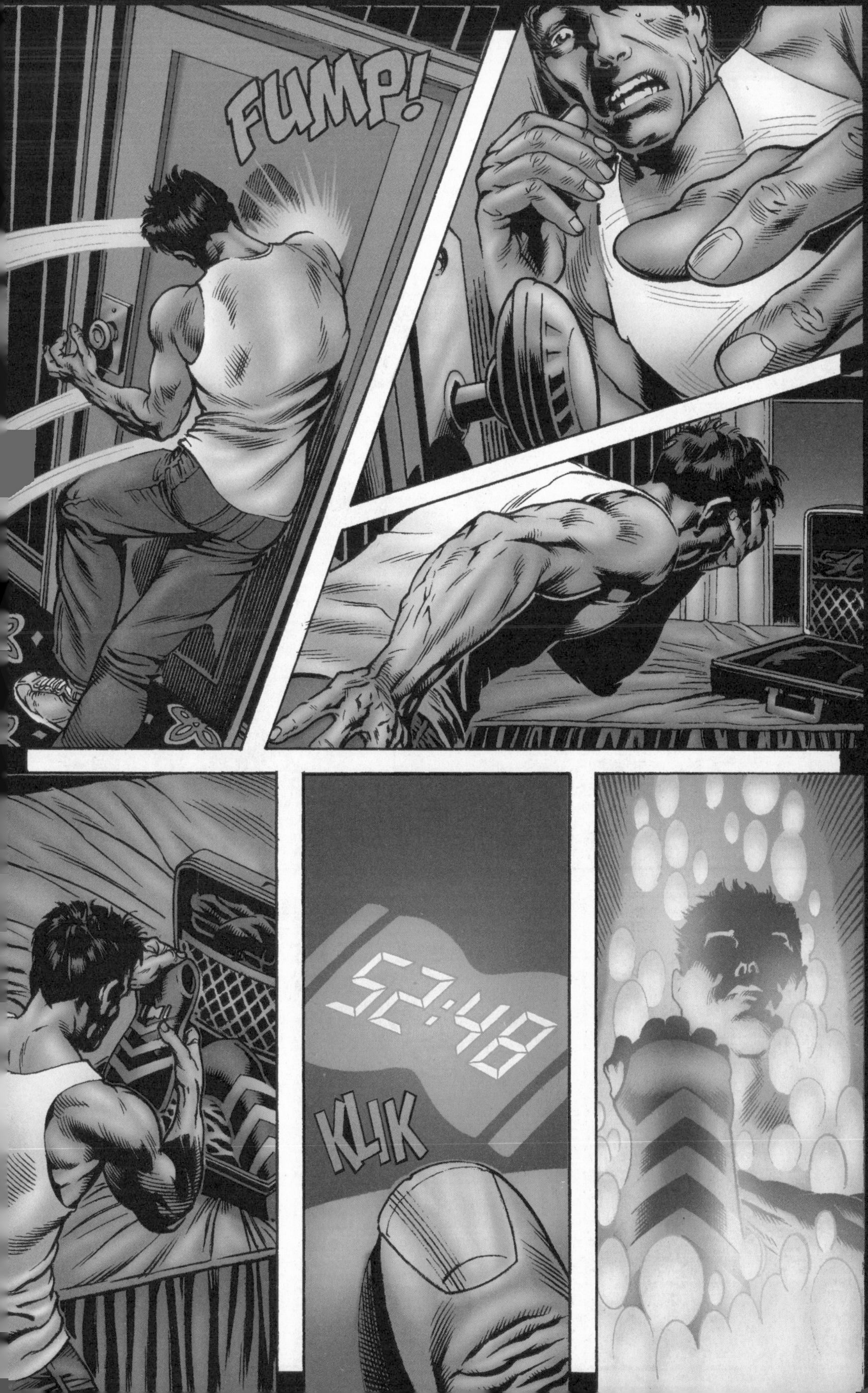
FUMP!
52:48
KLIK

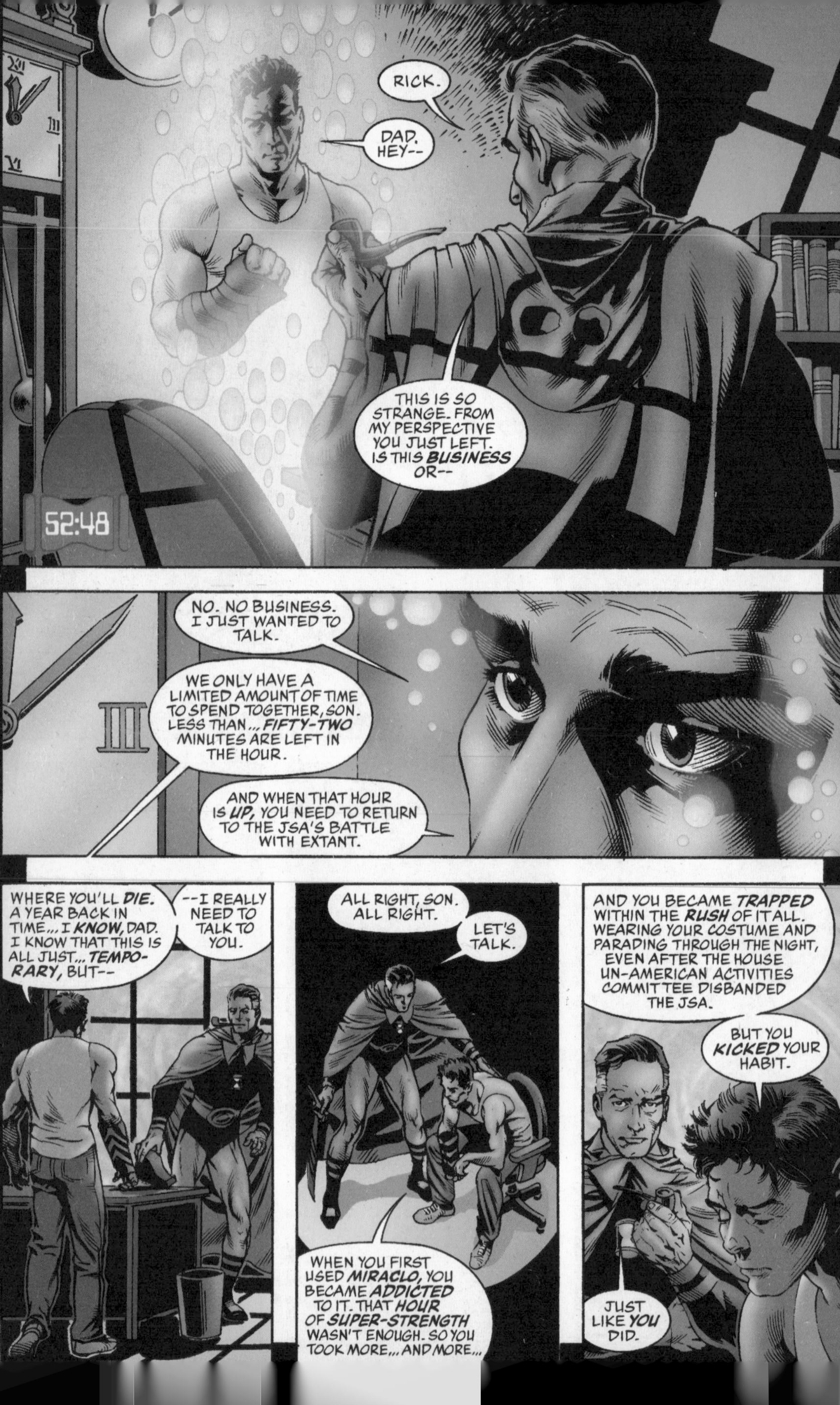
RICK.
DAD. HEY--
THIS IS SO STRANGE. FROM MY PERSPECTIVE YOU JUST LEFT. IS THIS BUSINESS OR--
52:48
NO. NO BUSINESS. I JUST WANTED TO TALK.
WE ONLY HAVE A LIMITED AMOUNT OF TIME TO SPEND TOGETHER, SON. LESS THAN... FIFTY-TWO MINUTES ARE LEFT IN THE HOUR.
AND WHEN THAT HOUR IS UP, YOU NEED TO RETURN TO THE JSA'S BATTLE WITH EXTANT.
WHERE YOU'LL DIE. A YEAR BACK IN TIME... I KNOW, DAD. I KNOW THAT THIS IS ALL JUST... TEMPORARY, BUT--
--I REALLY NEED TO TALK TO YOU.
ALL RIGHT, SON. ALL RIGHT.
LET'S TALK.
WHEN YOU FIRST USED MIRACLO, YOU BECAME ADDICTED TO IT. THAT HOUR OF SUPER-STRENGTH WASN'T ENOUGH. SO YOU TOOK MORE... AND MORE...
AND YOU BECAME TRAPPED WITHIN THE RUSH OF IT ALL. WEARING YOUR COSTUME AND PARADING THROUGH THE NIGHT, EVEN AFTER THE HOUSE UN-AMERICAN ACTIVITIES COMMITTEE DISBANDED THE JSA.
BUT YOU KICKED YOUR HABIT.
JUST LIKE YOU DID.

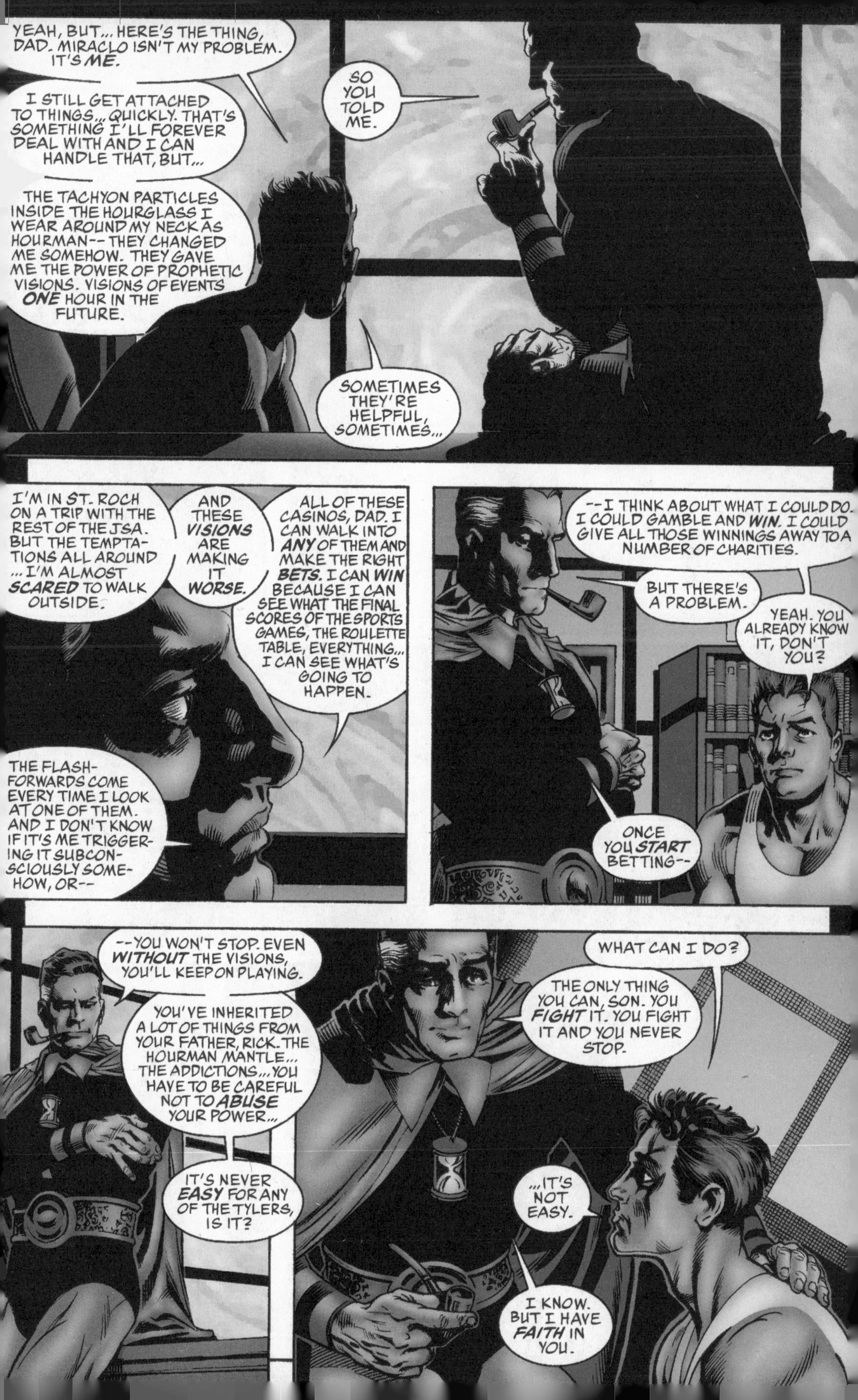
YEAH, BUT... HERE'S THE THING, DAD. MIRACLO ISN'T MY PROBLEM. IT'S ME.
I STILL GET ATTACHED TO THINGS... QUICKLY. THAT'S SOMETHING I'LL FOREVER DEAL WITH AND I CAN HANDLE THAT, BUT...
THE TACHYON PARTICLES INSIDE THE HOURGLASS I WEAR AROUND MY NECK AS HOURMAN-- THEY CHANGED ME SOMEHOW. THEY GAVE ME THE POWER OF PROPHETIC VISIONS. VISIONS OF EVENTS ONE HOUR IN THE FUTURE.
SO YOU TOLD ME.
SOMETIMES THEY'RE HELPFUL, SOMETIMES...
I'M IN ST. ROCH ON A TRIP WITH THE REST OF THE JSA. BUT THE TEMPTATIONS ALL AROUND ... I'M ALMOST SCARED TO WALK OUTSIDE.
AND THESE VISIONS ARE MAKING IT WORSE.
ALL OF THESE CASINOS, DAD. I CAN WALK INTO ANY OF THEM AND MAKE THE RIGHT BETS. I CAN WIN BECAUSE I CAN SEE WHAT THE FINAL SCORES OF THE SPORTS GAMES, THE ROULETTE TABLE, EVERYTHING... I CAN SEE WHAT'S GOING TO HAPPEN.
THE FLASH-FORWARDS COME EVERY TIME I LOOK AT ONE OF THEM. AND I DON'T KNOW IF IT'S ME TRIGGERING IT SUBCONSCIOUSLY SOMEHOW, OR--
--I THINK ABOUT WHAT I COULD DO. I COULD GAMBLE AND WIN. I COULD GIVE ALL THOSE WINNINGS AWAY TO A NUMBER OF CHARITIES.
BUT THERE'S A PROBLEM.
YEAH. YOU ALREADY KNOW IT, DON'T YOU?
ONCE YOU START BETTING--
--YOU WON'T STOP. EVEN WITHOUT THE VISIONS, YOU'LL KEEP ON PLAYING.
YOU'VE INHERITED A LOT OF THINGS FROM YOUR FATHER, RICK. THE HOURMAN MANTLE... THE ADDICTIONS... YOU HAVE TO BE CAREFUL NOT TO ABUSE YOUR POWER...
IT'S NEVER EASY FOR ANY OF THE TYLERS, IS IT?
WHAT CAN I DO?
THE ONLY THING YOU CAN, SON. YOU FIGHT IT. YOU FIGHT IT AND YOU NEVER STOP.
...IT'S NOT EASY.
I KNOW. BUT I HAVE FAITH IN YOU.

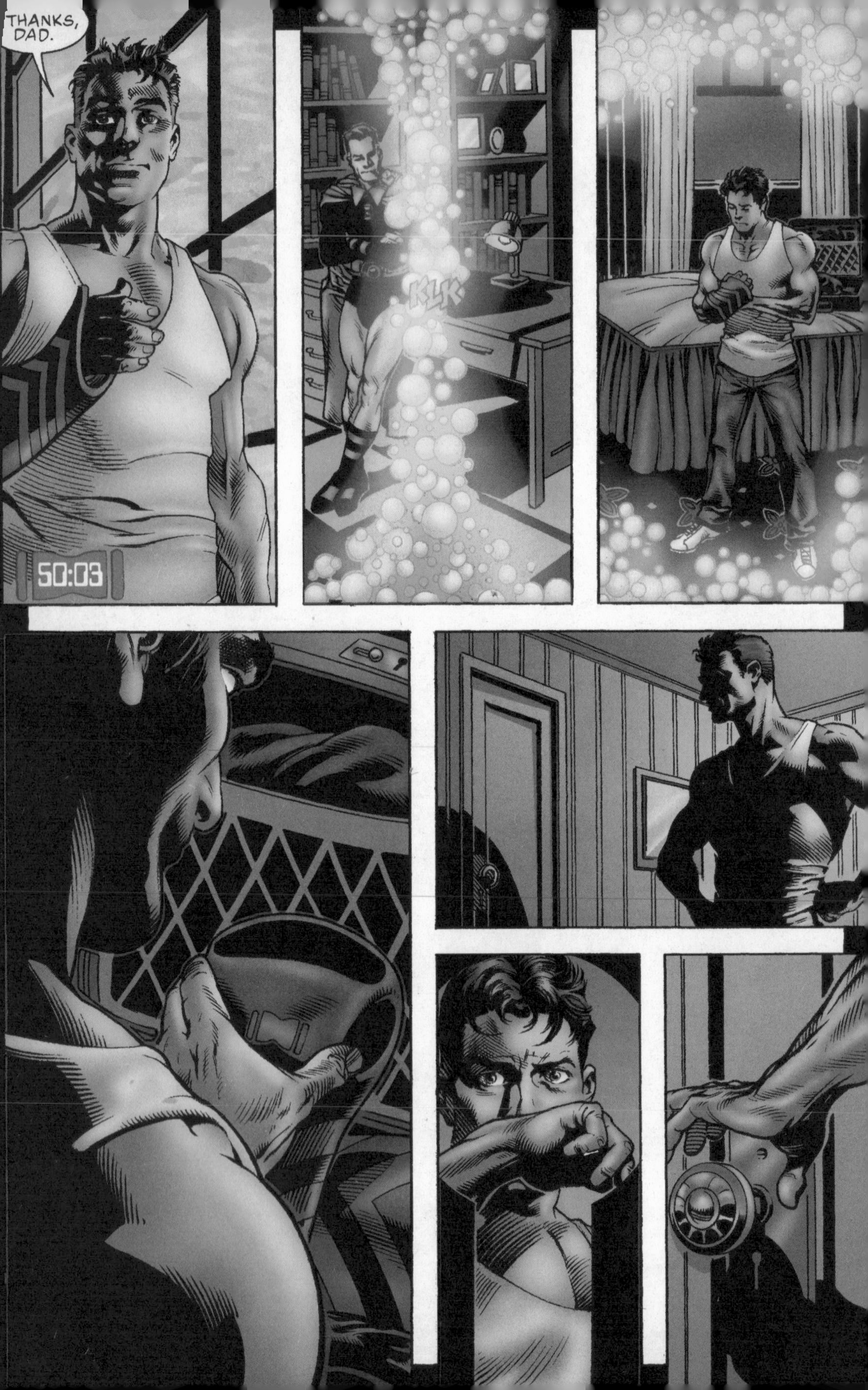
THANKS, DAD.
50:03
KLK

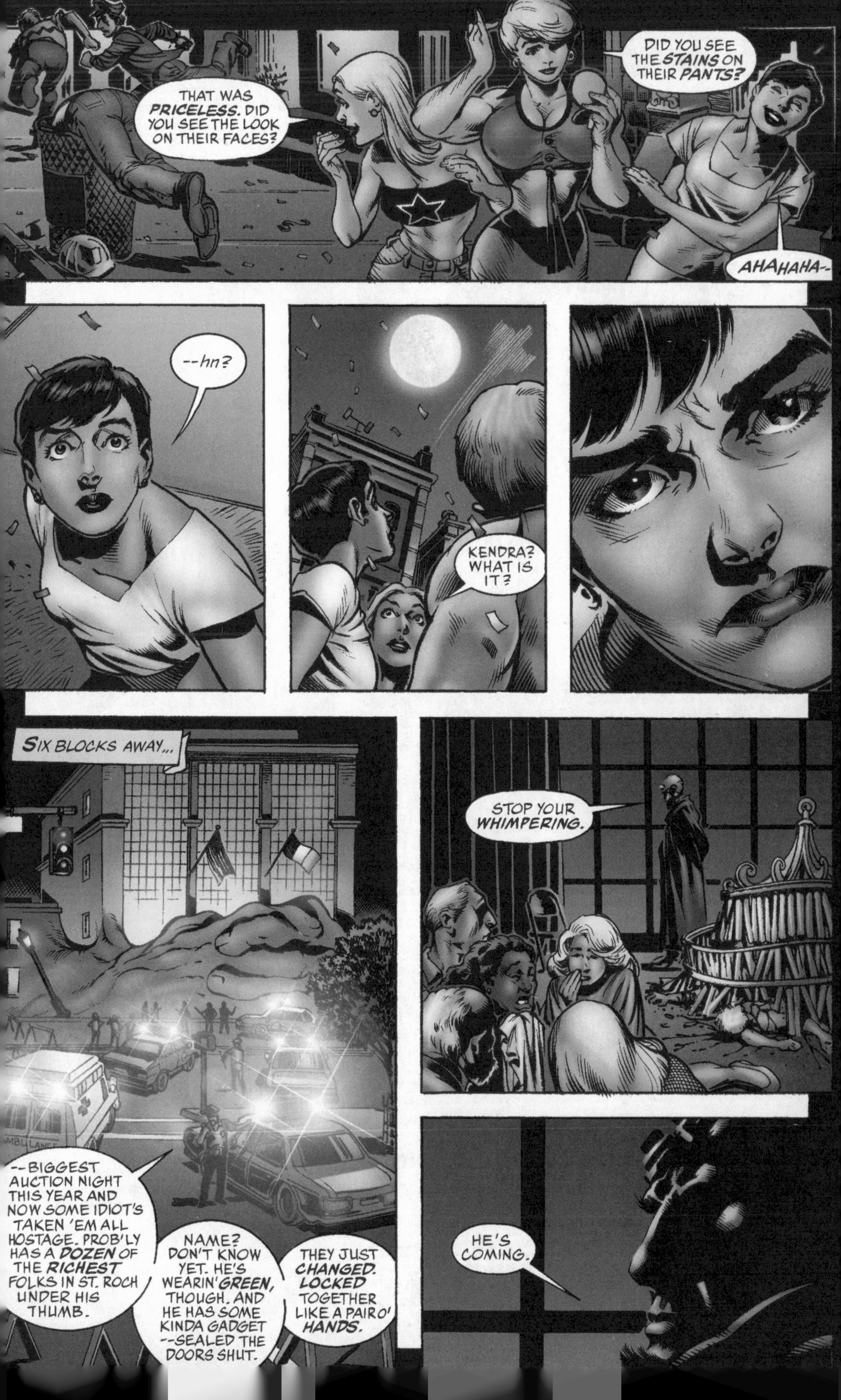
THAT WAS PRICELESS. DID YOU SEE THE LOOK ON THEIR FACES?
DID YOU SEE THE STAINS ON THEIR PANTS?
AHAHAHA--
--hn?
KENDRA? WHAT IS IT?
SIX BLOCKS AWAY...
--BIGGEST AUCTION NIGHT THIS YEAR AND NOW SOME IDIOT'S TAKEN 'EM ALL HOSTAGE. PROB'LY HAS A DOZEN OF THE RICHEST FOLKS IN ST. ROCH UNDER HIS THUMB.
NAME? DON'T KNOW YET. HE'S WEARIN' GREEN, THOUGH. AND HE HAS SOME KINDA GADGET --SEALED THE DOORS SHUT.
THEY JUST CHANGED. LOCKED TOGETHER LIKE A PAIR O' HANDS.
STOP YOUR WHIMPERING.
HE'S COMING.

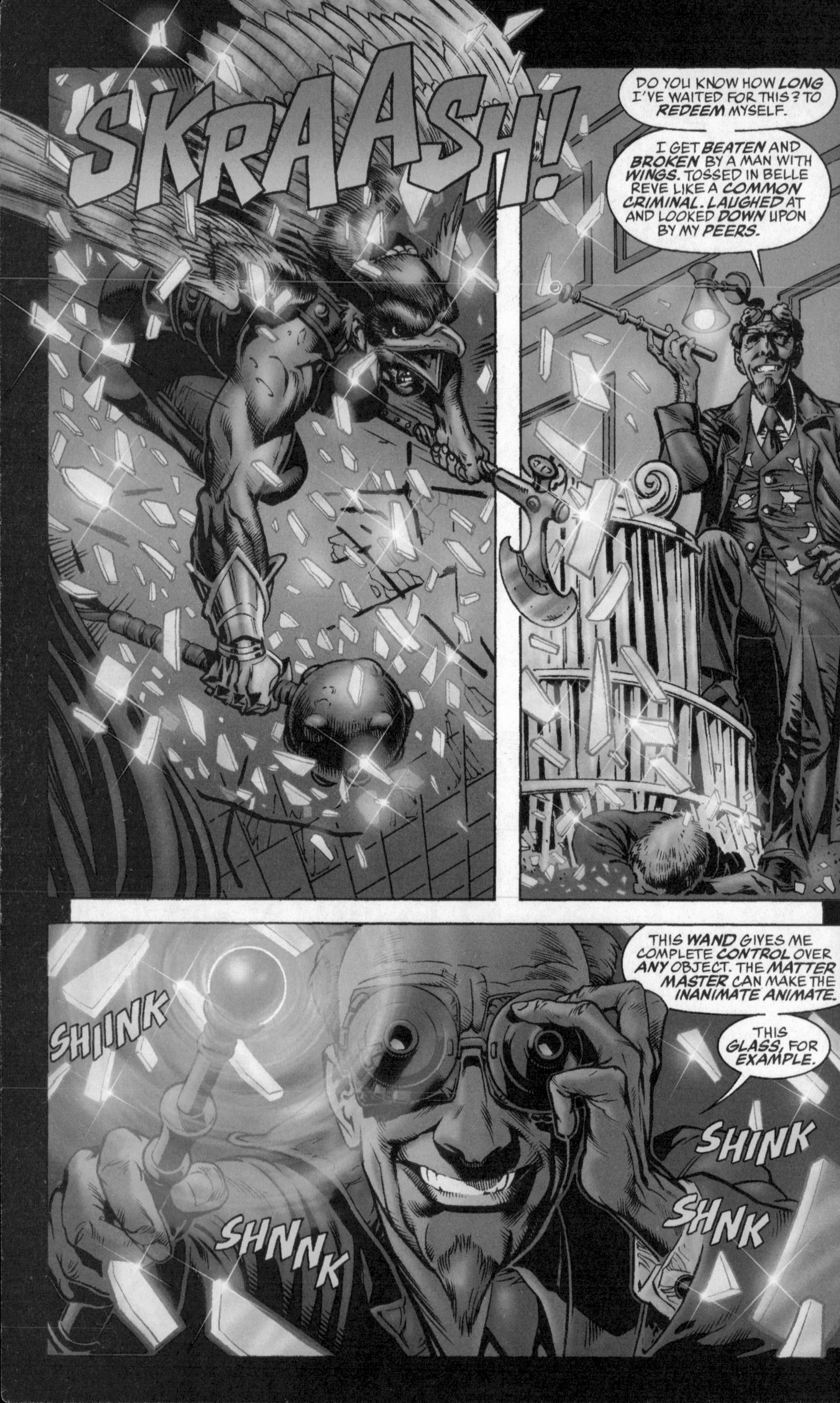
SKRAASH!
DO YOU KNOW HOW LONG I'VE WAITED FOR THIS? TO REDEEM MYSELF.
I GET BEATEN AND BROKEN BY A MAN WITH WINGS. TOSSED IN BELLE REVE LIKE A COMMON CRIMINAL. LAUGHED AT AND LOOKED DOWN UPON BY MY PEERS.
THIS WAND GIVES ME COMPLETE CONTROL OVER ANY OBJECT. THE MATTER MASTER CAN MAKE THE INANIMATE ANIMATE.
THIS GLASS, FOR EXAMPLE.
SHIINK
SHINK
SHNK
SHNNK

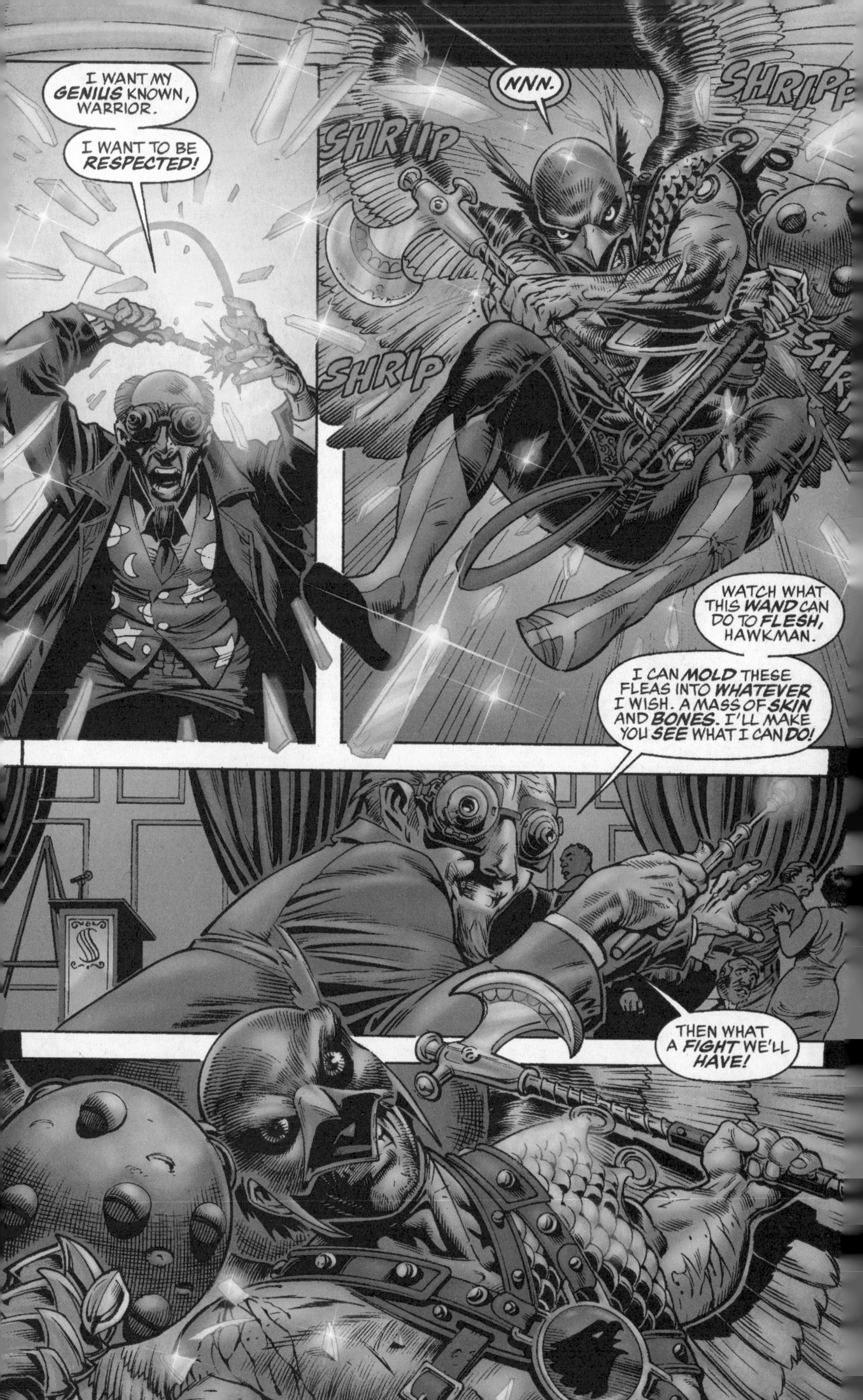
I WANT MY GENIUS KNOWN, WARRIOR.
I WANT TO BE RESPECTED!
NNN.
SHRIIP
SHRIPP
SHRIP
SHRI
WATCH WHAT THIS WAND CAN DO TO FLESH, HAWKMAN.
I CAN MOLD THESE FLEAS INTO WHATEVER I WISH. A MASS OF SKIN AND BONES. I'LL MAKE YOU SEE WHAT I CAN DO!
THEN WHAT A FIGHT WE'LL HAVE!

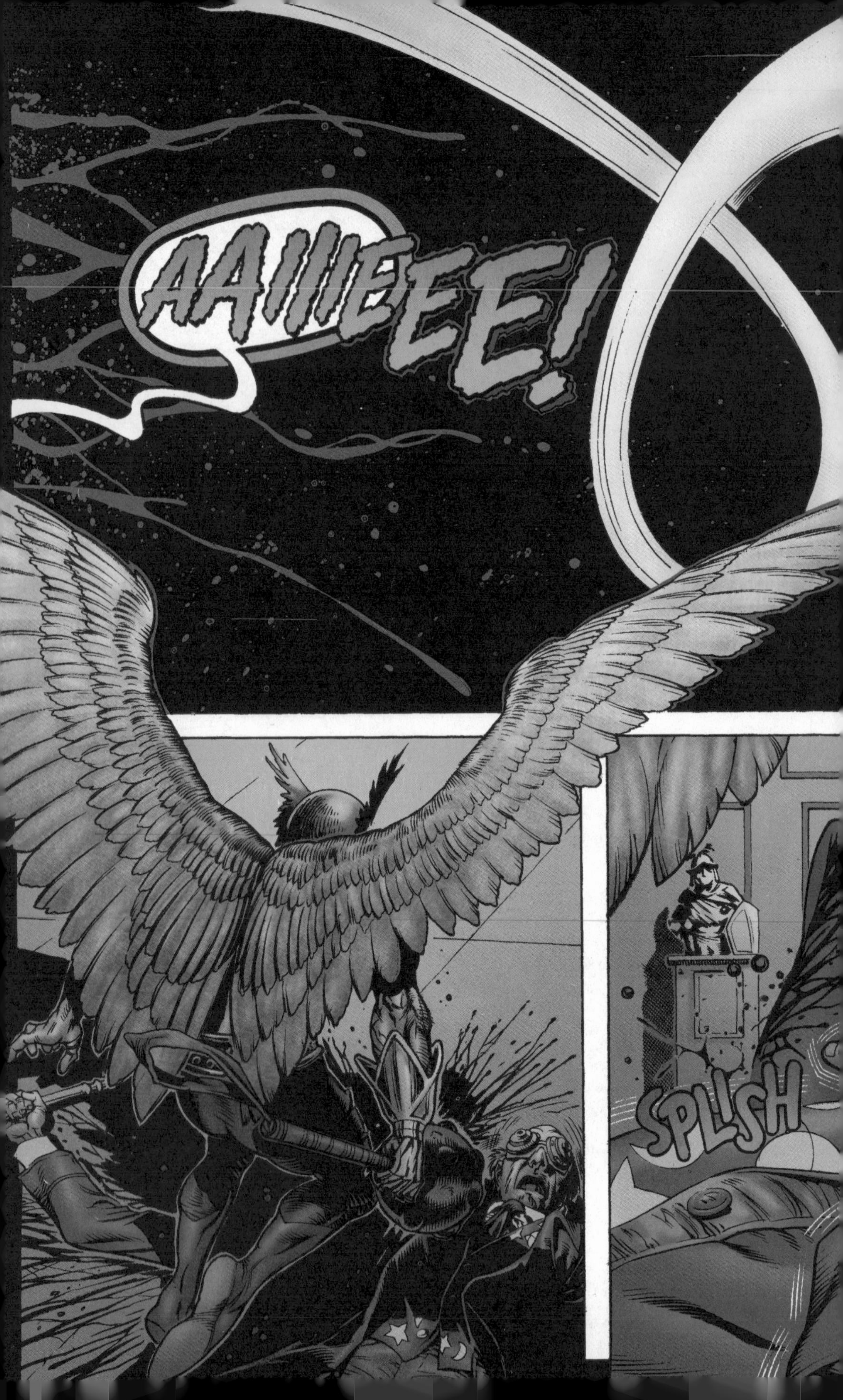
AAIIIEEEE!
SPLISH

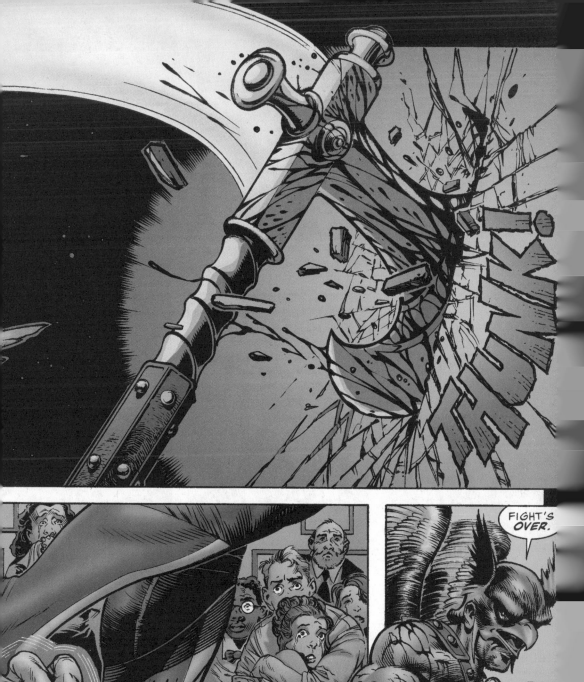

THUNK!

PLISH SPLISH

FIGHT'S OVER.

SHONK

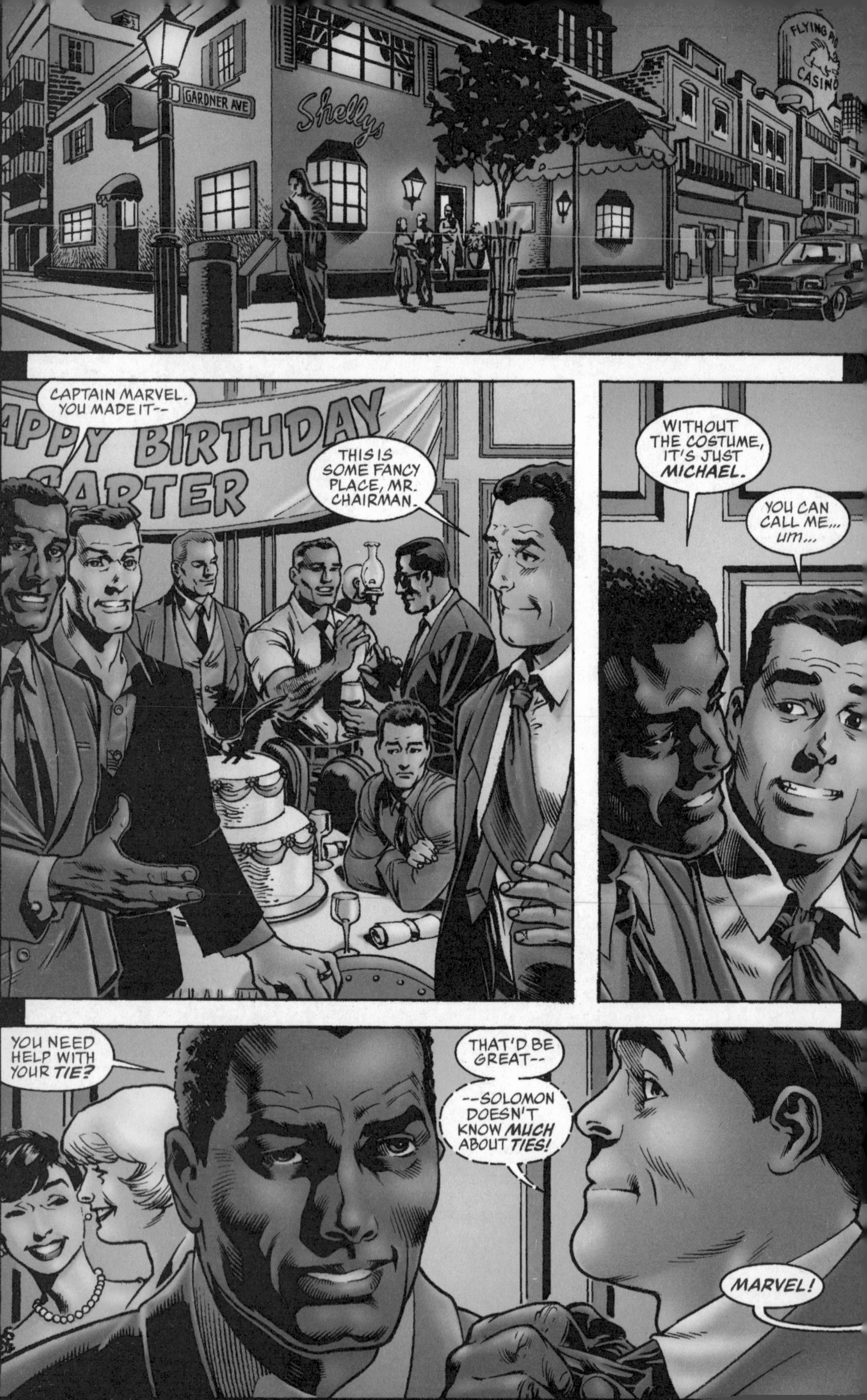
GARDNER AVE
Shellys
FLYING PO
CASINO
APPY BIRTHDAY CARTER
CAPTAIN MARVEL. YOU MADE IT--
THIS IS SOME FANCY PLACE, MR. CHAIRMAN.
WITHOUT THE COSTUME, IT'S JUST MICHAEL.
YOU CAN CALL ME... UM...
YOU NEED HELP WITH YOUR TIE?
THAT'D BE GREAT--
--SOLOMON DOESN'T KNOW MUCH ABOUT TIES!
MARVEL!

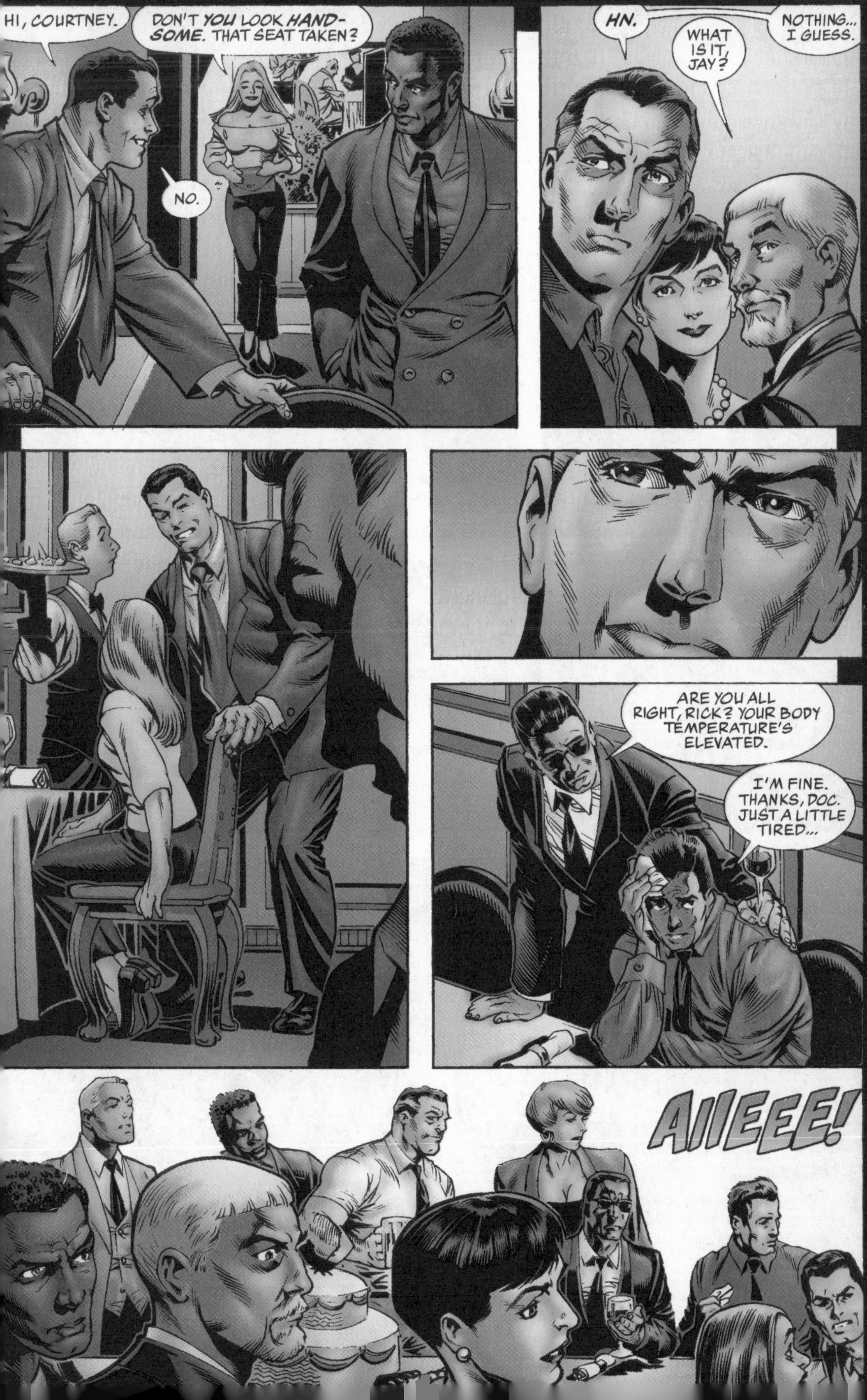
HI, COURTNEY.
DON'T YOU LOOK HAND-SOME. THAT SEAT TAKEN?
NO.
HN.
WHAT IS IT, JAY?
NOTHING... I GUESS.
ARE YOU ALL RIGHT, RICK? YOUR BODY TEMPERATURE'S ELEVATED.
I'M FINE. THANKS, DOC. JUST A LITTLE TIRED...
AIIEEE!

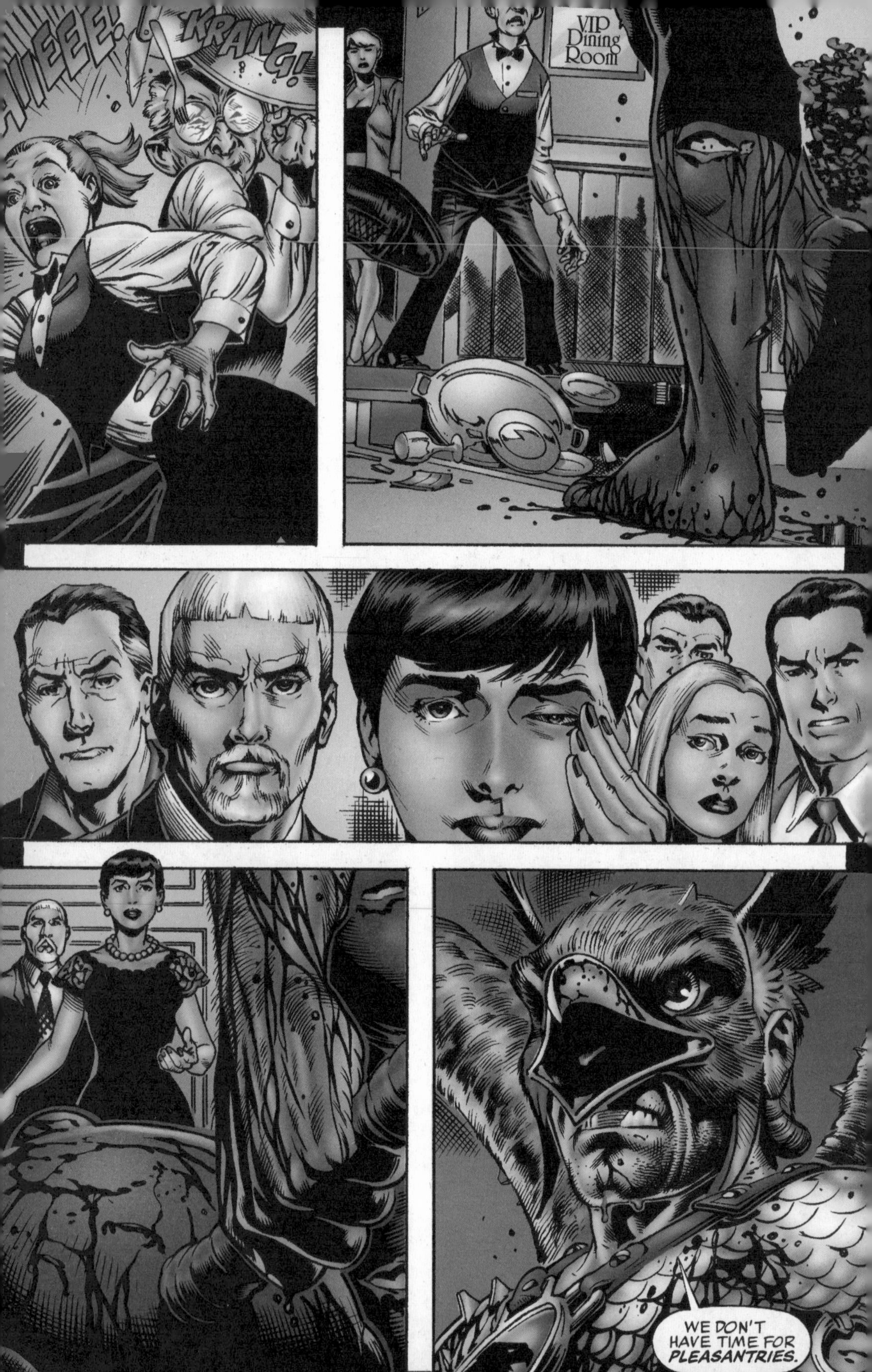
IIEEE!
KRANG!
VIP Dining Room
WE DON'T HAVE TIME FOR PLEASANTRIES.

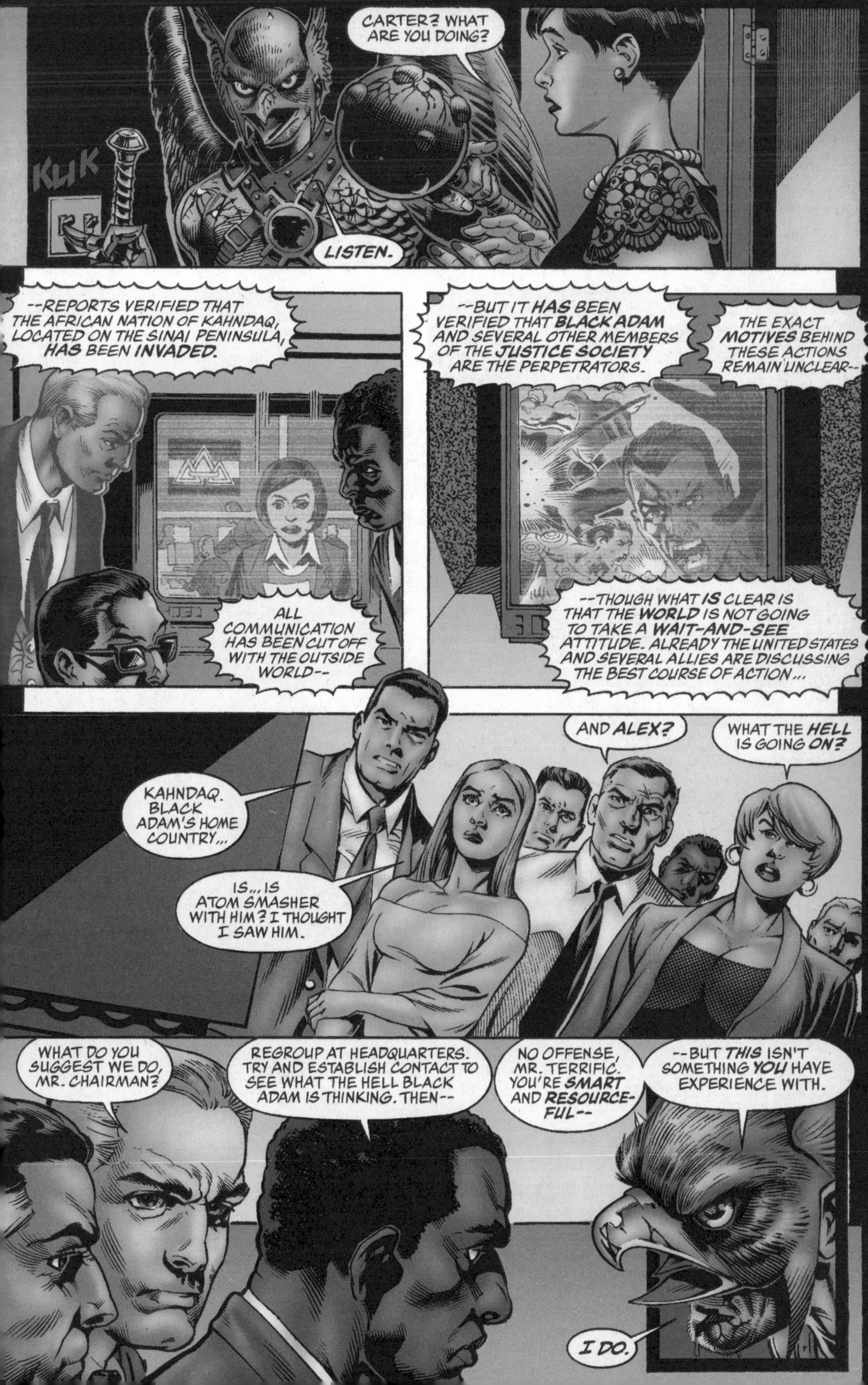
CARTER? WHAT ARE YOU DOING?
KLIK
LISTEN.
--REPORTS VERIFIED THAT THE AFRICAN NATION OF KAHNDAQ, LOCATED ON THE SINAI PENINSULA, HAS BEEN INVADED.
ALL COMMUNICATION HAS BEEN CUT OFF WITH THE OUTSIDE WORLD--
--BUT IT HAS BEEN VERIFIED THAT BLACK ADAM AND SEVERAL OTHER MEMBERS OF THE JUSTICE SOCIETY ARE THE PERPETRATORS.
THE EXACT MOTIVES BEHIND THESE ACTIONS REMAIN UNCLEAR--
--THOUGH WHAT IS CLEAR IS THAT THE WORLD IS NOT GOING TO TAKE A WAIT-AND-SEE ATTITUDE. ALREADY THE UNITED STATES AND SEVERAL ALLIES ARE DISCUSSING THE BEST COURSE OF ACTION...
KAHNDAQ. BLACK ADAM'S HOME COUNTRY...
IS... IS ATOM SMASHER WITH HIM? I THOUGHT I SAW HIM.
AND ALEX?
WHAT THE HELL IS GOING ON?
WHAT DO YOU SUGGEST WE DO, MR. CHAIRMAN?
REGROUP AT HEADQUARTERS. TRY AND ESTABLISH CONTACT TO SEE WHAT THE HELL BLACK ADAM IS THINKING. THEN--
NO OFFENSE, MR. TERRIFIC. YOU'RE SMART AND RESOURCE-FUL--
--BUT THIS ISN'T SOMETHING YOU HAVE EXPERIENCE WITH.
I DO.

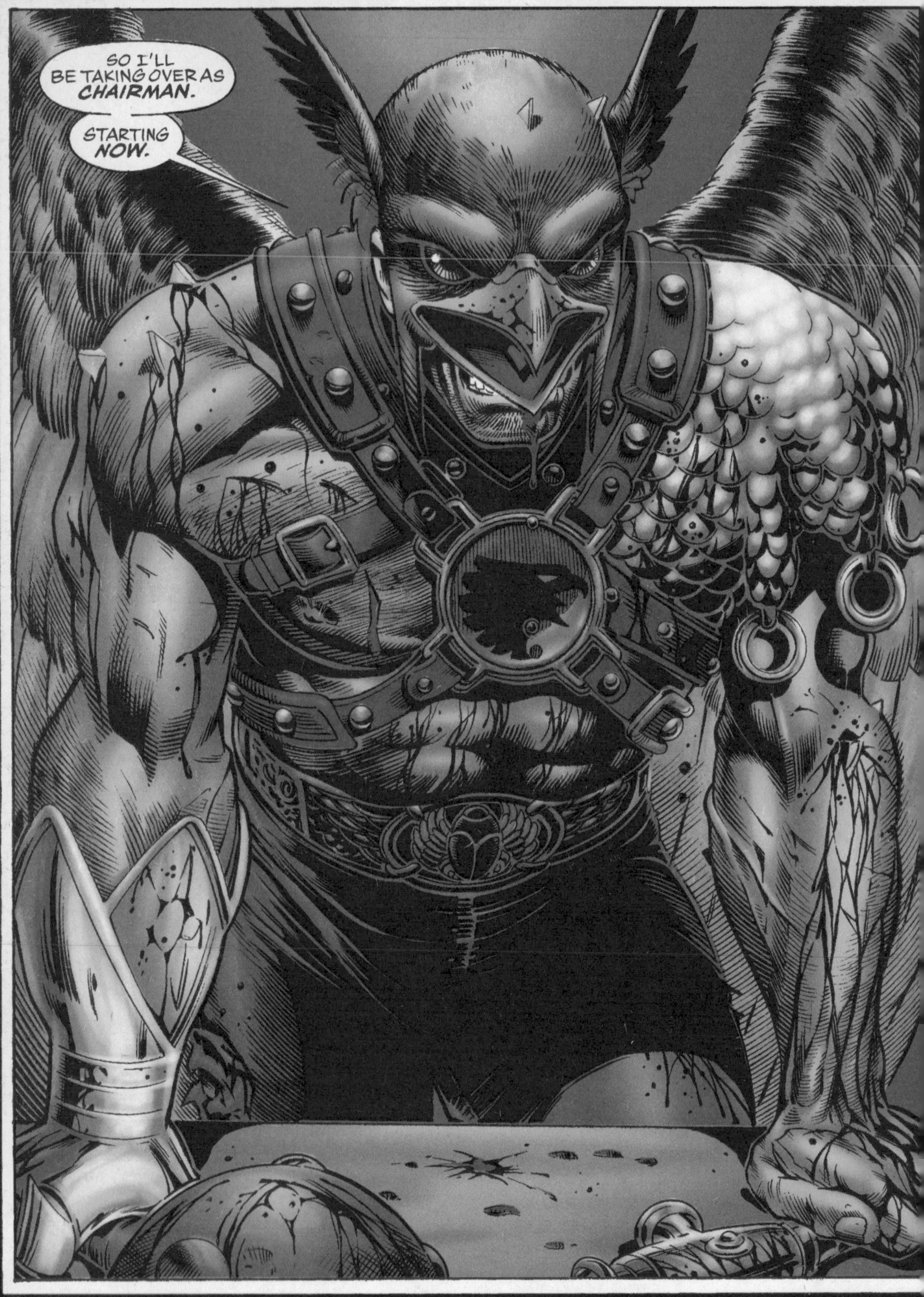
SO I'LL BE TAKING OVER AS CHAIRMAN.
STARTING NOW.

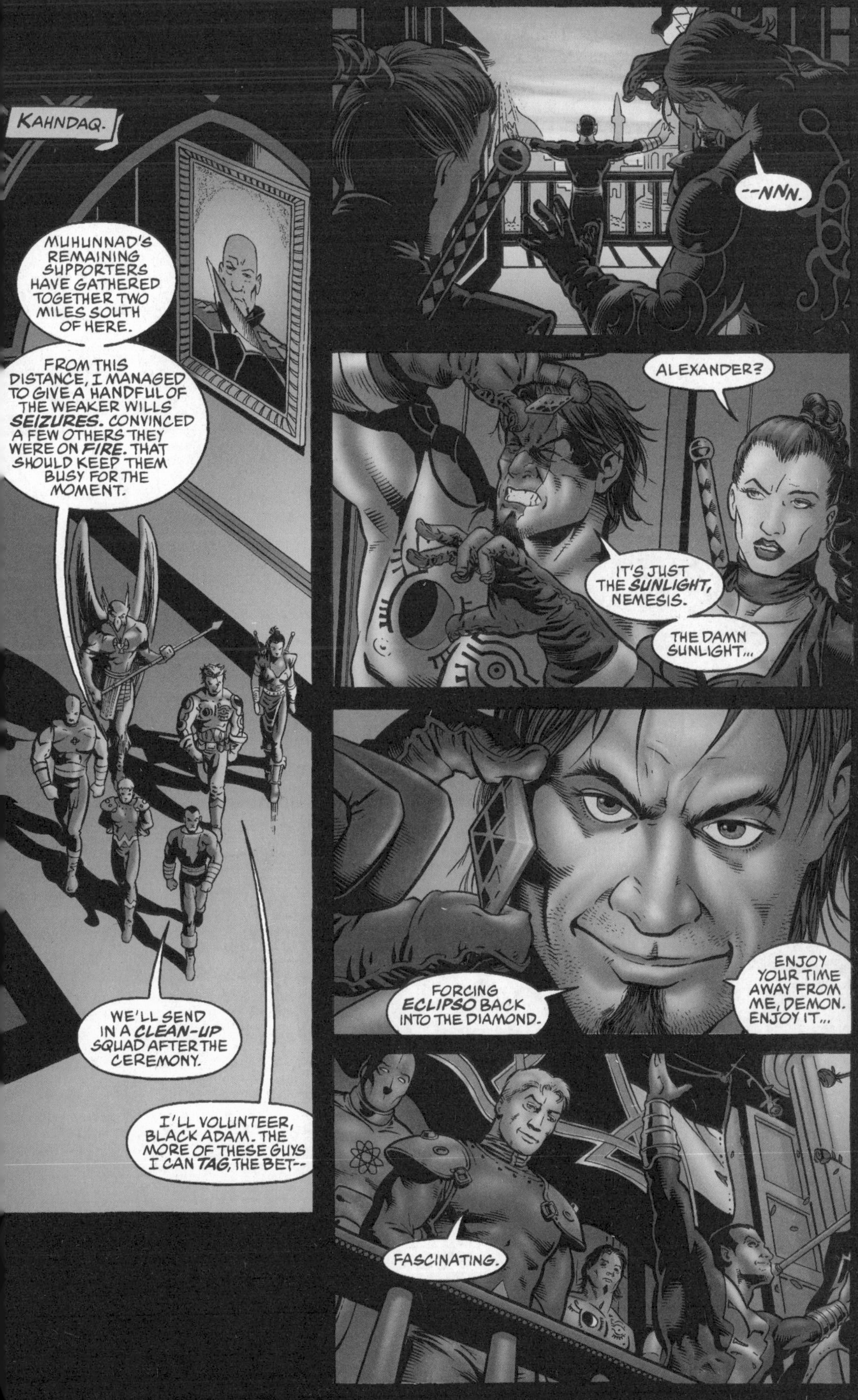
KAHNDAQ.
MUHUNNAD'S REMAINING SUPPORTERS HAVE GATHERED TOGETHER TWO MILES SOUTH OF HERE.
FROM THIS DISTANCE, I MANAGED TO GIVE A HANDFUL OF THE WEAKER WILLS SEIZURES. CONVINCED A FEW OTHERS THEY WERE ON FIRE. THAT SHOULD KEEP THEM BUSY FOR THE MOMENT.
WE'LL SEND IN A CLEAN-UP SQUAD AFTER THE CEREMONY.
I'LL VOLUNTEER, BLACK ADAM. THE MORE OF THESE GUYS I CAN TAG, THE BET--
--NNN.
ALEXANDER?
IT'S JUST THE SUNLIGHT, NEMESIS.
THE DAMN SUNLIGHT...
FORCING ECLIPSO BACK INTO THE DIAMOND.
ENJOY YOUR TIME AWAY FROM ME, DEMON. ENJOY IT...
FASCINATING.

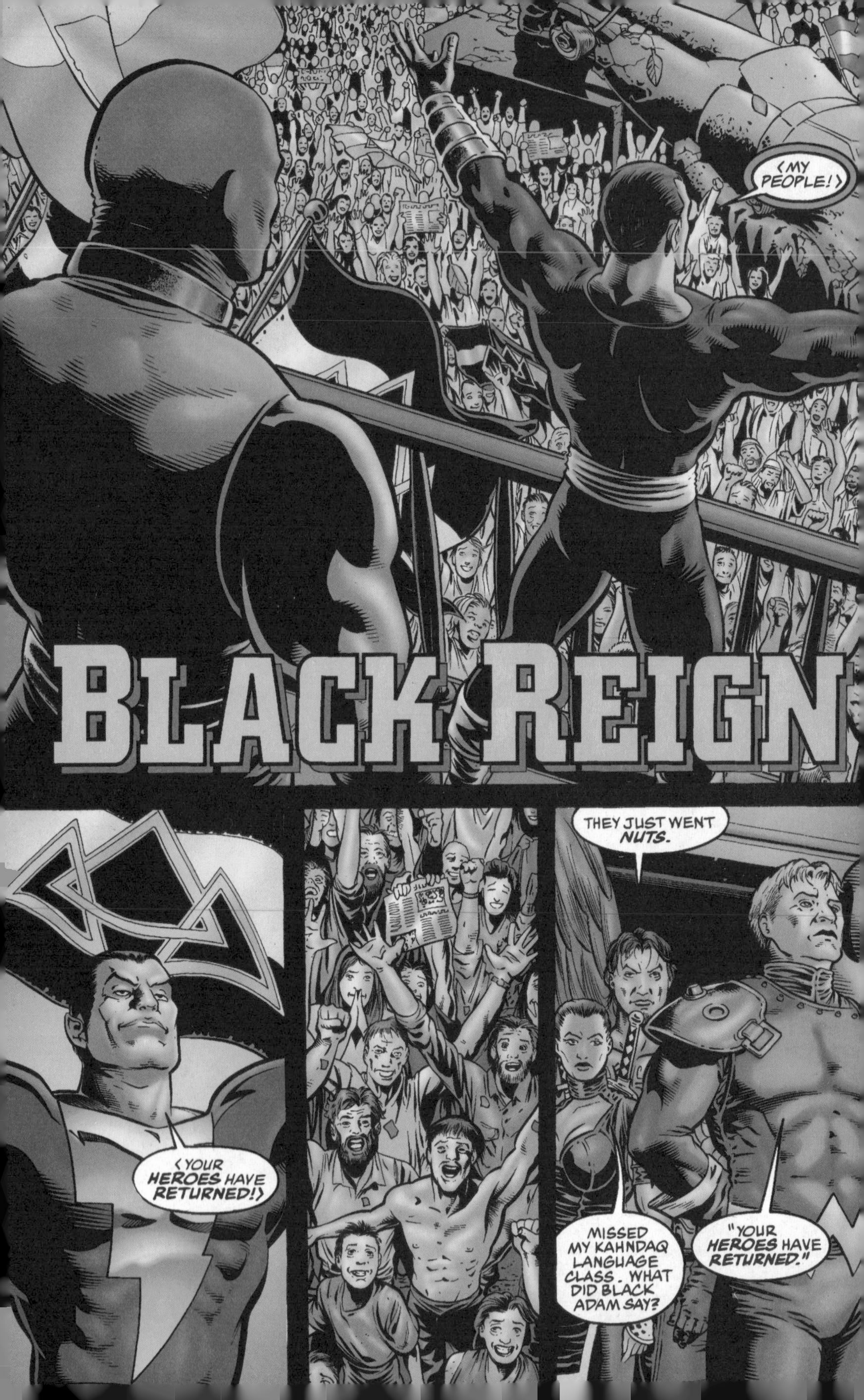
‹MY PEOPLE!›
BLACK REIGN
‹YOUR HEROES HAVE RETURNED!›
THEY JUST WENT NUTS.
MISSED MY KAHNDAQ LANGUAGE CLASS. WHAT DID BLACK ADAM SAY?
"YOUR HEROES HAVE RETURNED."

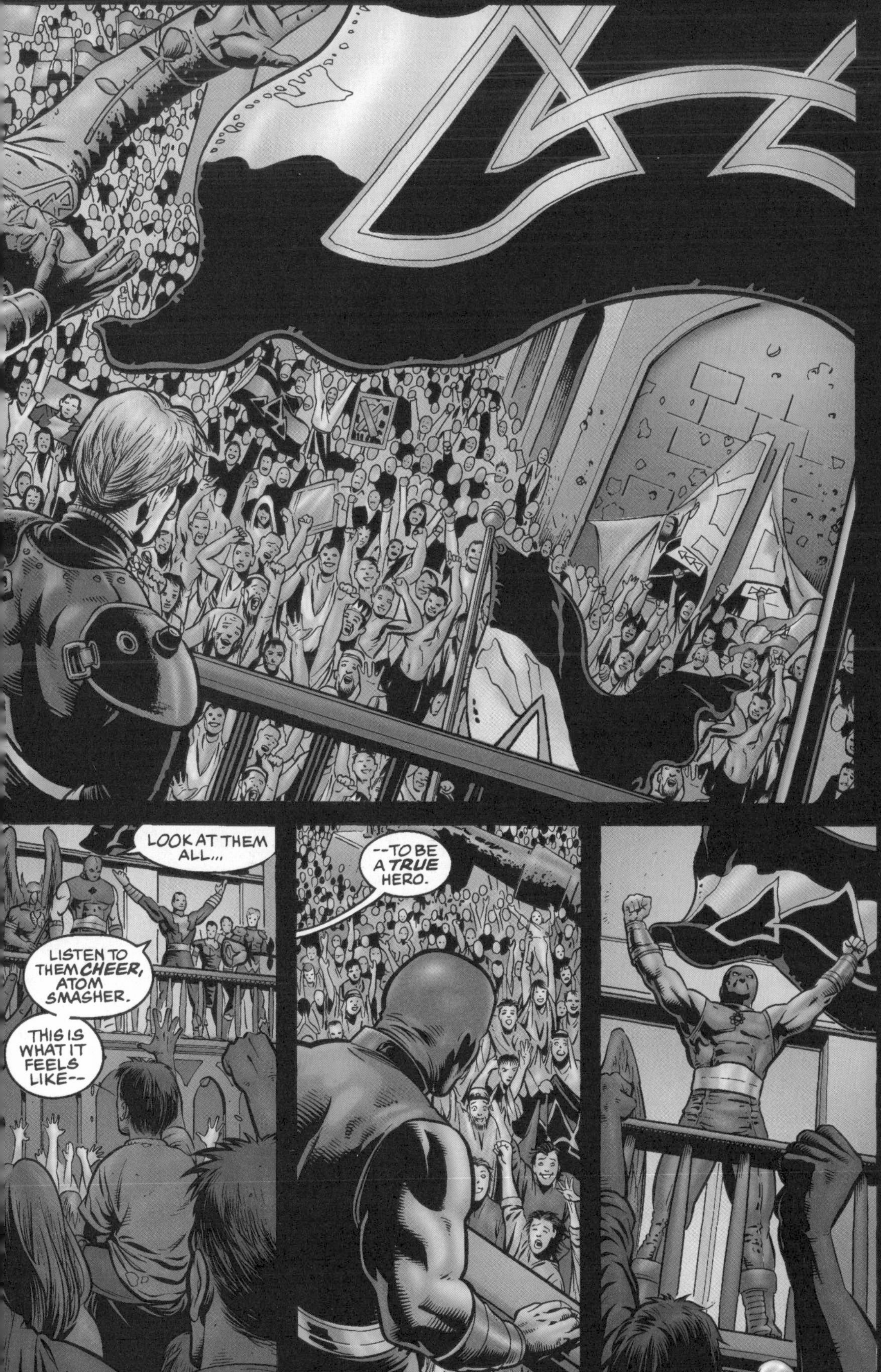
LOOK AT THEM ALL...
LISTEN TO THEM CHEER, ATOM SMASHER.
THIS IS WHAT IT FEELS LIKE--
--TO BE A TRUE HERO.

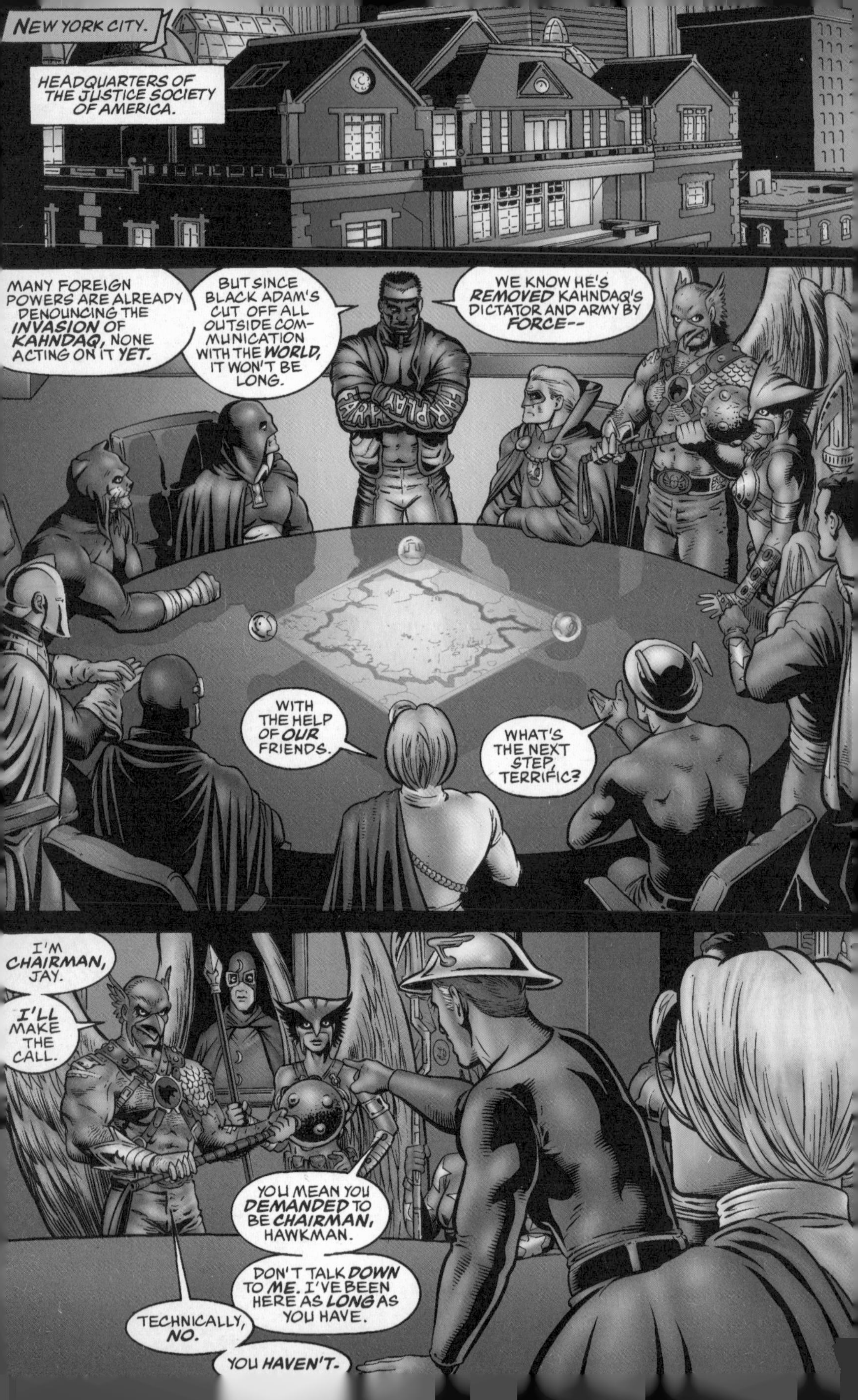
NEW YORK CITY.
HEADQUARTERS OF THE JUSTICE SOCIETY OF AMERICA.
MANY FOREIGN POWERS ARE ALREADY DENOUNCING THE INVASION OF KAHNDAQ, NONE ACTING ON IT YET.
BUT SINCE BLACK ADAM'S CUT OFF ALL OUTSIDE COM-MUNICATION WITH THE WORLD, IT WON'T BE LONG.
WE KNOW HE'S REMOVED KAHNDAQ'S DICTATOR AND ARMY BY FORCE--
FAIRPLAY
WITH THE HELP OF OUR FRIENDS.
WHAT'S THE NEXT STEP, TERRIFIC?
I'M CHAIRMAN, JAY.
I'LL MAKE THE CALL.
YOU MEAN YOU DEMANDED TO BE CHAIRMAN, HAWKMAN.
DON'T TALK DOWN TO ME. I'VE BEEN HERE AS LONG AS YOU HAVE.
TECHNICALLY, NO.
YOU HAVEN'T.

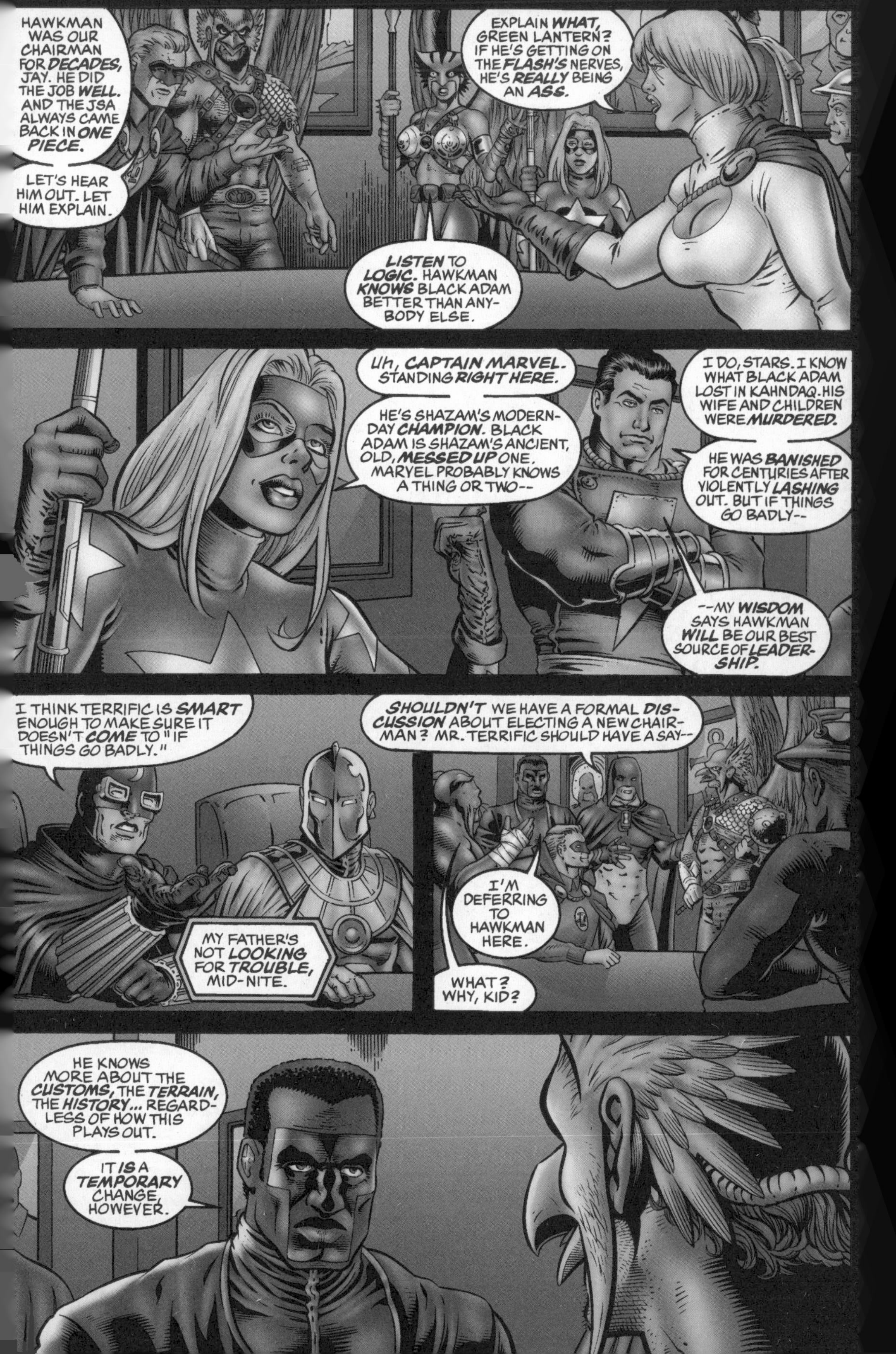
HAWKMAN WAS OUR CHAIRMAN FOR DECADES, JAY. HE DID THE JOB WELL. AND THE JSA ALWAYS CAME BACK IN ONE PIECE.
LET'S HEAR HIM OUT. LET HIM EXPLAIN.
EXPLAIN WHAT, GREEN LANTERN? IF HE'S GETTING ON THE FLASH'S NERVES, HE'S REALLY BEING AN ASS.
LISTEN TO LOGIC. HAWKMAN KNOWS BLACK ADAM BETTER THAN ANYBODY ELSE.
Uh, CAPTAIN MARVEL. STANDING RIGHT HERE.
HE'S SHAZAM'S MODERN-DAY CHAMPION. BLACK ADAM IS SHAZAM'S ANCIENT, OLD, MESSED UP ONE. MARVEL PROBABLY KNOWS A THING OR TWO--
I DO, STARS. I KNOW WHAT BLACK ADAM LOST IN KAHNDAQ. HIS WIFE AND CHILDREN WERE MURDERED.
HE WAS BANISHED FOR CENTURIES AFTER VIOLENTLY LASHING OUT. BUT IF THINGS GO BADLY--
--MY WISDOM SAYS HAWKMAN WILL BE OUR BEST SOURCE OF LEADERSHIP.
I THINK TERRIFIC IS SMART ENOUGH TO MAKE SURE IT DOESN'T COME TO "IF THINGS GO BADLY."
MY FATHER'S NOT LOOKING FOR TROUBLE, MID-NITE.
SHOULDN'T WE HAVE A FORMAL DISCUSSION ABOUT ELECTING A NEW CHAIRMAN? MR. TERRIFIC SHOULD HAVE A SAY--
I'M DEFERRING TO HAWKMAN HERE.
WHAT? WHY, KID?
HE KNOWS MORE ABOUT THE CUSTOMS, THE TERRAIN, THE HISTORY... REGARDLESS OF HOW THIS PLAYS OUT.
IT IS A TEMPORARY CHANGE, HOWEVER.

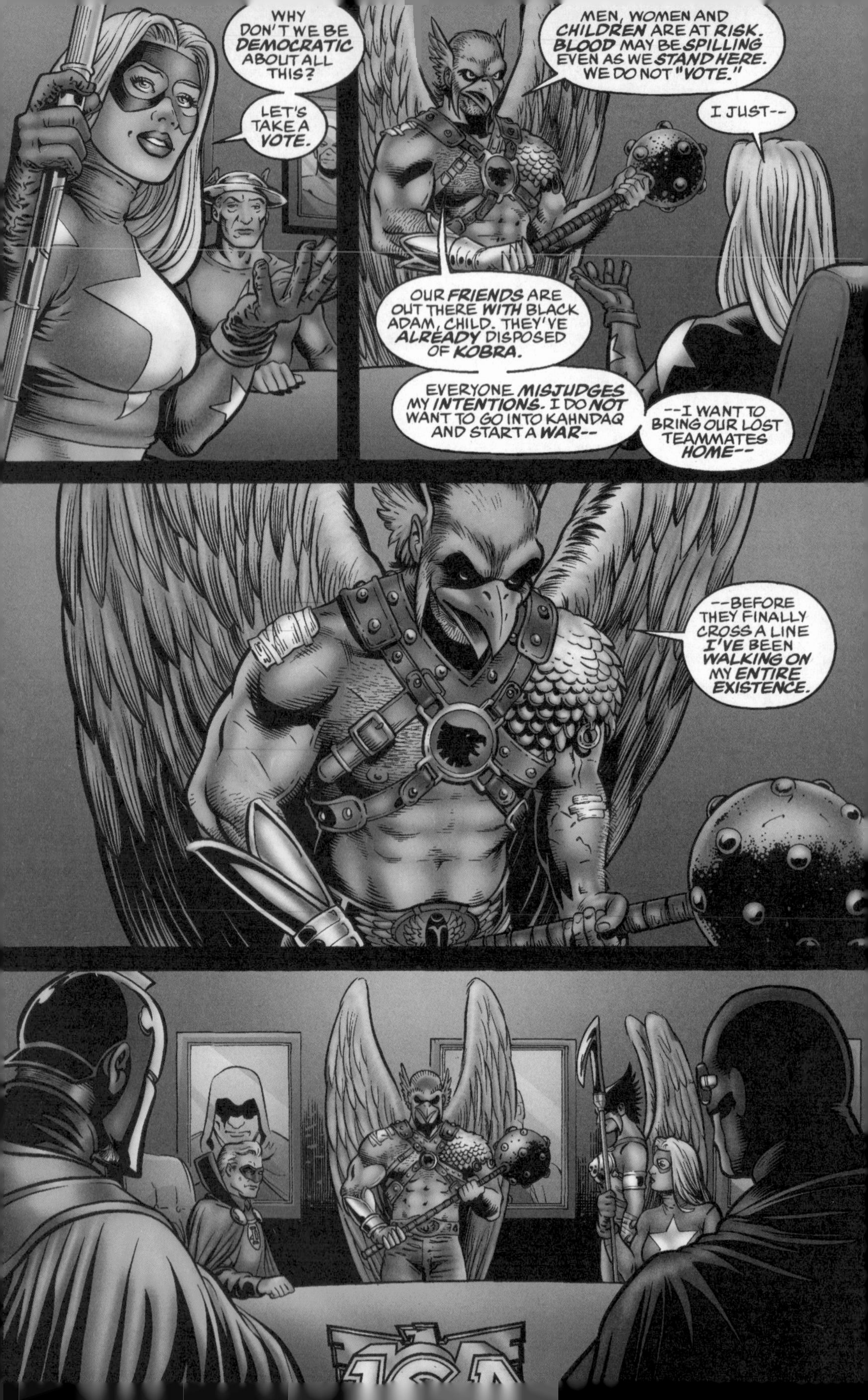
WHY DON'T WE BE DEMOCRATIC ABOUT ALL THIS?
LET'S TAKE A VOTE.
MEN, WOMEN AND CHILDREN ARE AT RISK. BLOOD MAY BE SPILLING EVEN AS WE STAND HERE. WE DO NOT "VOTE."
I JUST--
OUR FRIENDS ARE OUT THERE WITH BLACK ADAM, CHILD. THEY'VE ALREADY DISPOSED OF KOBRA.
EVERYONE MISJUDGES MY INTENTIONS. I DO NOT WANT TO GO INTO KAHNDAQ AND START A WAR--
--I WANT TO BRING OUR LOST TEAMMATES HOME--
--BEFORE THEY FINALLY CROSS A LINE I'VE BEEN WALKING ON MY ENTIRE EXISTENCE.

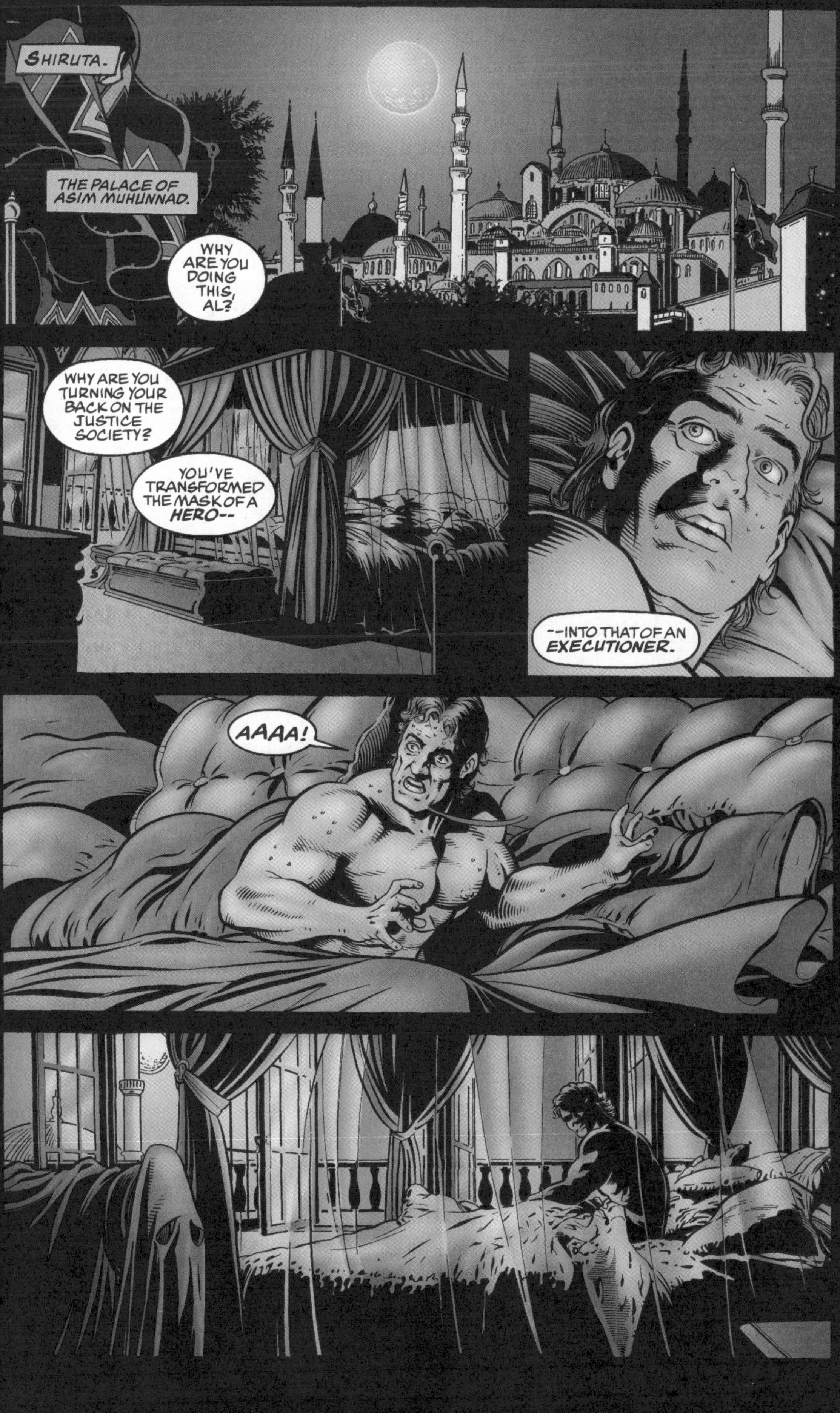
SHIRUTA.
THE PALACE OF ASIM MUHUNNAD.
WHY ARE YOU DOING THIS, AL?
WHY ARE YOU TURNING YOUR BACK ON THE JUSTICE SOCIETY?
YOU'VE TRANSFORMED THE MASK OF A HERO--
--INTO THAT OF AN EXECUTIONER.
AAAA!

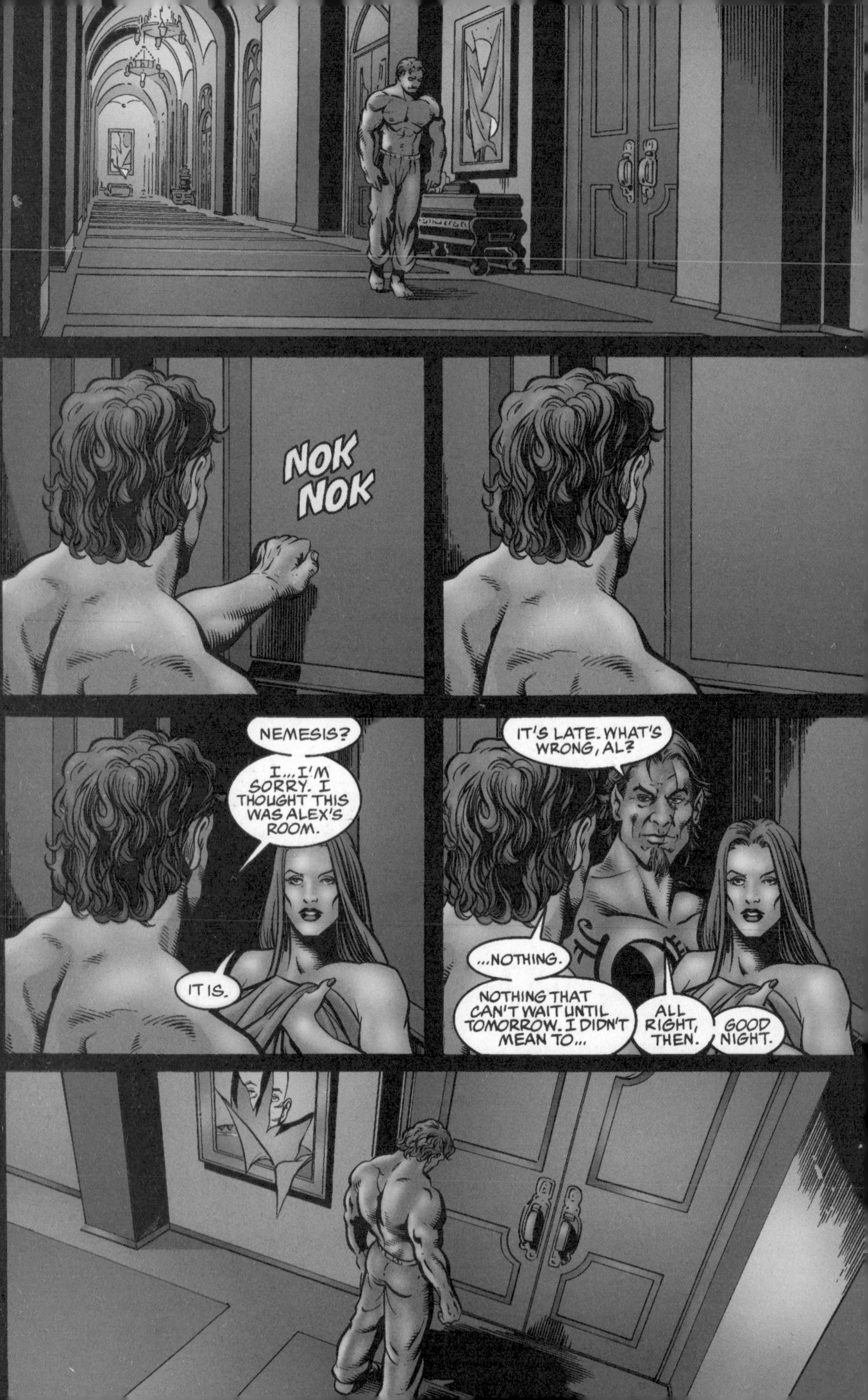
NOK NOK
NEMESIS?
I... I'M SORRY. I THOUGHT THIS WAS ALEX'S ROOM.
IT IS.
IT'S LATE. WHAT'S WRONG, AL?
...NOTHING.
NOTHING THAT CAN'T WAIT UNTIL TOMORROW. I DIDN'T MEAN TO...
ALL RIGHT, THEN.
GOOD NIGHT.

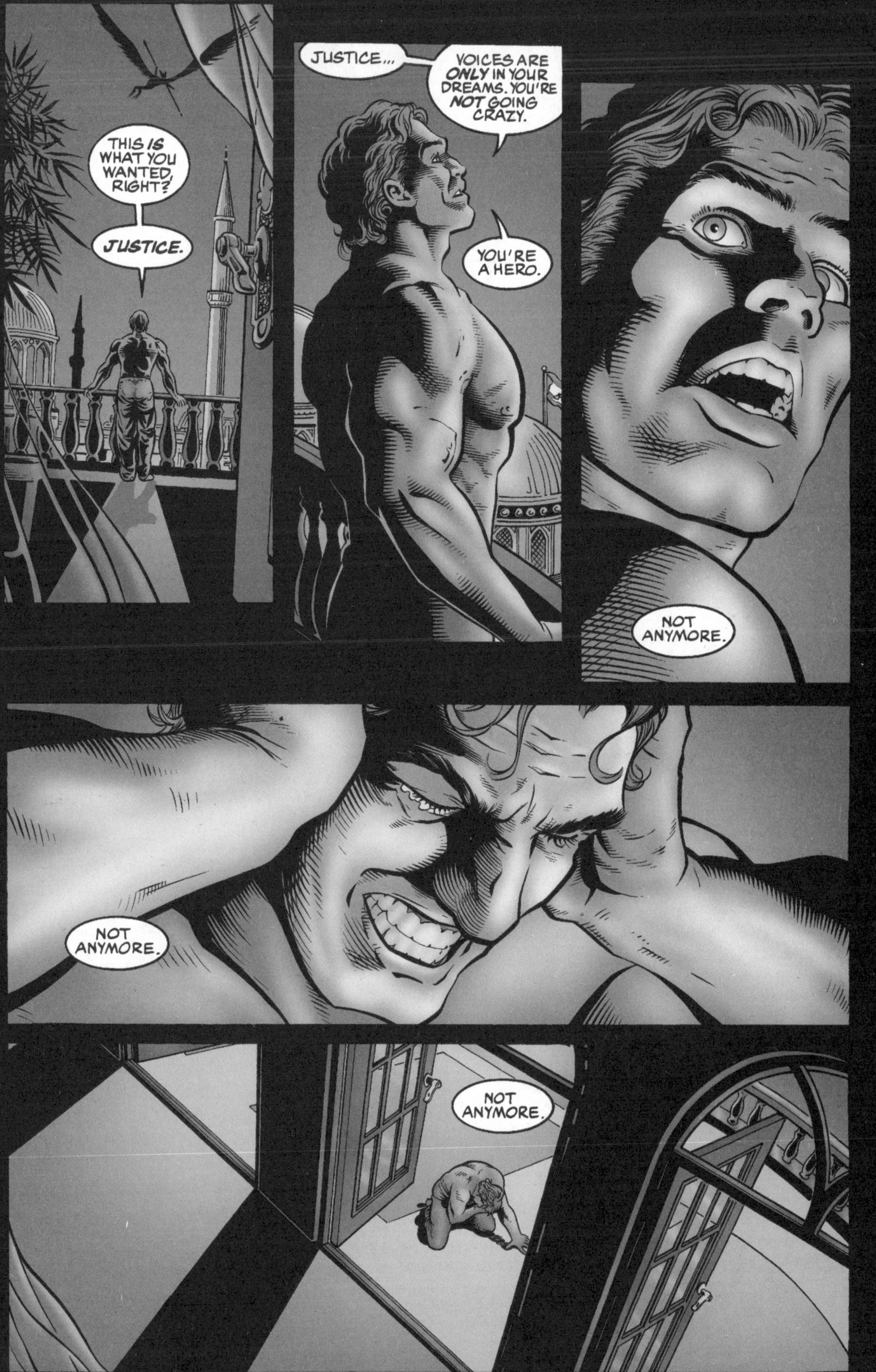
THIS IS WHAT YOU WANTED, RIGHT?
JUSTICE.
JUSTICE...
VOICES ARE ONLY IN YOUR DREAMS. YOU'RE NOT GOING CRAZY.
YOU'RE A HERO.
NOT ANYMORE.
NOT ANYMORE.
NOT ANYMORE.

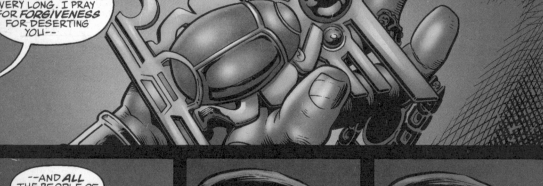

SHIRUTA. AND MY *SONS*. GON. HURUT.

I OFFER YOU THE *SCARAB* I WAS *ENTOMBED* IN FOR SO VERY LONG. I PRAY FOR *FORGIVENESS* FOR DESERTING YOU--

--AND *ALL* THE PEOPLE OF *KAHNDAQ.*

SHUMP

I *MISS* YOU.

YOU WANT THEM TO *RESPOND,* BUT YOU KNOW THEY WILL NOT.

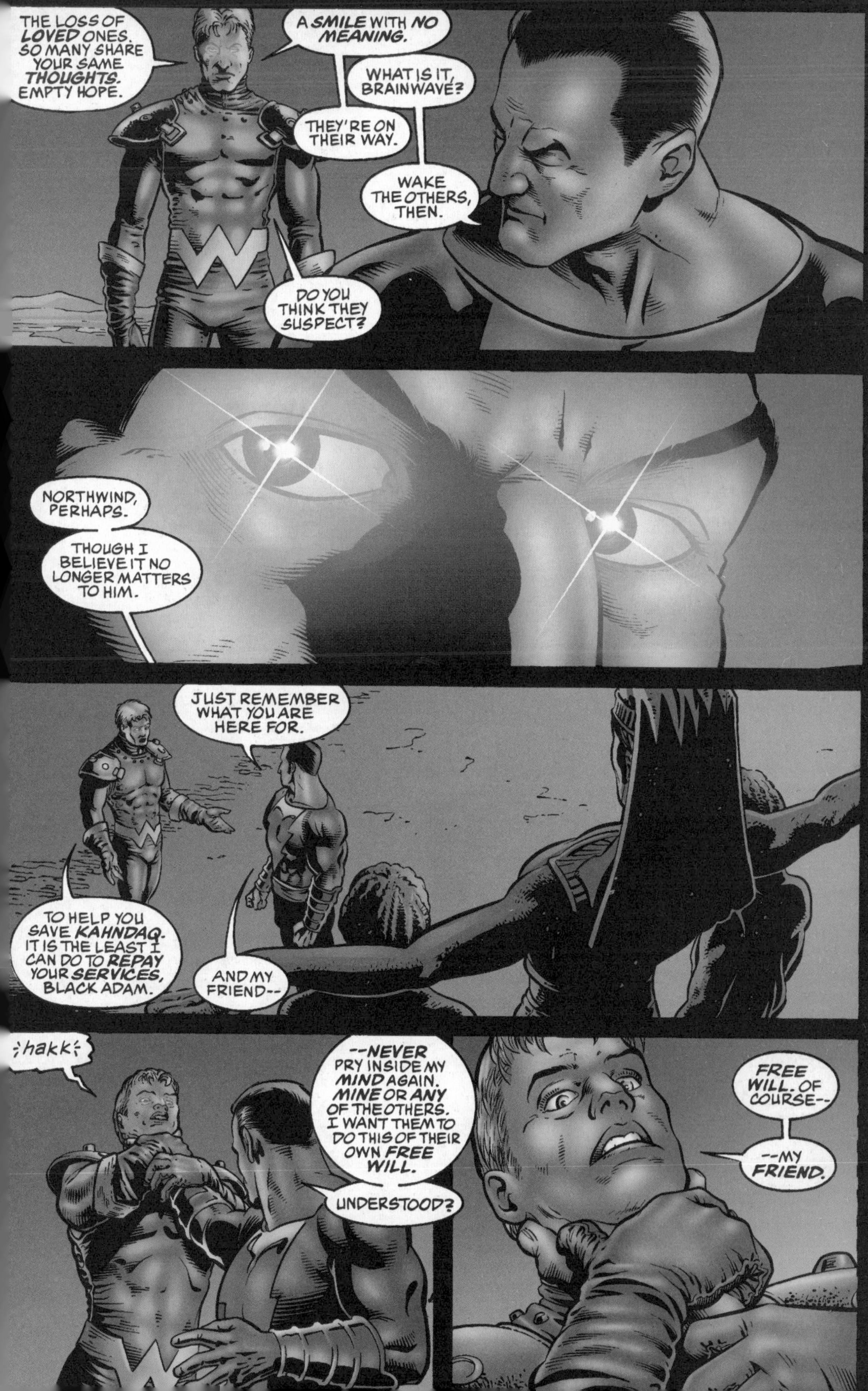
THE LOSS OF LOVED ONES. SO MANY SHARE YOUR SAME THOUGHTS. EMPTY HOPE.
A SMILE WITH NO MEANING.
WHAT IS IT, BRAINWAVE?
THEY'RE ON THEIR WAY.
WAKE THE OTHERS, THEN.
DO YOU THINK THEY SUSPECT?
NORTHWIND, PERHAPS.
THOUGH I BELIEVE IT NO LONGER MATTERS TO HIM.
JUST REMEMBER WHAT YOU ARE HERE FOR.
TO HELP YOU SAVE KAHNDAQ. IT IS THE LEAST I CAN DO TO REPAY YOUR SERVICES, BLACK ADAM.
AND MY FRIEND--
;hakk;
--NEVER PRY INSIDE MY MIND AGAIN. MINE OR ANY OF THE OTHERS. I WANT THEM TO DO THIS OF THEIR OWN FREE WILL.
UNDERSTOOD?
FREE WILL. OF COURSE--
--MY FRIEND.

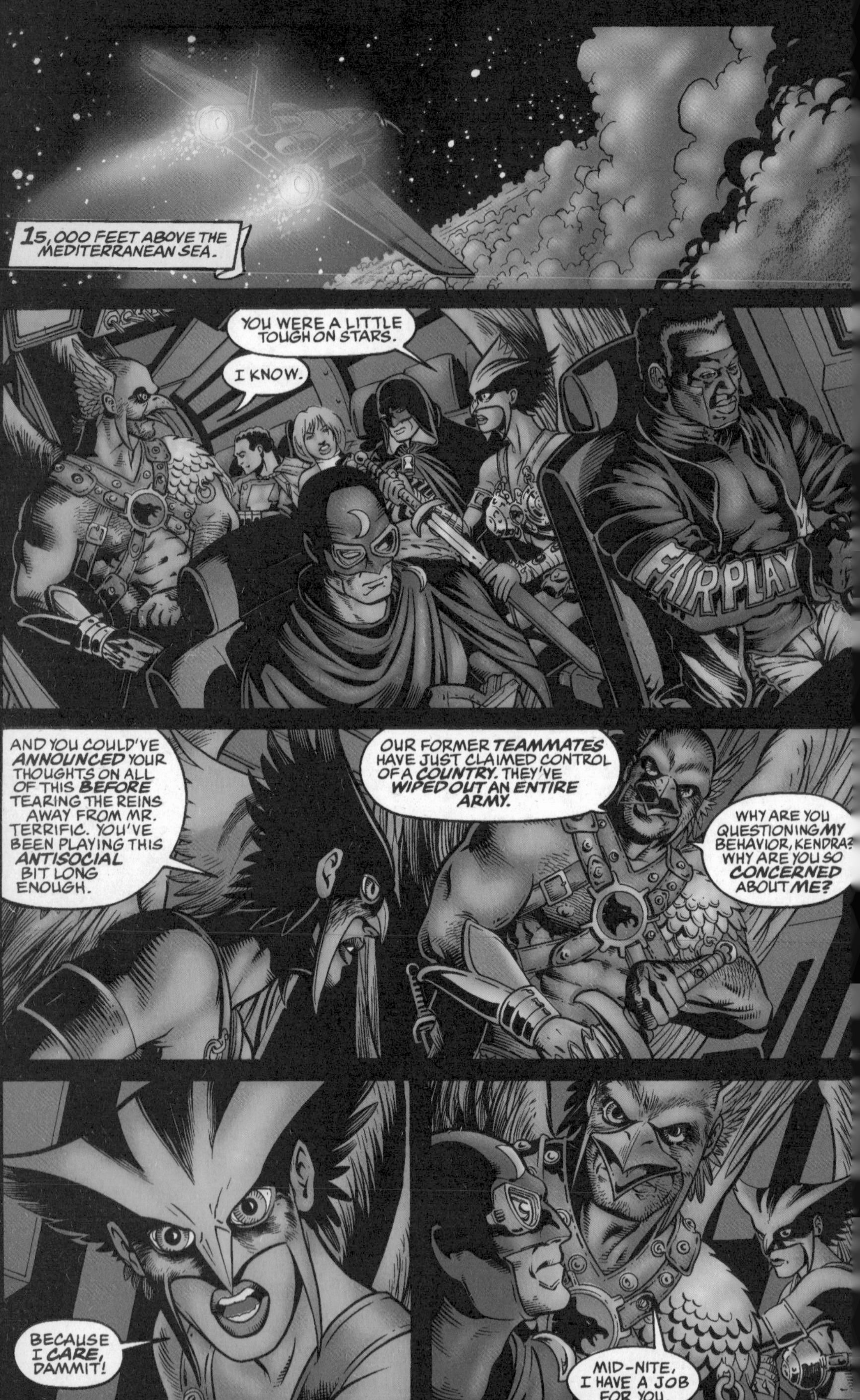
15,000 FEET ABOVE THE MEDITERRANEAN SEA.
YOU WERE A LITTLE TOUGH ON STARS.
I KNOW.
FAIR PLAY
AND YOU COULD'VE ANNOUNCED YOUR THOUGHTS ON ALL OF THIS BEFORE TEARING THE REINS AWAY FROM MR. TERRIFIC. YOU'VE BEEN PLAYING THIS ANTISOCIAL BIT LONG ENOUGH.
OUR FORMER TEAMMATES HAVE JUST CLAIMED CONTROL OF A COUNTRY. THEY'VE WIPED OUT AN ENTIRE ARMY.
WHY ARE YOU QUESTIONING MY BEHAVIOR, KENDRA? WHY ARE YOU SO CONCERNED ABOUT ME?
BECAUSE I CARE, DAMMIT!
MID-NITE, I HAVE A JOB FOR YOU.

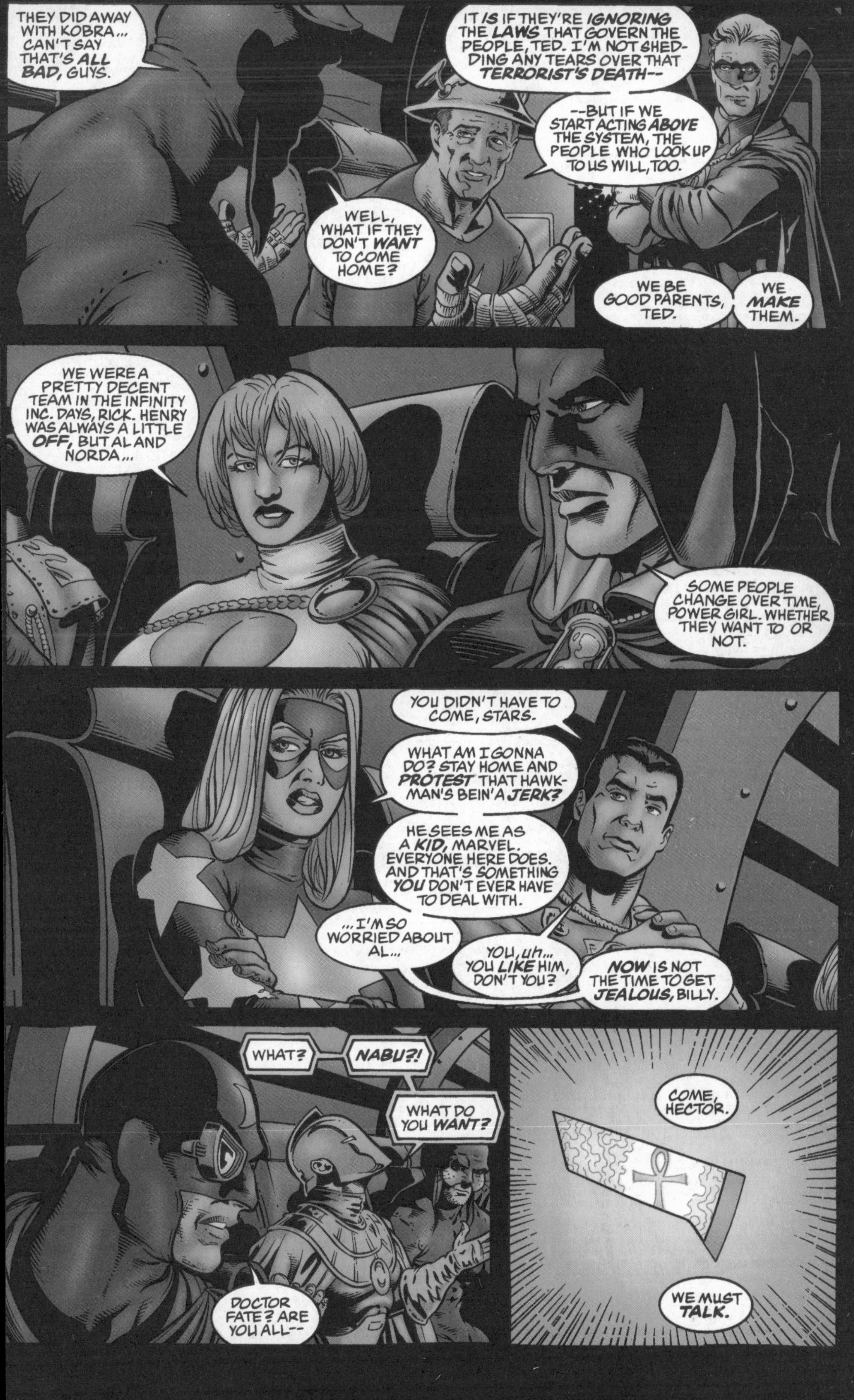
THEY DID AWAY WITH KOBRA... CAN'T SAY THAT'S ALL BAD, GUYS.
IT IS IF THEY'RE IGNORING THE LAWS THAT GOVERN THE PEOPLE, TED. I'M NOT SHEDDING ANY TEARS OVER THAT TERRORIST'S DEATH--
--BUT IF WE START ACTING ABOVE THE SYSTEM, THE PEOPLE WHO LOOK UP TO US WILL, TOO.
WELL, WHAT IF THEY DON'T WANT TO COME HOME?
WE BE GOOD PARENTS, TED.
WE MAKE THEM.
WE WERE A PRETTY DECENT TEAM IN THE INFINITY INC. DAYS, RICK. HENRY WAS ALWAYS A LITTLE OFF, BUT AL AND NORDA...
SOME PEOPLE CHANGE OVER TIME, POWER GIRL. WHETHER THEY WANT TO OR NOT.
YOU DIDN'T HAVE TO COME, STARS.
WHAT AM I GONNA DO? STAY HOME AND PROTEST THAT HAWKMAN'S BEIN' A JERK?
HE SEES ME AS A KID, MARVEL. EVERYONE HERE DOES. AND THAT'S SOMETHING YOU DON'T EVER HAVE TO DEAL WITH.
...I'M SO WORRIED ABOUT AL...
YOU, uh... YOU LIKE HIM, DON'T YOU?
NOW IS NOT THE TIME TO GET JEALOUS, BILLY.
WHAT?
NABU?!
WHAT DO YOU WANT?
DOCTOR FATE? ARE YOU ALL--
COME, HECTOR.
WE MUST TALK.

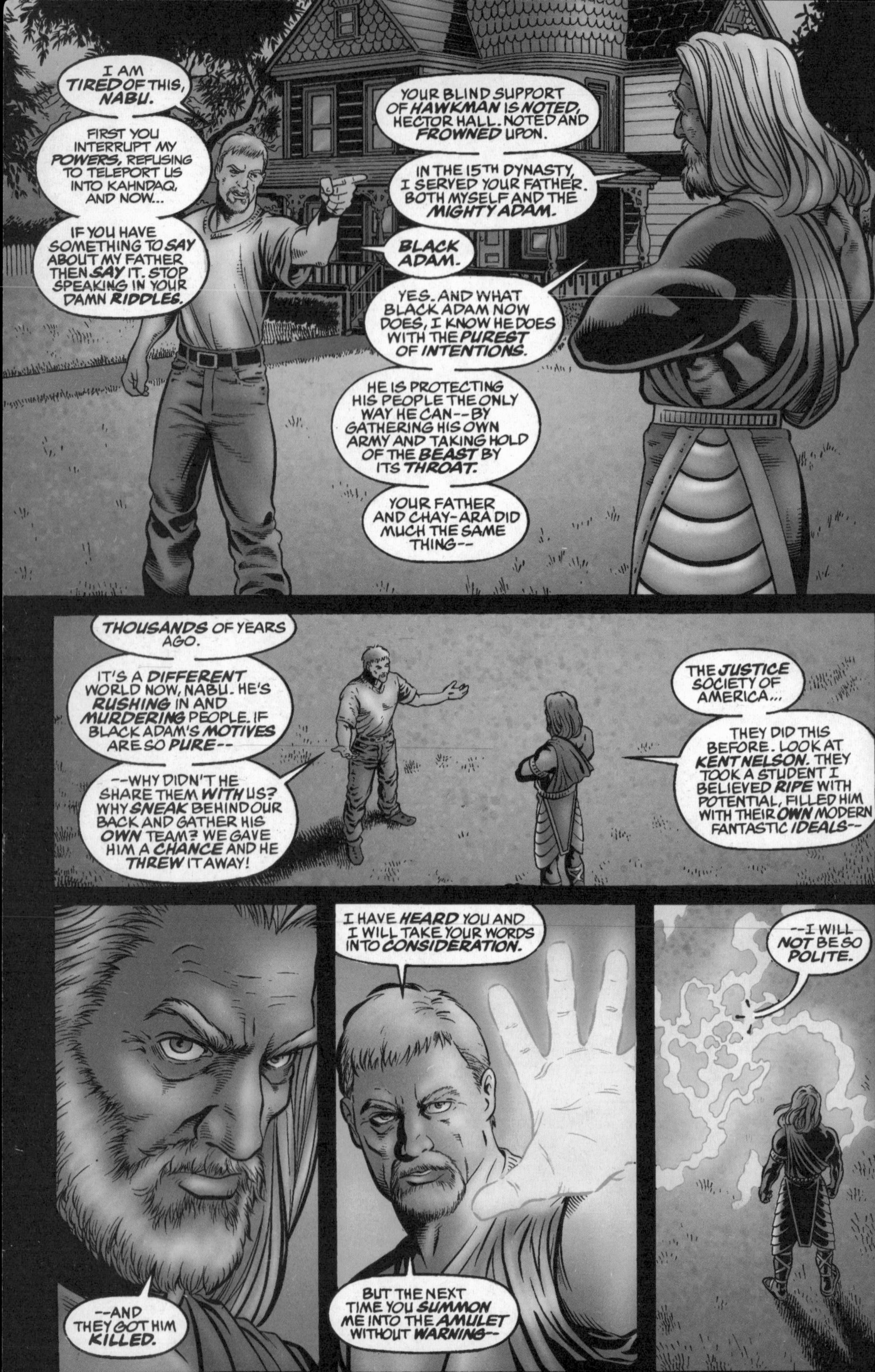
I AM TIRED OF THIS, NABU.
FIRST YOU INTERRUPT MY POWERS, REFUSING TO TELEPORT US INTO KAHNDAQ, AND NOW...
IF YOU HAVE SOMETHING TO SAY ABOUT MY FATHER THEN SAY IT. STOP SPEAKING IN YOUR DAMN RIDDLES.
YOUR BLIND SUPPORT OF HAWKMAN IS NOTED, HECTOR HALL. NOTED AND FROWNED UPON.
IN THE 15TH DYNASTY, I SERVED YOUR FATHER. BOTH MYSELF AND THE MIGHTY ADAM.
BLACK ADAM.
YES. AND WHAT BLACK ADAM NOW DOES, I KNOW HE DOES WITH THE PUREST OF INTENTIONS.
HE IS PROTECTING HIS PEOPLE THE ONLY WAY HE CAN--BY GATHERING HIS OWN ARMY AND TAKING HOLD OF THE BEAST BY ITS THROAT.
YOUR FATHER AND CHAY-ARA DID MUCH THE SAME THING--
THOUSANDS OF YEARS AGO.
IT'S A DIFFERENT WORLD NOW, NABU. HE'S RUSHING IN AND MURDERING PEOPLE. IF BLACK ADAM'S MOTIVES ARE SO PURE--
--WHY DIDN'T HE SHARE THEM WITH US? WHY SNEAK BEHIND OUR BACK AND GATHER HIS OWN TEAM? WE GAVE HIM A CHANCE AND HE THREW IT AWAY!
THE JUSTICE SOCIETY OF AMERICA...
THEY DID THIS BEFORE. LOOK AT KENT NELSON. THEY TOOK A STUDENT I BELIEVED RIPE WITH POTENTIAL, FILLED HIM WITH THEIR OWN MODERN FANTASTIC IDEALS--
--AND THEY GOT HIM KILLED.
I HAVE HEARD YOU AND I WILL TAKE YOUR WORDS INTO CONSIDERATION.
BUT THE NEXT TIME YOU SUMMON ME INTO THE AMULET WITHOUT WARNING--
--I WILL NOT BE SO POLITE.

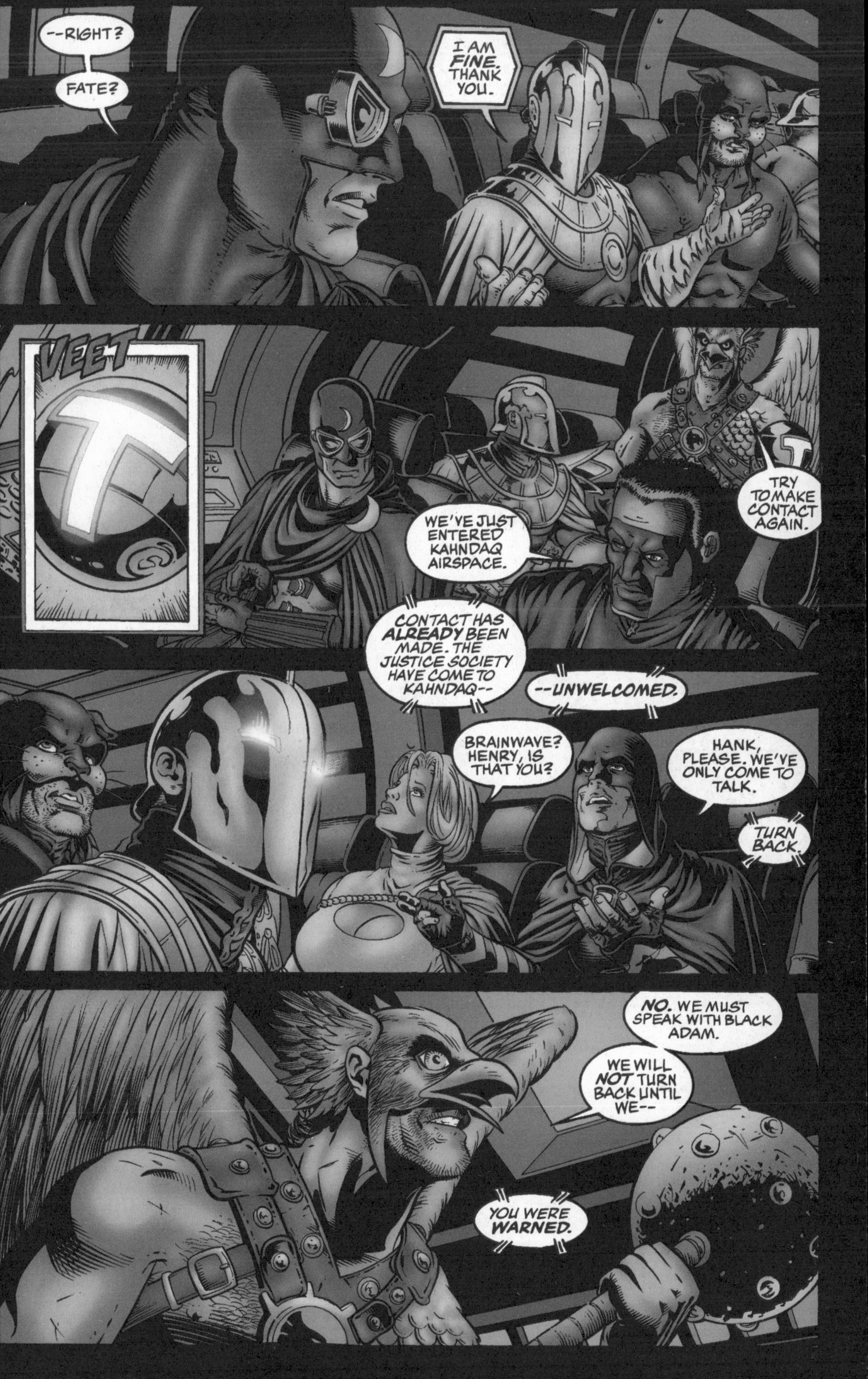

--RIGHT?
FATE?
I AM FINE. THANK YOU.
VEET
WE'VE JUST ENTERED KAHNDAQ AIRSPACE.
TRY TO MAKE CONTACT AGAIN.
CONTACT HAS ALREADY BEEN MADE. THE JUSTICE SOCIETY HAVE COME TO KAHNDAQ--
--UNWELCOMED.
BRAINWAVE? HENRY, IS THAT YOU?
HANK, PLEASE. WE'VE ONLY COME TO TALK.
TURN BACK.
NO. WE MUST SPEAK WITH BLACK ADAM.
WE WILL NOT TURN BACK UNTIL WE--
YOU WERE WARNED.

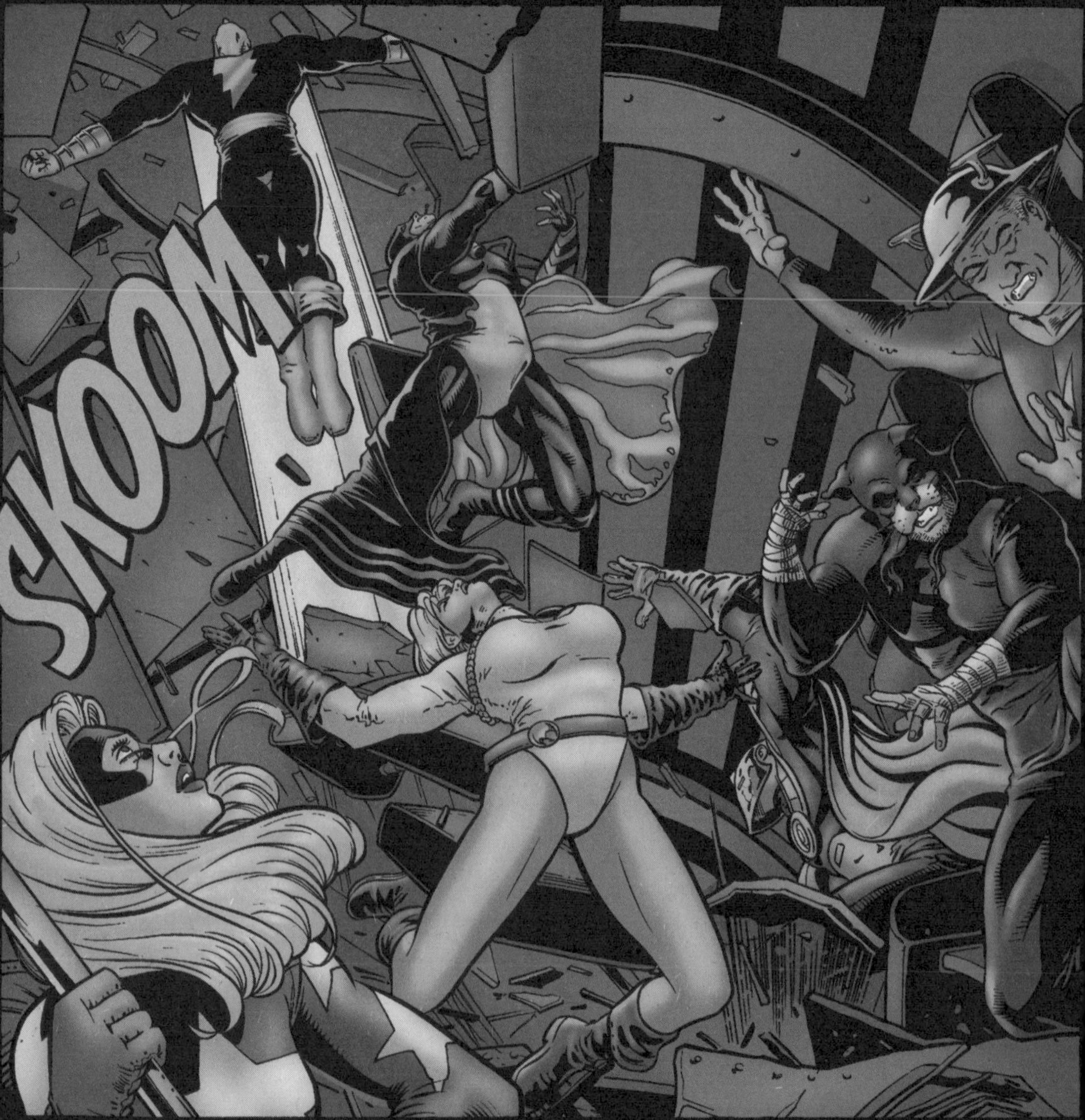
SKOOM

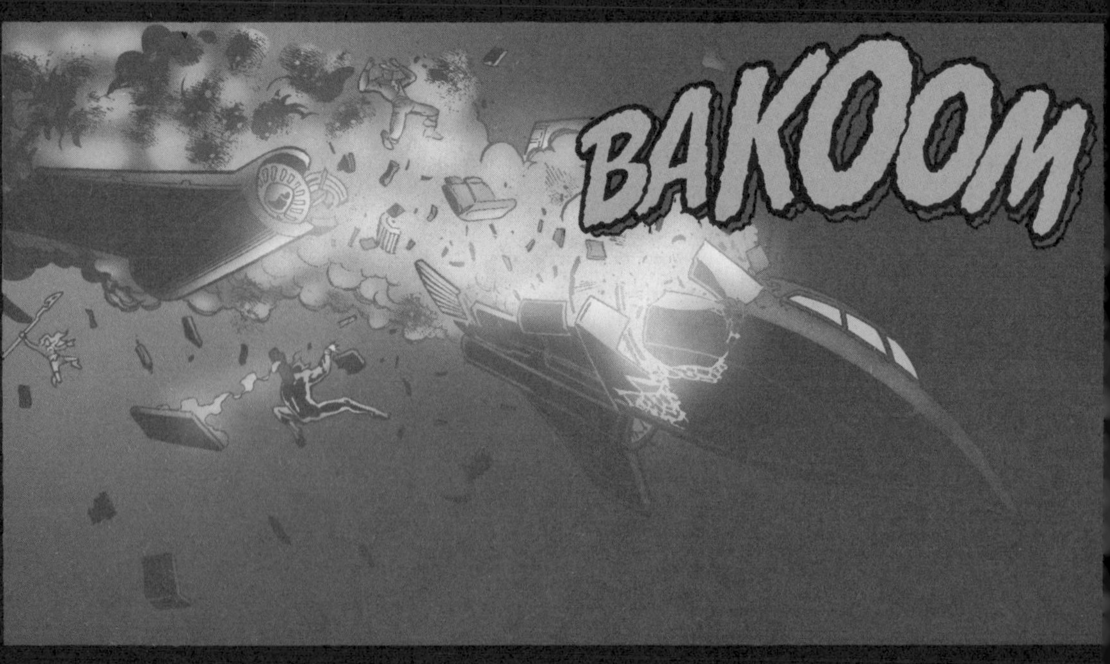
BAKOOM

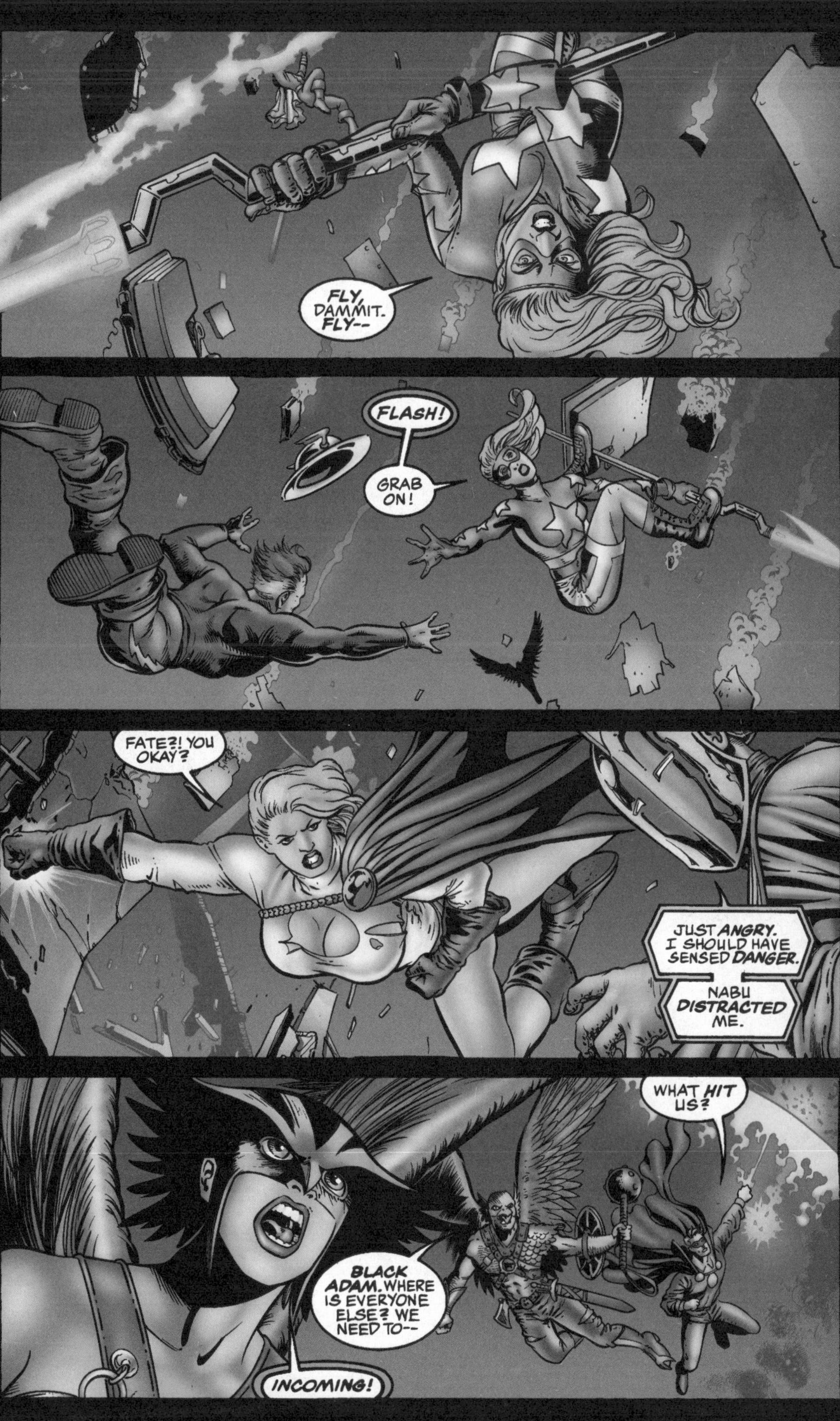
FLY, DAMMIT. FLY--
FLASH!
GRAB ON!
FATE?! YOU OKAY?
JUST ANGRY. I SHOULD HAVE SENSED DANGER.
NABU DISTRACTED ME.
WHAT HIT US?
BLACK ADAM. WHERE IS EVERYONE ELSE? WE NEED TO--
INCOMING!

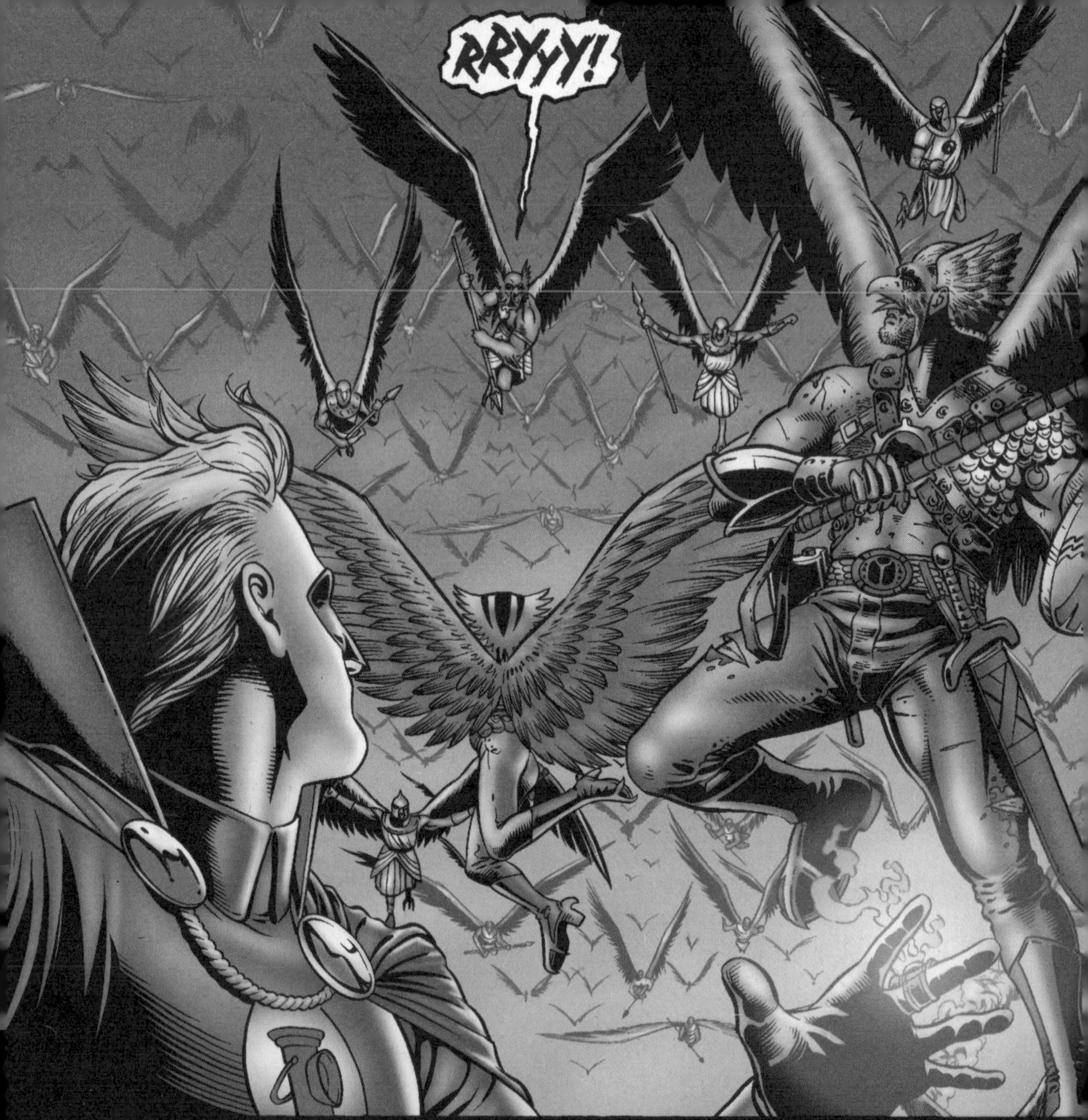
RRYYY!

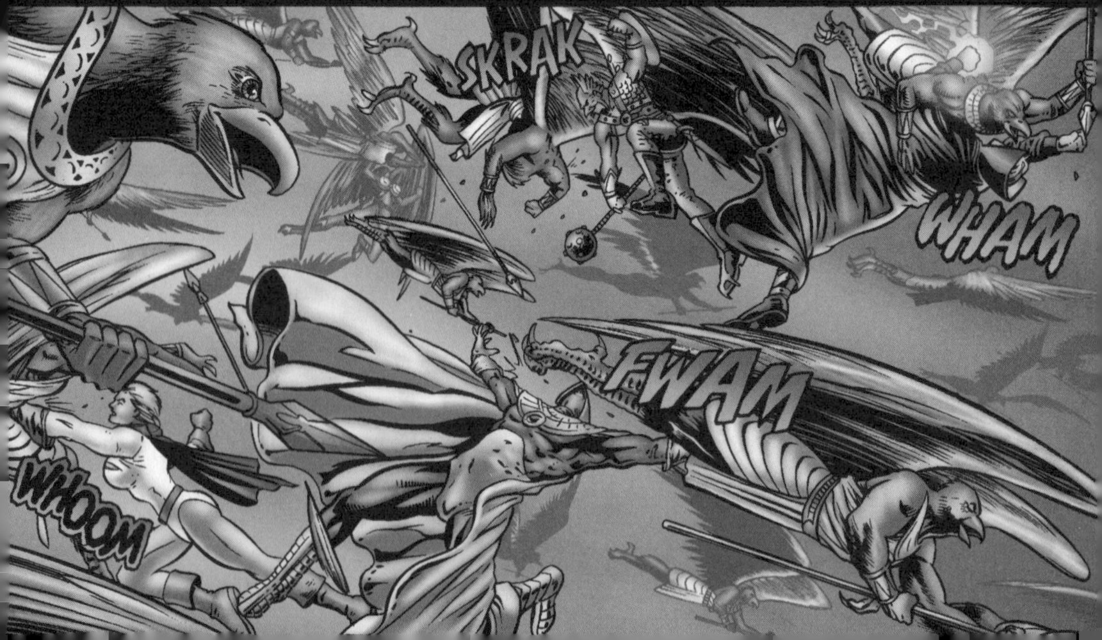
SKRAK
WHAM
FWAM
WHOOM

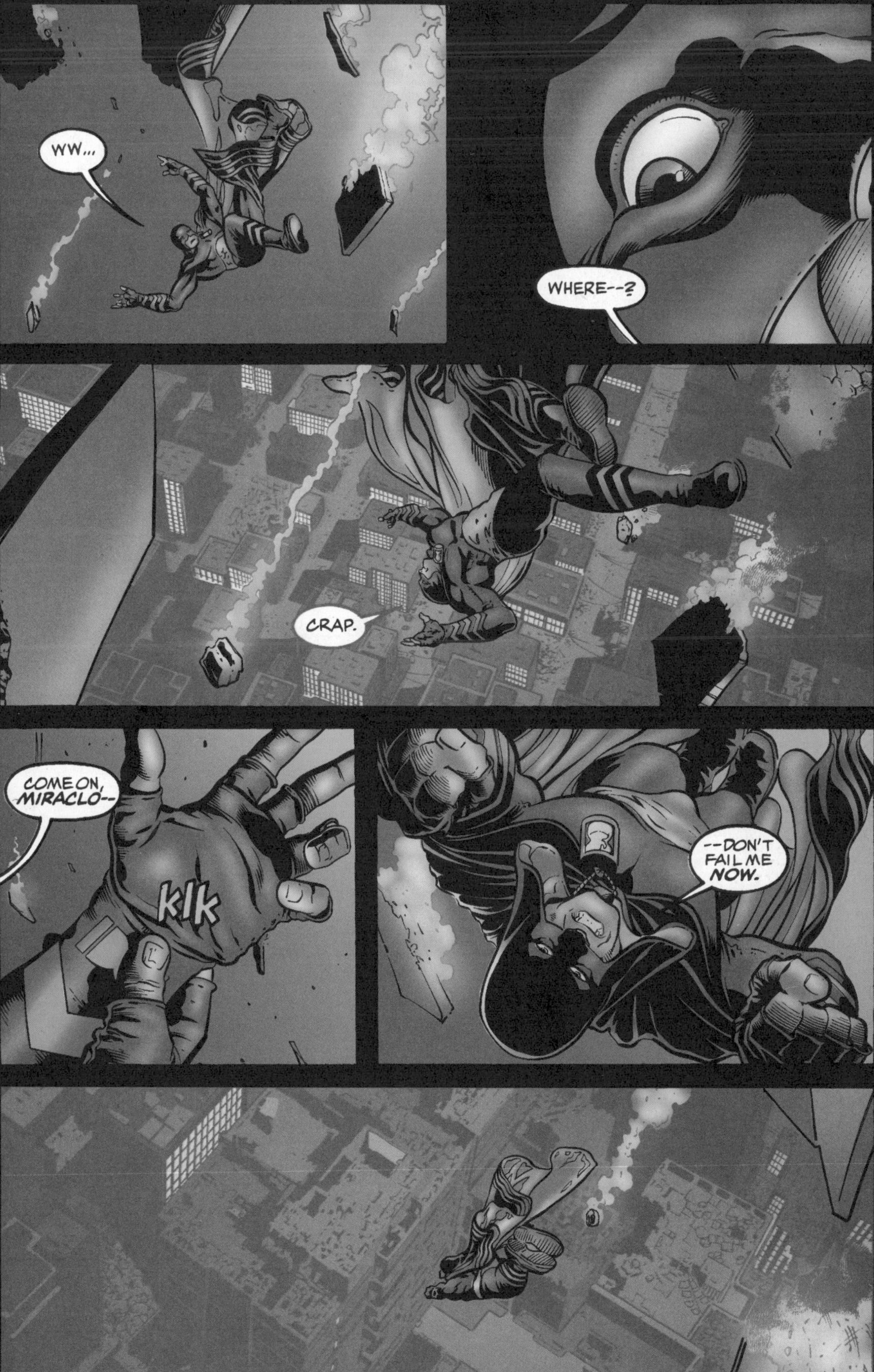

WW...
WHERE--?
CRAP.
COME ON, MIRACLO--
KLK
--DON'T FAIL ME NOW.

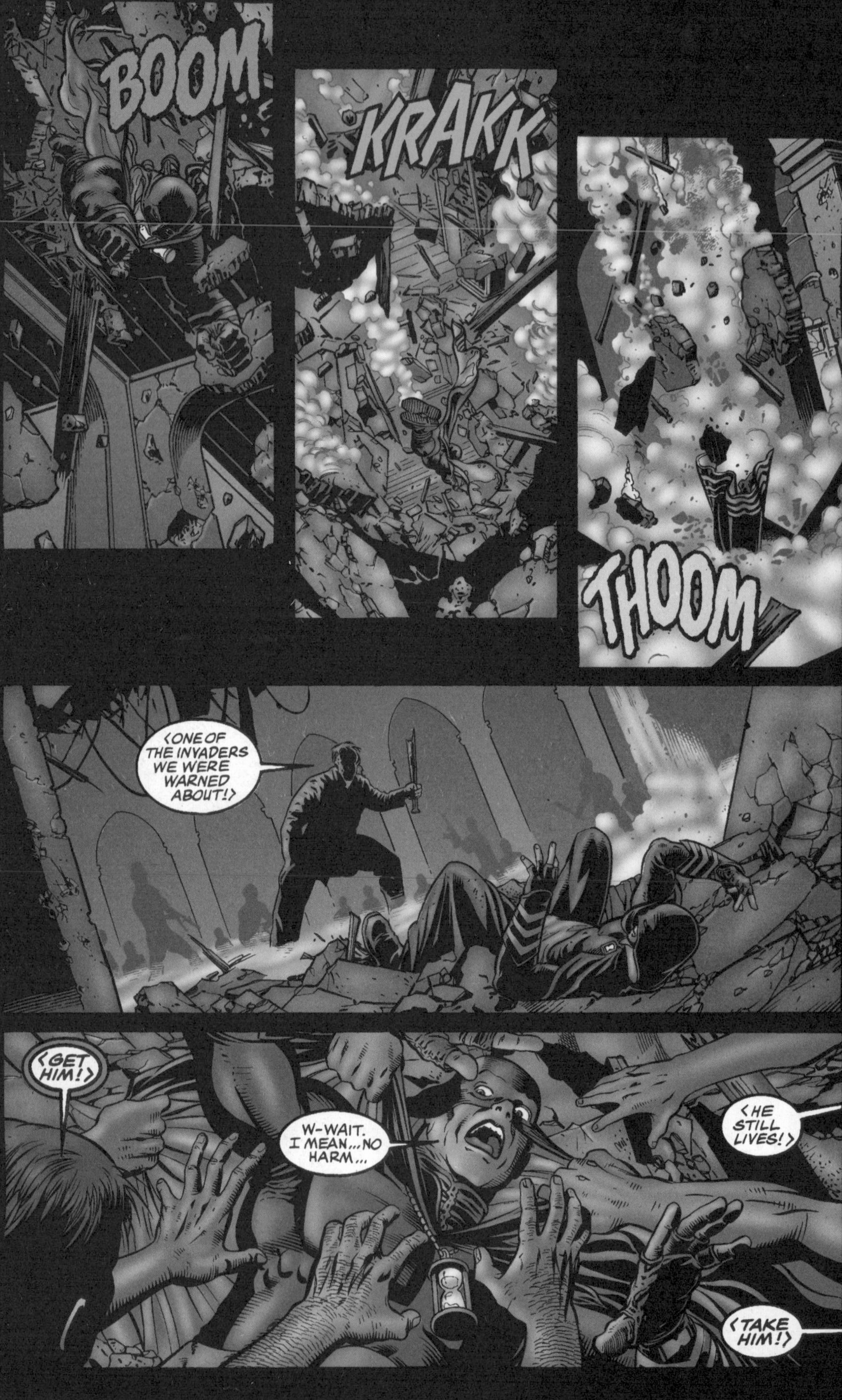
BOOM
KRAKK
THOOM
<ONE OF THE INVADERS WE WERE WARNED ABOUT!>
<GET HIM!>
W-WAIT. I MEAN... NO HARM...
<HE STILL LIVES!>
<TAKE HIM!>

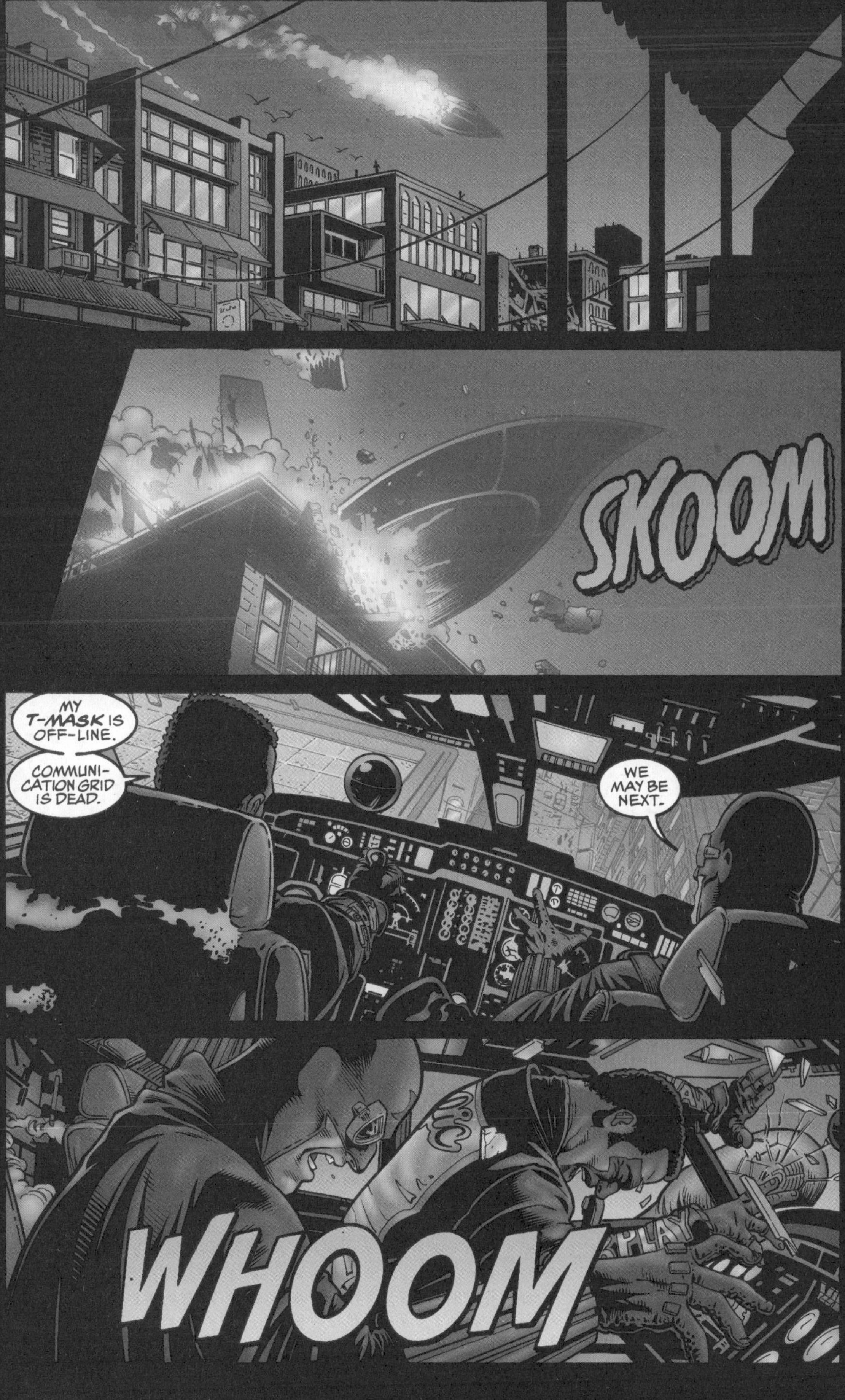
SKOOM
MY T-MASK IS OFF-LINE.
COMMUNICATION GRID IS DEAD.
WE MAY BE NEXT.
WHOOM
PLAY

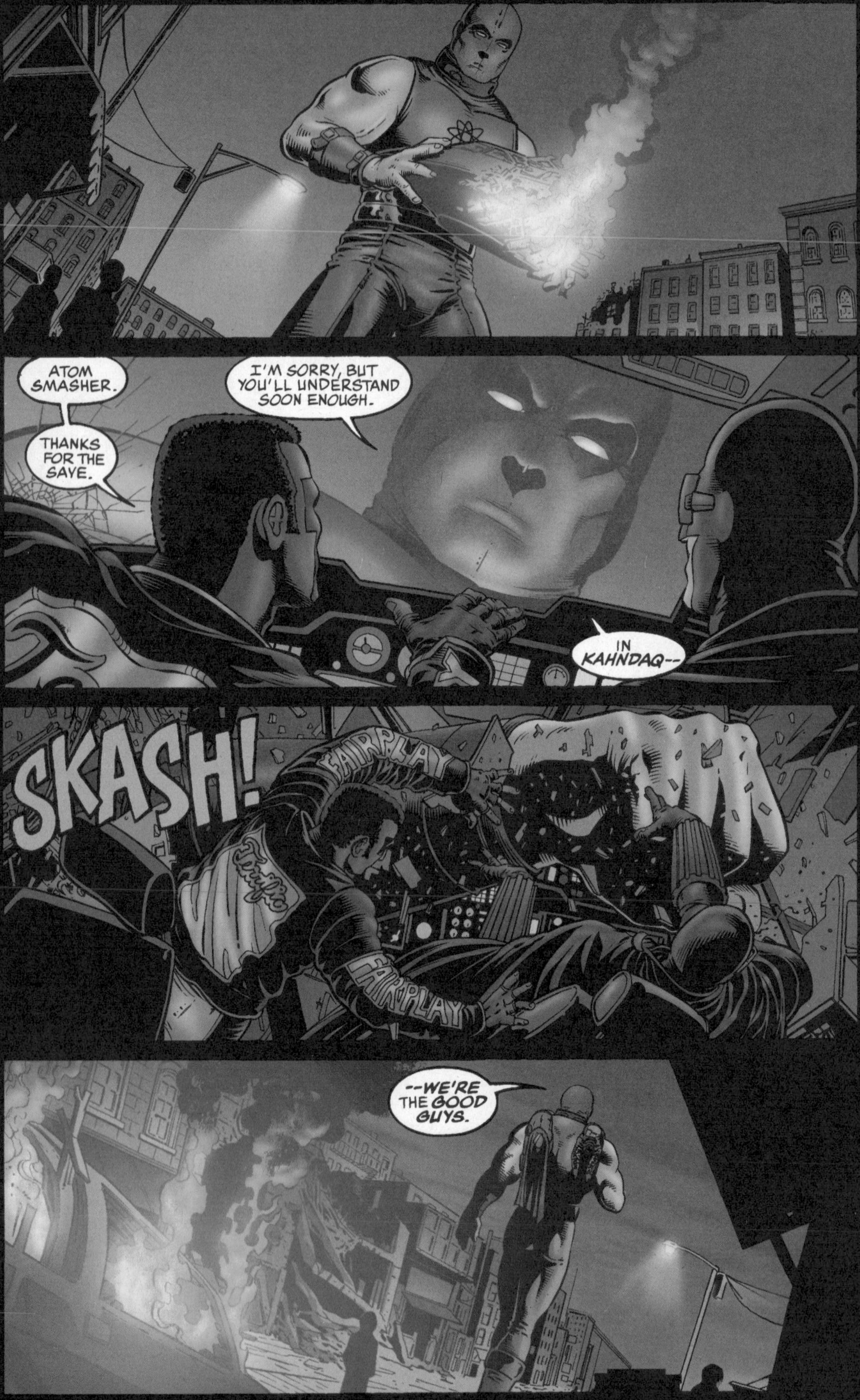
ATOM SMASHER.
THANKS FOR THE SAVE.
I'M SORRY, BUT YOU'LL UNDERSTAND SOON ENOUGH.
IN KAHNDAQ--
SKASH!
FAIRPLAY
FAIRPLAY
--WE'RE THE GOOD GUYS.

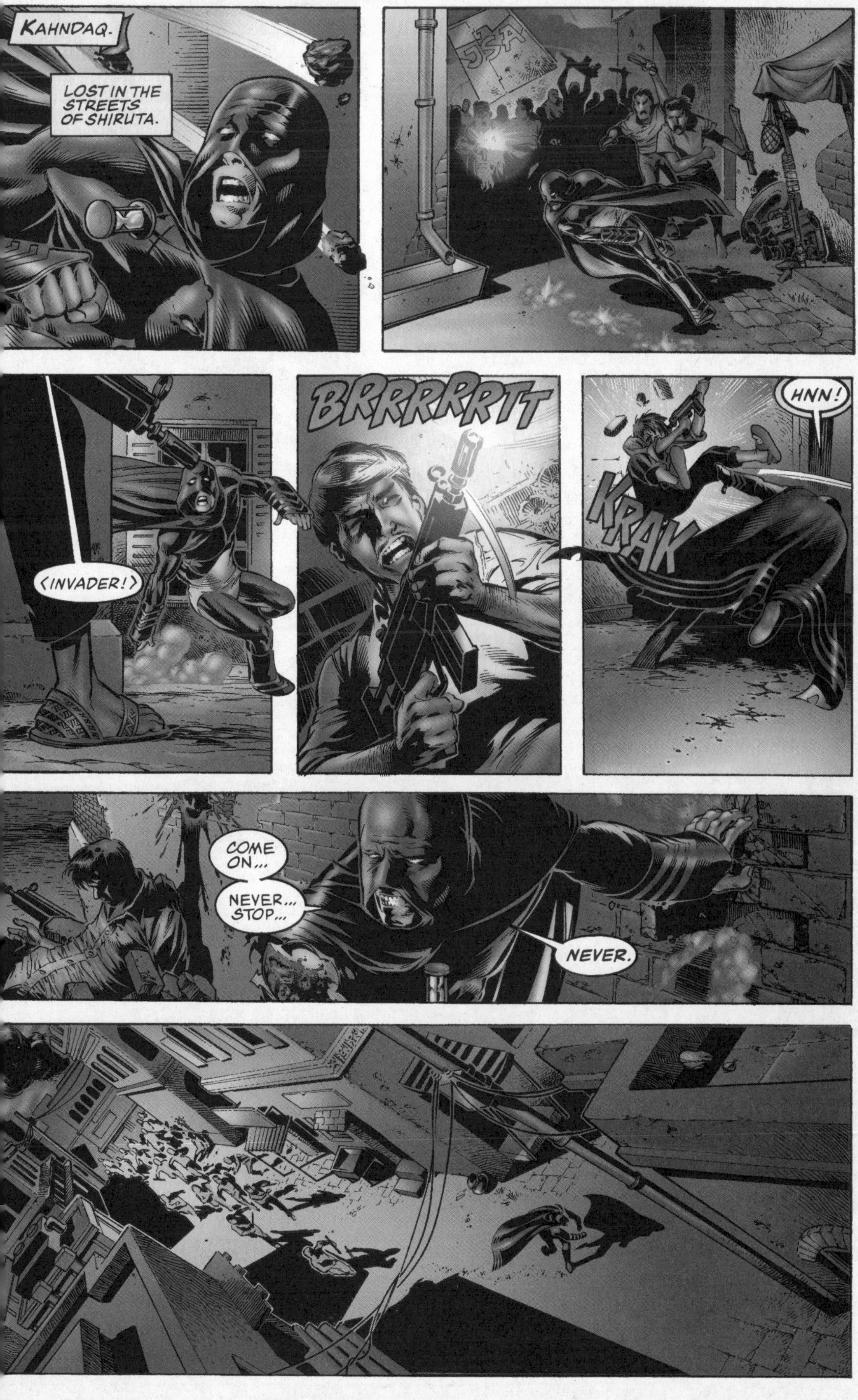
KAHNDAQ.
LOST IN THE STREETS OF SHIRUTA.
JSA
<INVADER!>
BRRRRRRTT
HNN!
KRAK
COME ON...
NEVER... STOP...
NEVER.

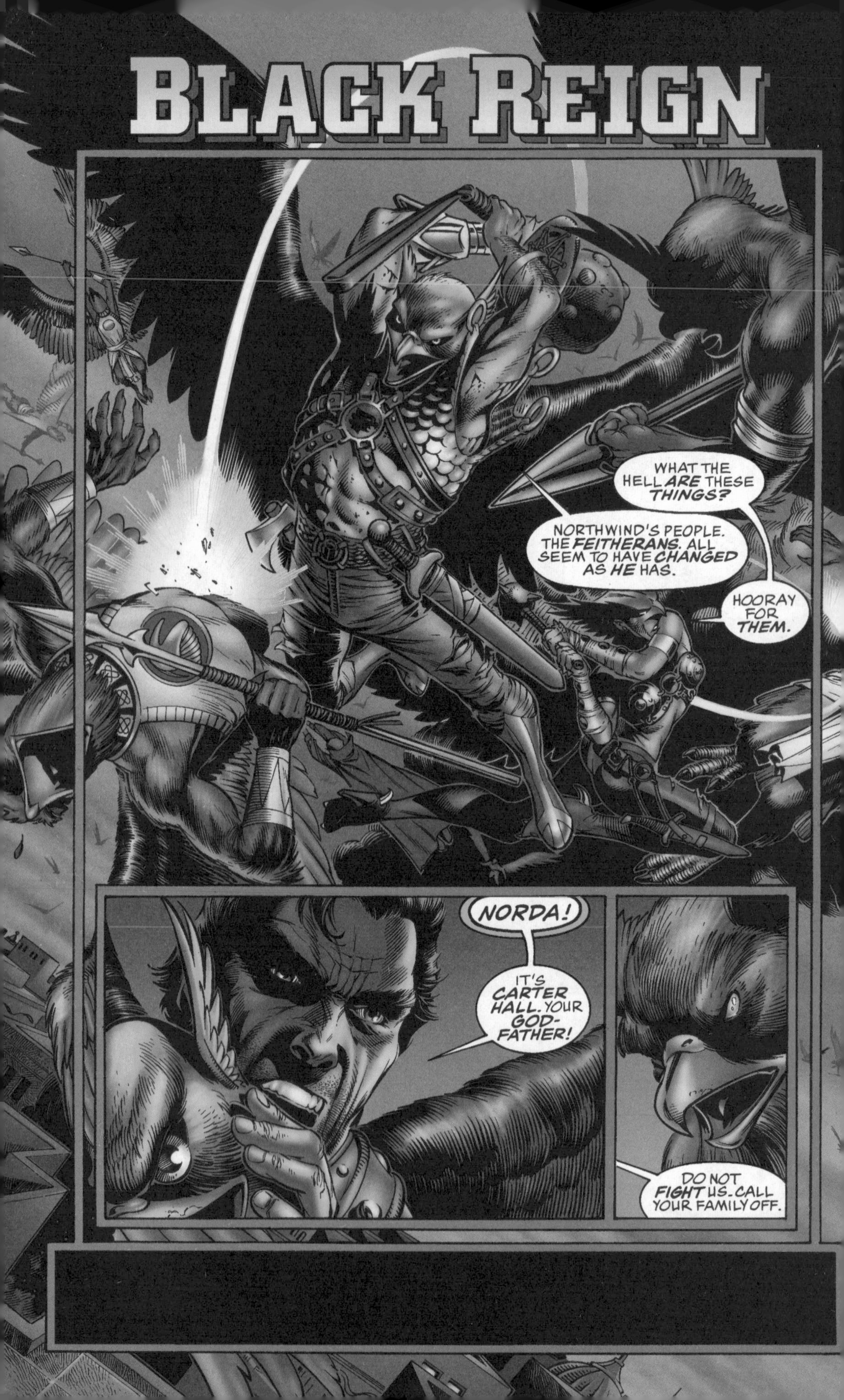
BLACK REIGN
WHAT THE HELL ARE THESE THINGS?
NORTHWIND'S PEOPLE. THE FEITHERANS. ALL SEEM TO HAVE CHANGED AS HE HAS.
HOORAY FOR THEM.
NORDA!
IT'S CARTER HALL. YOUR GOD-FATHER!
DO NOT FIGHT US. CALL YOUR FAMILY OFF.

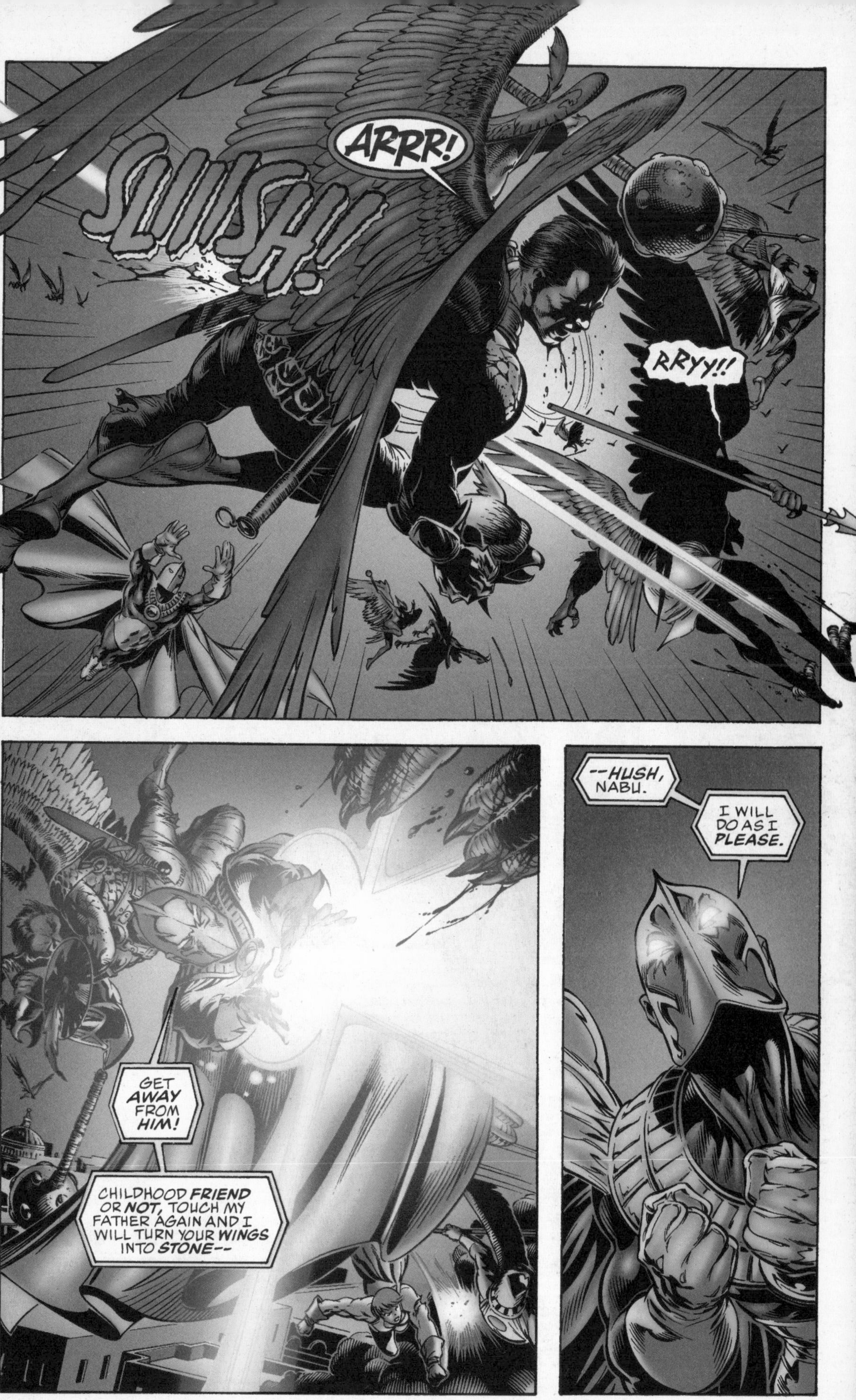

SLUISH!!
ARRR!
RRYY!!
GET AWAY FROM HIM!
CHILDHOOD FRIEND OR NOT, TOUCH MY FATHER AGAIN AND I WILL TURN YOUR WINGS INTO STONE--
--HUSH, NABU.
I WILL DO AS I PLEASE.

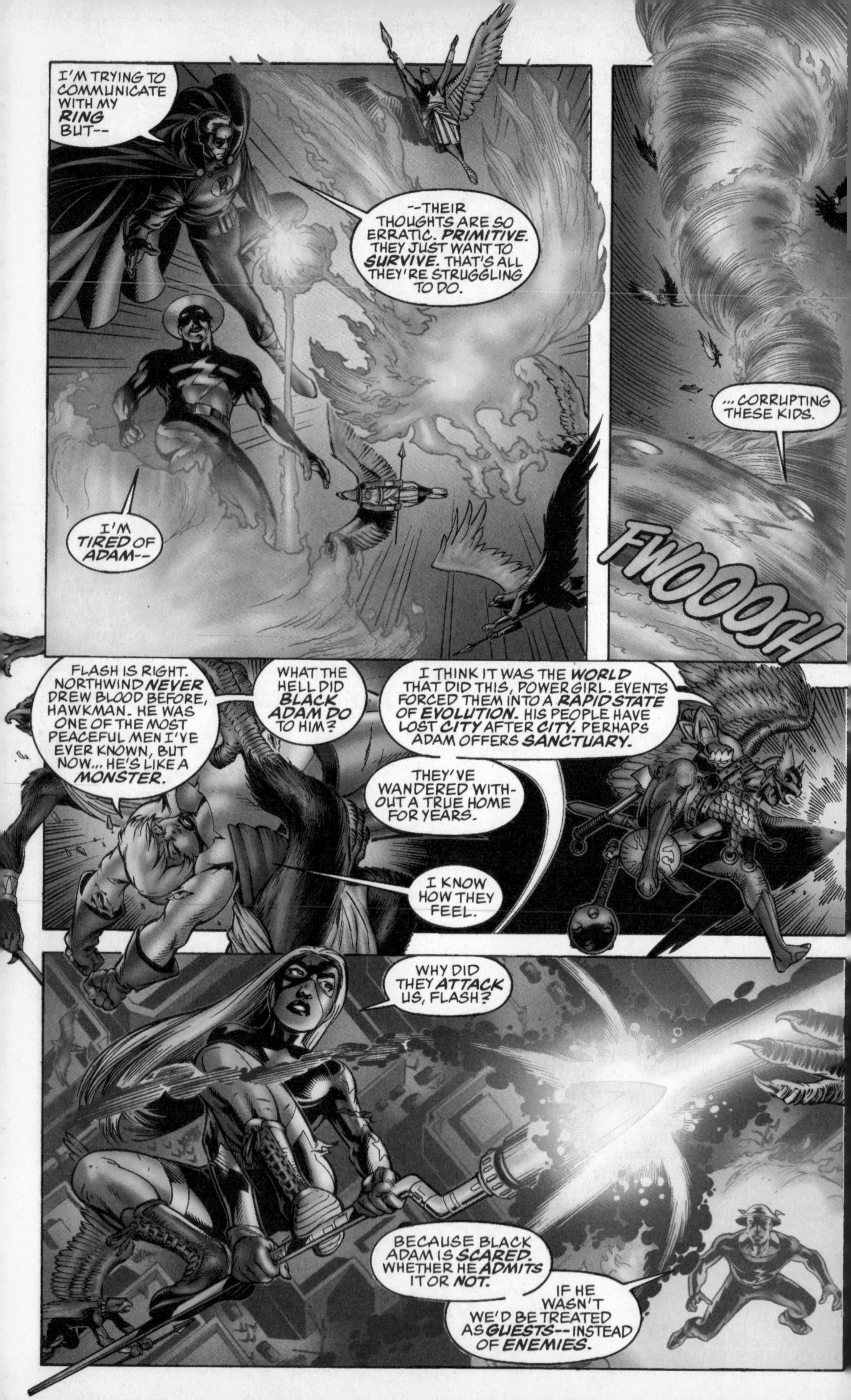

I'M TRYING TO COMMUNICATE WITH MY RING BUT--
--THEIR THOUGHTS ARE SO ERRATIC. PRIMITIVE. THEY JUST WANT TO SURVIVE. THAT'S ALL THEY'RE STRUGGLING TO DO.
I'M TIRED OF ADAM--
...CORRUPTING THESE KIDS.
FWOOOSH
FLASH IS RIGHT. NORTHWIND NEVER DREW BLOOD BEFORE, HAWKMAN. HE WAS ONE OF THE MOST PEACEFUL MEN I'VE EVER KNOWN, BUT NOW... HE'S LIKE A MONSTER.
WHAT THE HELL DID BLACK ADAM DO TO HIM?
I THINK IT WAS THE WORLD THAT DID THIS, POWER GIRL. EVENTS FORCED THEM INTO A RAPID STATE OF EVOLUTION. HIS PEOPLE HAVE LOST CITY AFTER CITY. PERHAPS ADAM OFFERS SANCTUARY.
THEY'VE WANDERED WITHOUT A TRUE HOME FOR YEARS.
I KNOW HOW THEY FEEL.
WHY DID THEY ATTACK US, FLASH?
BECAUSE BLACK ADAM IS SCARED. WHETHER HE ADMITS IT OR NOT.
IF HE WASN'T WE'D BE TREATED AS GUESTS--INSTEAD OF ENEMIES.

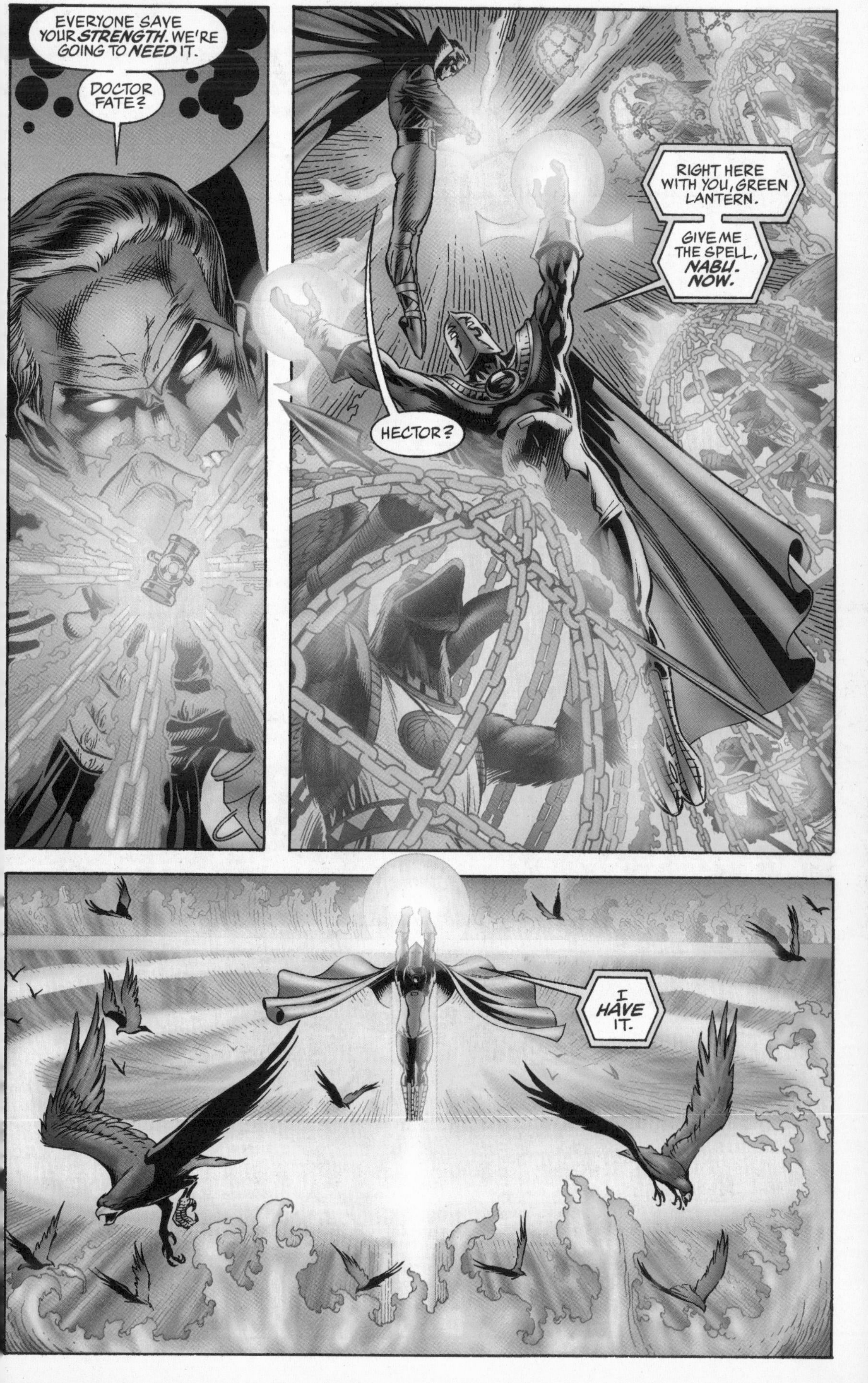
EVERYONE SAVE YOUR STRENGTH. WE'RE GOING TO NEED IT.
DOCTOR FATE?
RIGHT HERE WITH YOU, GREEN LANTERN.
GIVE ME THE SPELL, NABU. NOW.
HECTOR?
I HAVE IT.

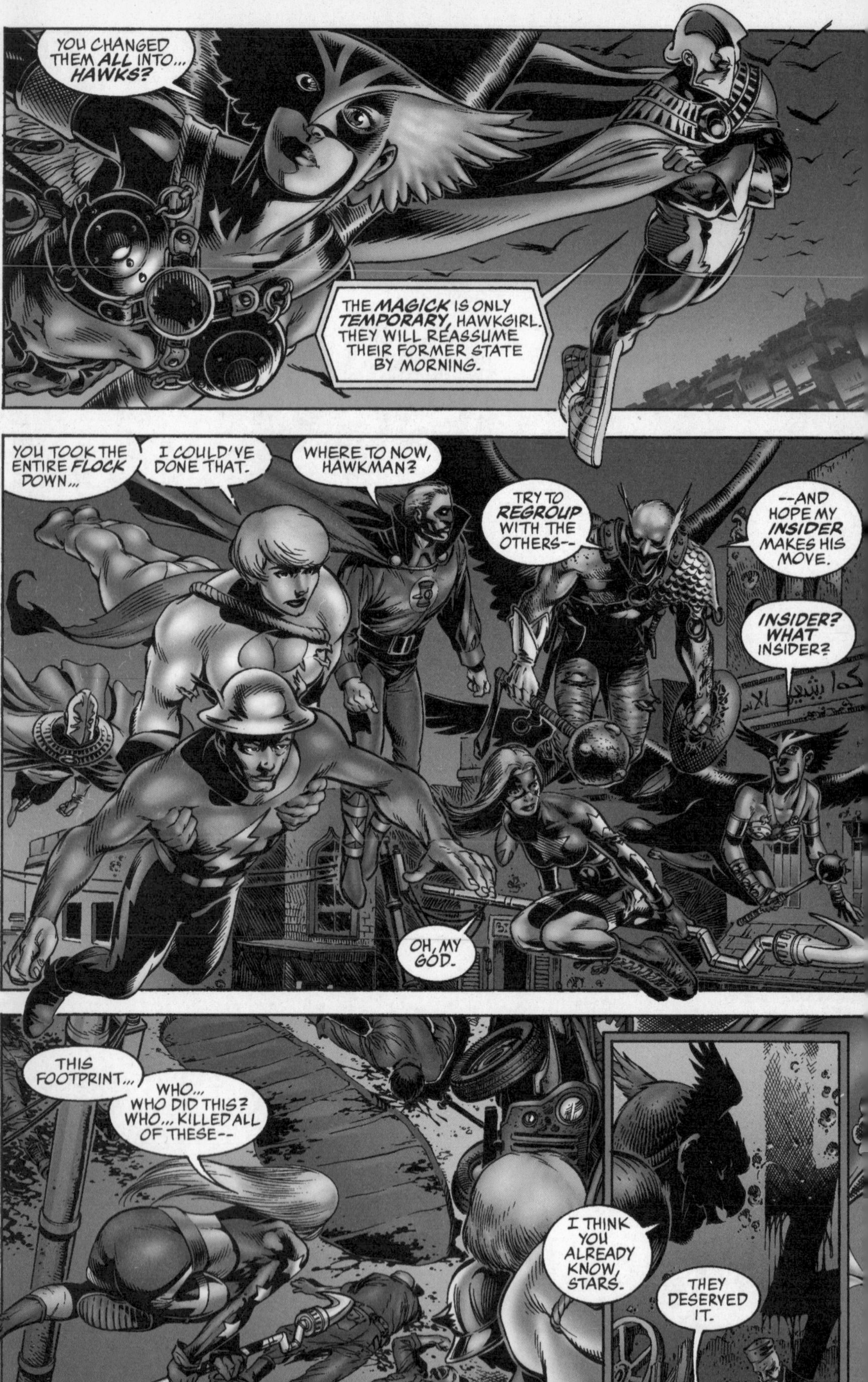
YOU CHANGED THEM ALL INTO... HAWKS?
THE MAGICK IS ONLY TEMPORARY, HAWKGIRL. THEY WILL REASSUME THEIR FORMER STATE BY MORNING.
YOU TOOK THE ENTIRE FLOCK DOWN...
I COULD'VE DONE THAT.
WHERE TO NOW, HAWKMAN?
TRY TO REGROUP WITH THE OTHERS--
--AND HOPE MY INSIDER MAKES HIS MOVE.
INSIDER? WHAT INSIDER?
OH, MY GOD.
THIS FOOTPRINT...
WHO... WHO DID THIS? WHO... KILLED ALL OF THESE--
I THINK YOU ALREADY KNOW, STARS.
THEY DESERVED IT.

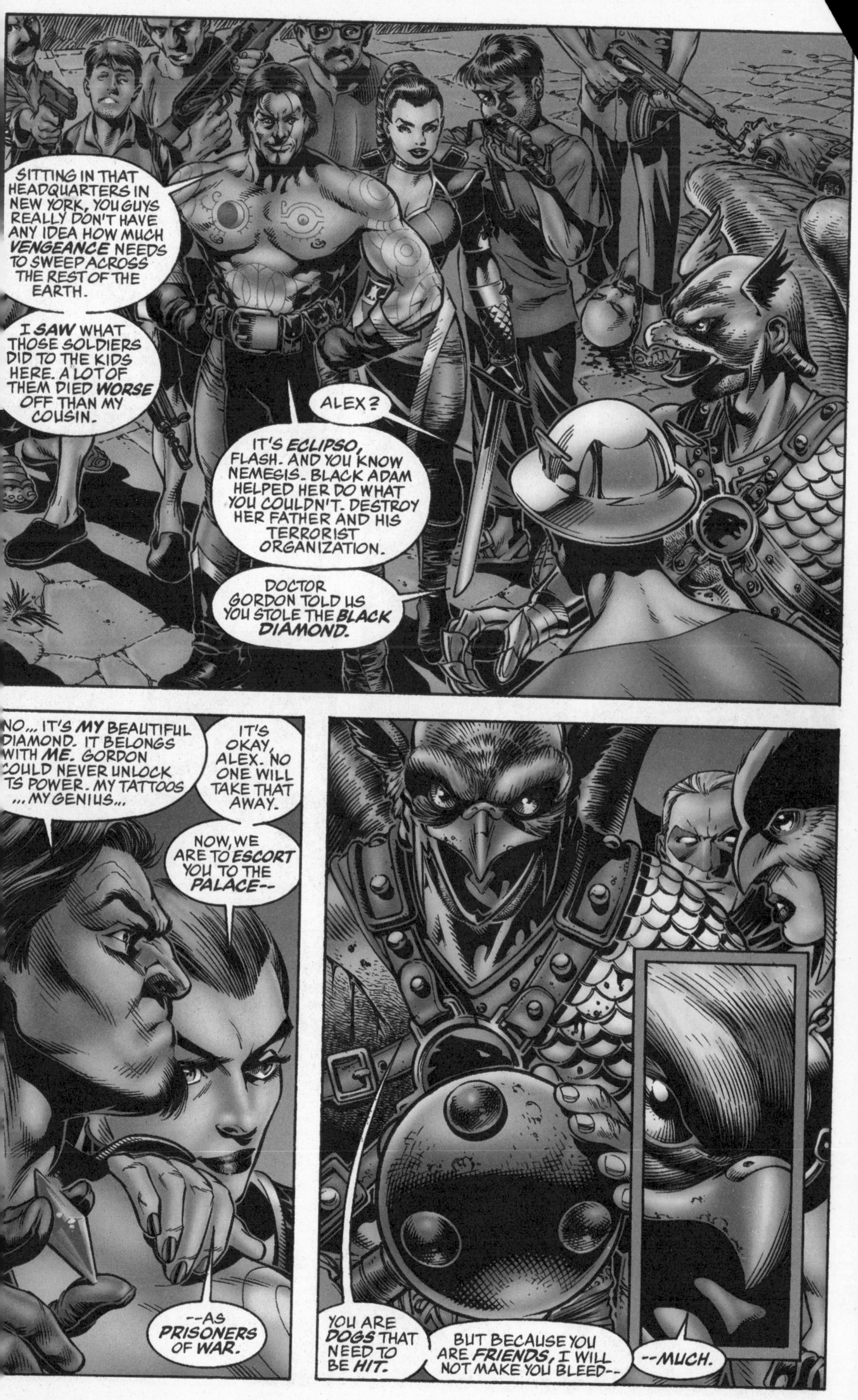
SITTING IN THAT HEADQUARTERS IN NEW YORK, YOU GUYS REALLY DON'T HAVE ANY IDEA HOW MUCH VENGEANCE NEEDS TO SWEEP ACROSS THE REST OF THE EARTH.
I SAW WHAT THOSE SOLDIERS DID TO THE KIDS HERE. A LOT OF THEM DIED WORSE OFF THAN MY COUSIN.
ALEX?
IT'S ECLIPSO, FLASH. AND YOU KNOW NEMESIS. BLACK ADAM HELPED HER DO WHAT YOU COULDN'T. DESTROY HER FATHER AND HIS TERRORIST ORGANIZATION.
DOCTOR GORDON TOLD US YOU STOLE THE BLACK DIAMOND.
NO... IT'S MY BEAUTIFUL DIAMOND. IT BELONGS WITH ME. GORDON COULD NEVER UNLOCK ITS POWER. MY TATTOOS ...MY GENIUS...
IT'S OKAY, ALEX. NO ONE WILL TAKE THAT AWAY.
NOW, WE ARE TO ESCORT YOU TO THE PALACE--
--AS PRISONERS OF WAR.
YOU ARE DOGS THAT NEED TO BE HIT.
BUT BECAUSE YOU ARE FRIENDS, I WILL NOT MAKE YOU BLEED--
--MUCH.

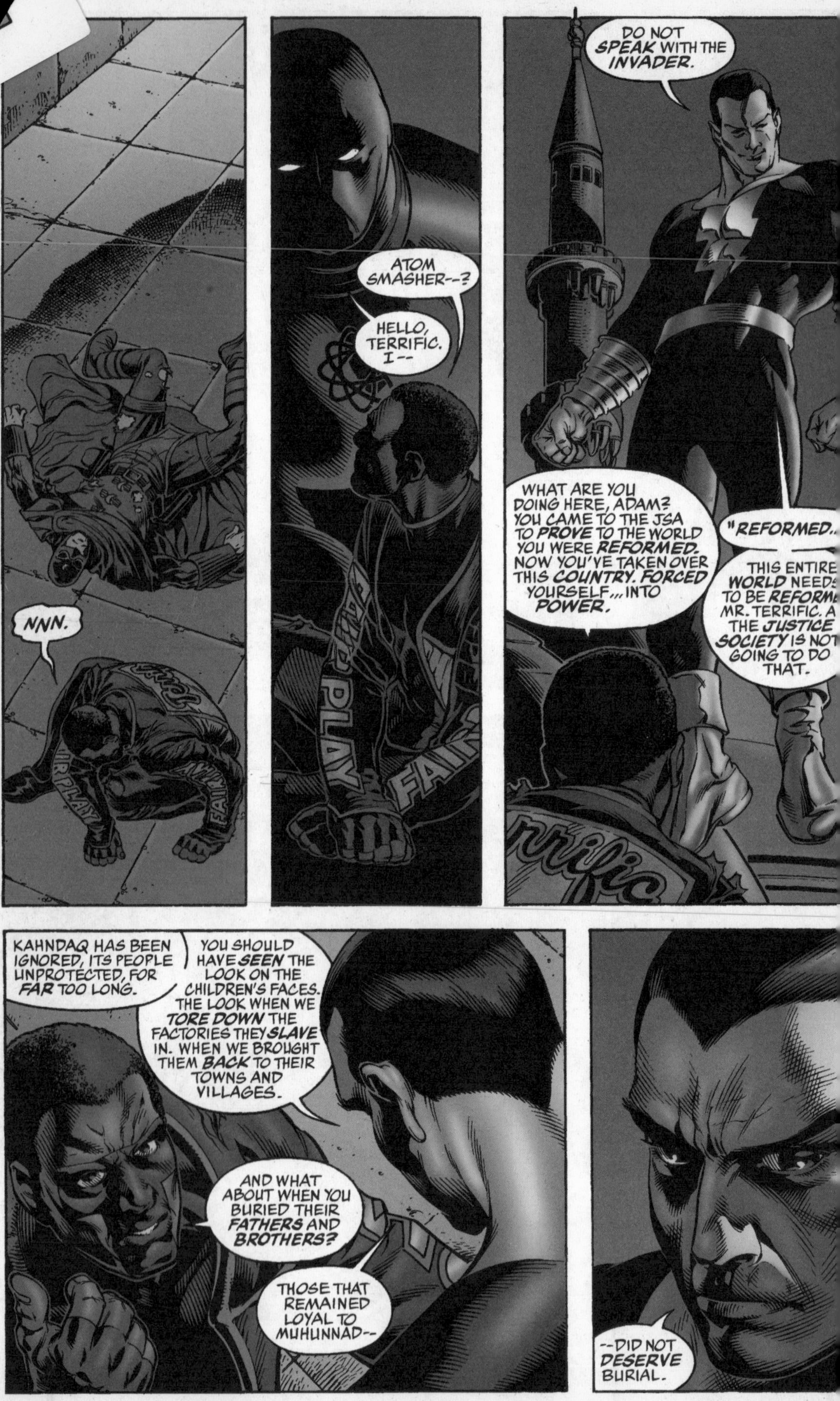
NNN.
ATOM SMASHER--?
HELLO, TERRIFIC. I--
DO NOT SPEAK WITH THE INVADER.
WHAT ARE YOU DOING HERE, ADAM? YOU CAME TO THE JSA TO PROVE TO THE WORLD YOU WERE REFORMED. NOW YOU'VE TAKEN OVER THIS COUNTRY. FORCED YOURSELF... INTO POWER.
"REFORMED..
THIS ENTIRE WORLD NEEDS TO BE REFORM MR. TERRIFIC. A THE JUSTICE SOCIETY IS NOT GOING TO DO THAT.
KAHNDAQ HAS BEEN IGNORED, ITS PEOPLE UNPROTECTED, FOR FAR TOO LONG.
YOU SHOULD HAVE SEEN THE LOOK ON THE CHILDREN'S FACES. THE LOOK WHEN WE TORE DOWN THE FACTORIES THEY SLAVE IN. WHEN WE BROUGHT THEM BACK TO THEIR TOWNS AND VILLAGES.
AND WHAT ABOUT WHEN YOU BURIED THEIR FATHERS AND BROTHERS?
THOSE THAT REMAINED LOYAL TO MUHUNNAD--
--DID NOT DESERVE BURIAL.

YOU OF ALL PEOPLE *MUST* UNDERSTAND. YOUR WIFE WAS *KILLED* BY A PATHETIC MAN WHO FAILED TO OBEY A SIMPLE *TRAFFIC LAW.*

AND HE'S SERVING TIME FOR *MANSLAUGHTER.*

BUT YOU *KNOW* THE PAIN I FEEL, MICHAEL. THE EMPTINESS AND HELPLESSNESS. THE *FRUSTRATION.*

I... I DO.

WE SIMPLY WISH THAT *PAIN* TO FALL UPON *NO OTHERS.* DAMN *OURSELVES.* WE'RE GOING TO *SAVE* THE *WORLD* BY *DESTROYING* ANYONE WHO BRINGS *VIOLENCE* INTO OUR *LANDS.*

WHEN KAHNDAQ BECOMES THE *PARADISE* IT IS *DESTINED* TO BE, WE WILL TURN OUR ATTENTION TO THE COUNTRIES *BORDERING* US. EGYPT. ISRAEL. AND THEN THE LANDS *BEYOND* THAT... AND BEYOND *THAT.*

AND YOU THINK *THOSE* PEOPLE WILL *WORSHIP* YOU LIKE A *GOD?*

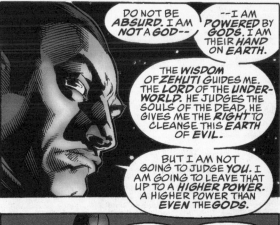

DO NOT BE *ABSURD.* I AM *NOT A GOD—*

—I AM *POWERED* BY *GODS.* I AM THEIR *HAND* ON *EARTH.*

THE *WISDOM* OF *ZEHUTI* GUIDES ME. THE *LORD* OF THE *UNDERWORLD.* HE JUDGES THE SOULS OF THE DEAD, HE GIVES ME THE *RIGHT* TO CLEANSE THIS *EARTH* OF EVIL.

BUT I AM NOT GOING TO JUDGE *YOU.* I AM GOING TO LEAVE THAT UP TO A *HIGHER POWER.* A HIGHER POWER THAN *EVEN* THE *GODS.*

ATOM SMASHER—

—TURN THEM OVER TO *THE PEOPLE.*

POK

I KNOW WHAT YOU WANT, BUT YOU CAN'T *END* LIVES TO *SAVE* THEM!

ADAM!

AL...

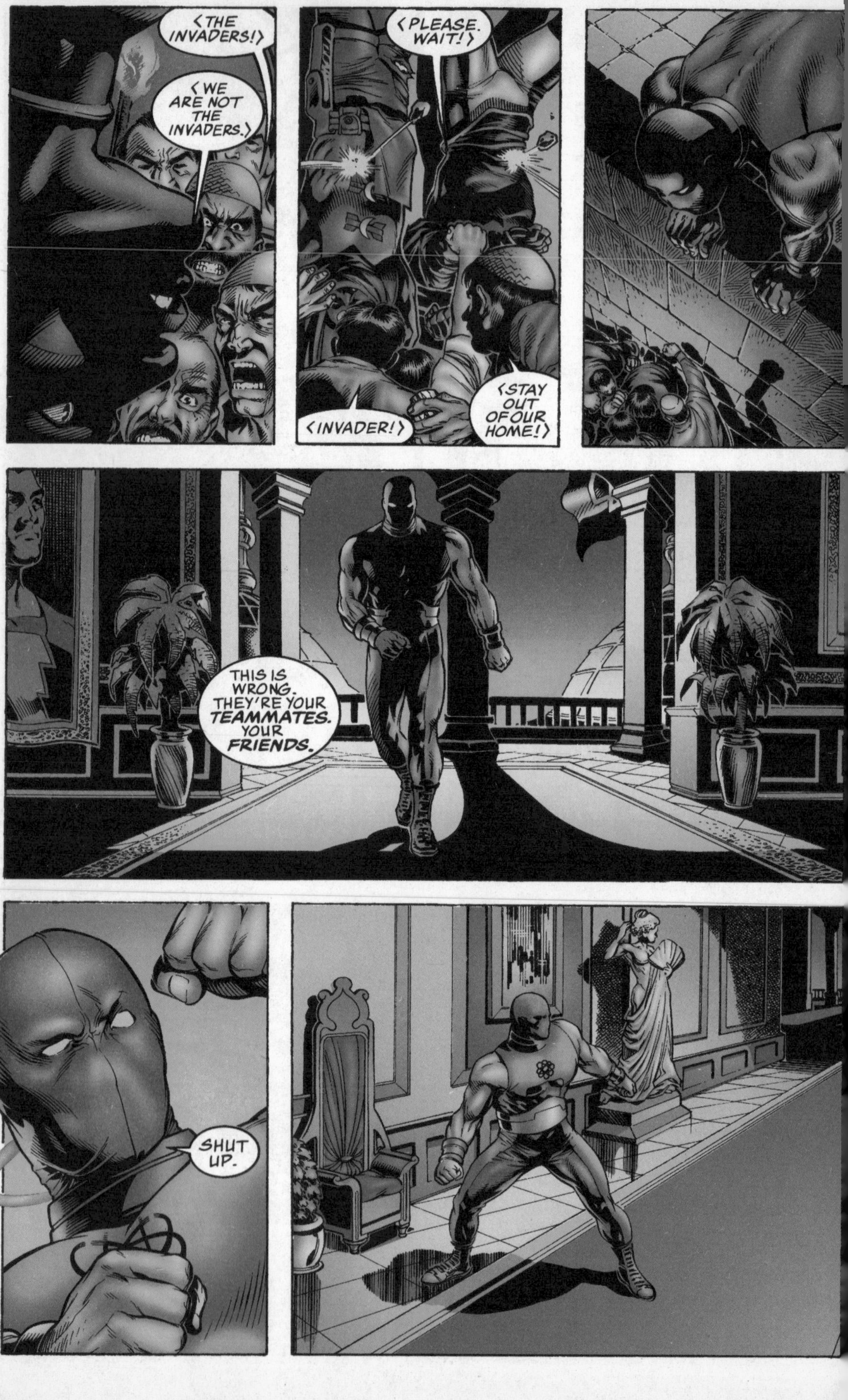
<THE INVADERS!>
<WE ARE NOT THE INVADERS.>
<PLEASE. WAIT!>
<INVADER!>
<STAY OUT OF OUR HOME!>
THIS IS WRONG. THEY'RE YOUR *TEAMMATES.* YOUR *FRIENDS.*
SHUT UP.

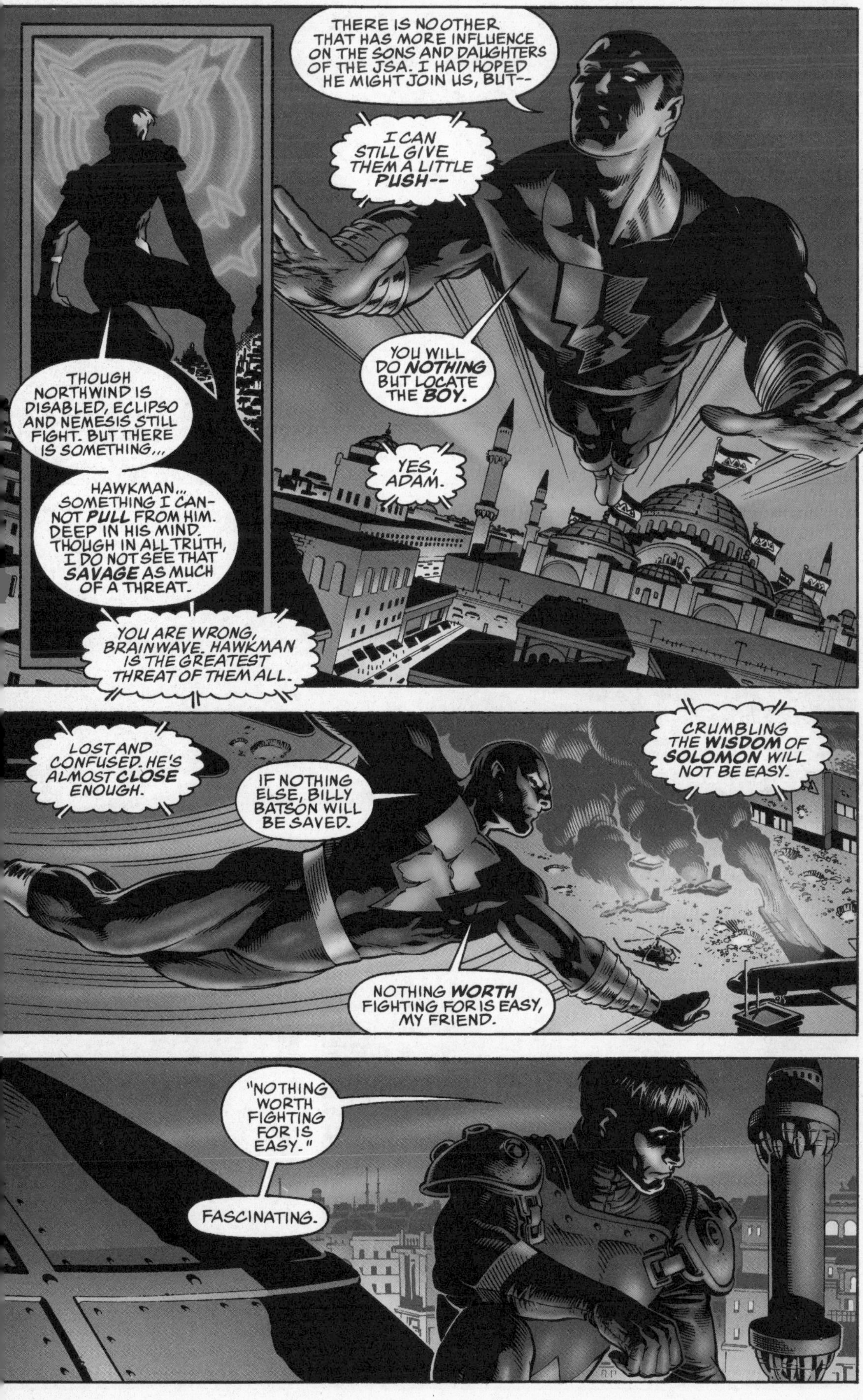
THERE IS NO OTHER THAT HAS MORE INFLUENCE ON THE SONS AND DAUGHTERS OF THE JSA. I HAD HOPED HE MIGHT JOIN US, BUT--
I CAN STILL GIVE THEM A LITTLE PUSH--
YOU WILL DO NOTHING BUT LOCATE THE BOY.
YES, ADAM.
THOUGH NORTHWIND IS DISABLED, ECLIPSO AND NEMESIS STILL FIGHT. BUT THERE IS SOMETHING...
HAWKMAN... SOMETHING I CANNOT PULL FROM HIM. DEEP IN HIS MIND. THOUGH IN ALL TRUTH, I DO NOT SEE THAT SAVAGE AS MUCH OF A THREAT.
YOU ARE WRONG, BRAINWAVE. HAWKMAN IS THE GREATEST THREAT OF THEM ALL.
LOST AND CONFUSED. HE'S ALMOST CLOSE ENOUGH.
IF NOTHING ELSE, BILLY BATSON WILL BE SAVED.
CRUMBLING THE WISDOM OF SOLOMON WILL NOT BE EASY.
NOTHING WORTH FIGHTING FOR IS EASY, MY FRIEND.
"NOTHING WORTH FIGHTING FOR IS EASY."
FASCINATING.

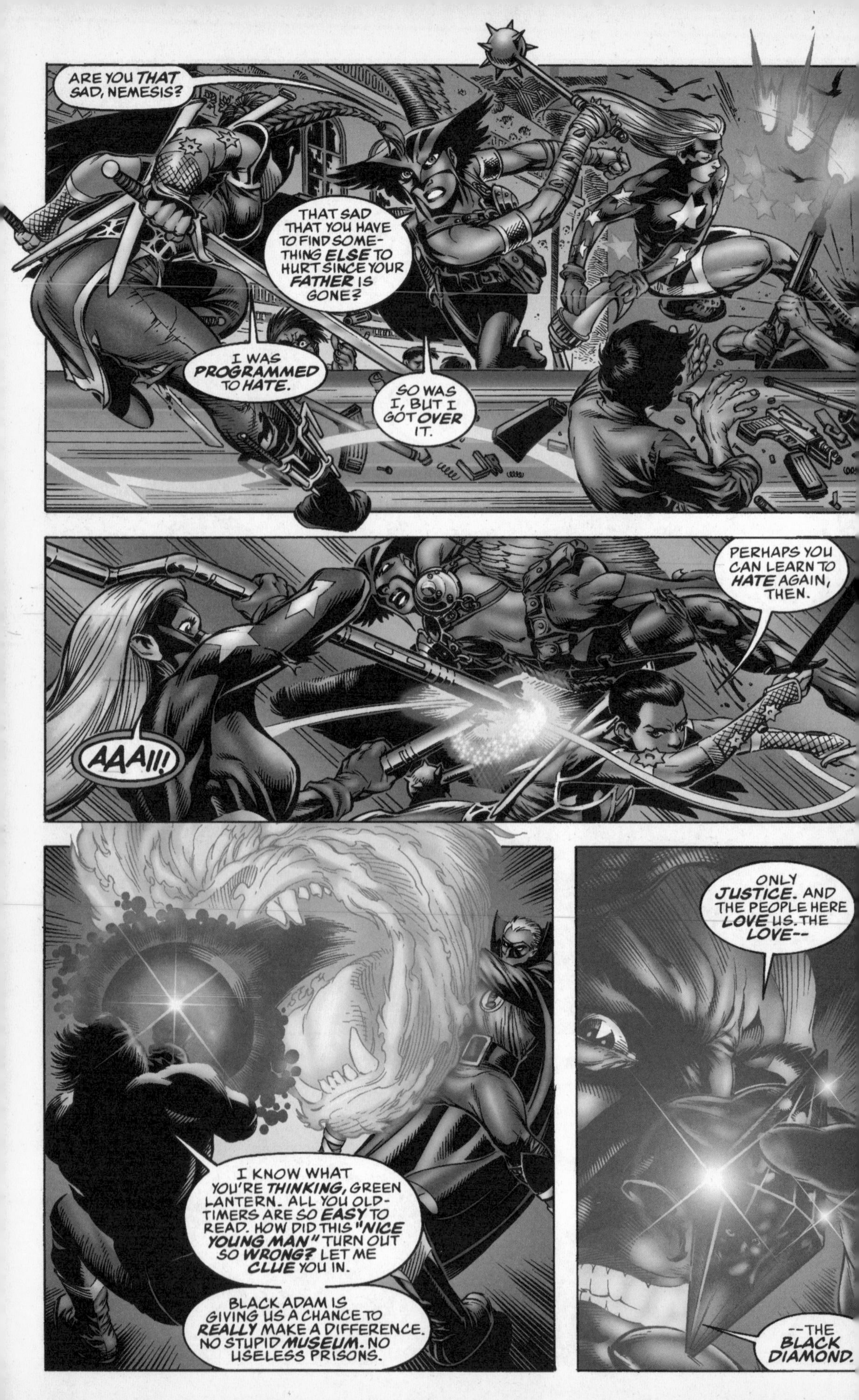
ARE YOU THAT SAD, NEMESIS?
THAT SAD THAT YOU HAVE TO FIND SOME-THING ELSE TO HURT SINCE YOUR FATHER IS GONE?
I WAS PROGRAMMED TO HATE.
SO WAS I, BUT I GOT OVER IT.
PERHAPS YOU CAN LEARN TO HATE AGAIN, THEN.
AAAII!
I KNOW WHAT YOU'RE THINKING, GREEN LANTERN. ALL YOU OLD-TIMERS ARE SO EASY TO READ. HOW DID THIS "NICE YOUNG MAN" TURN OUT SO WRONG? LET ME CLUE YOU IN.
BLACK ADAM IS GIVING US A CHANCE TO REALLY MAKE A DIFFERENCE. NO STUPID MUSEUM. NO USELESS PRISONS.
ONLY JUSTICE. AND THE PEOPLE HERE LOVE US. THE LOVE--
--THE BLACK DIAMOND.

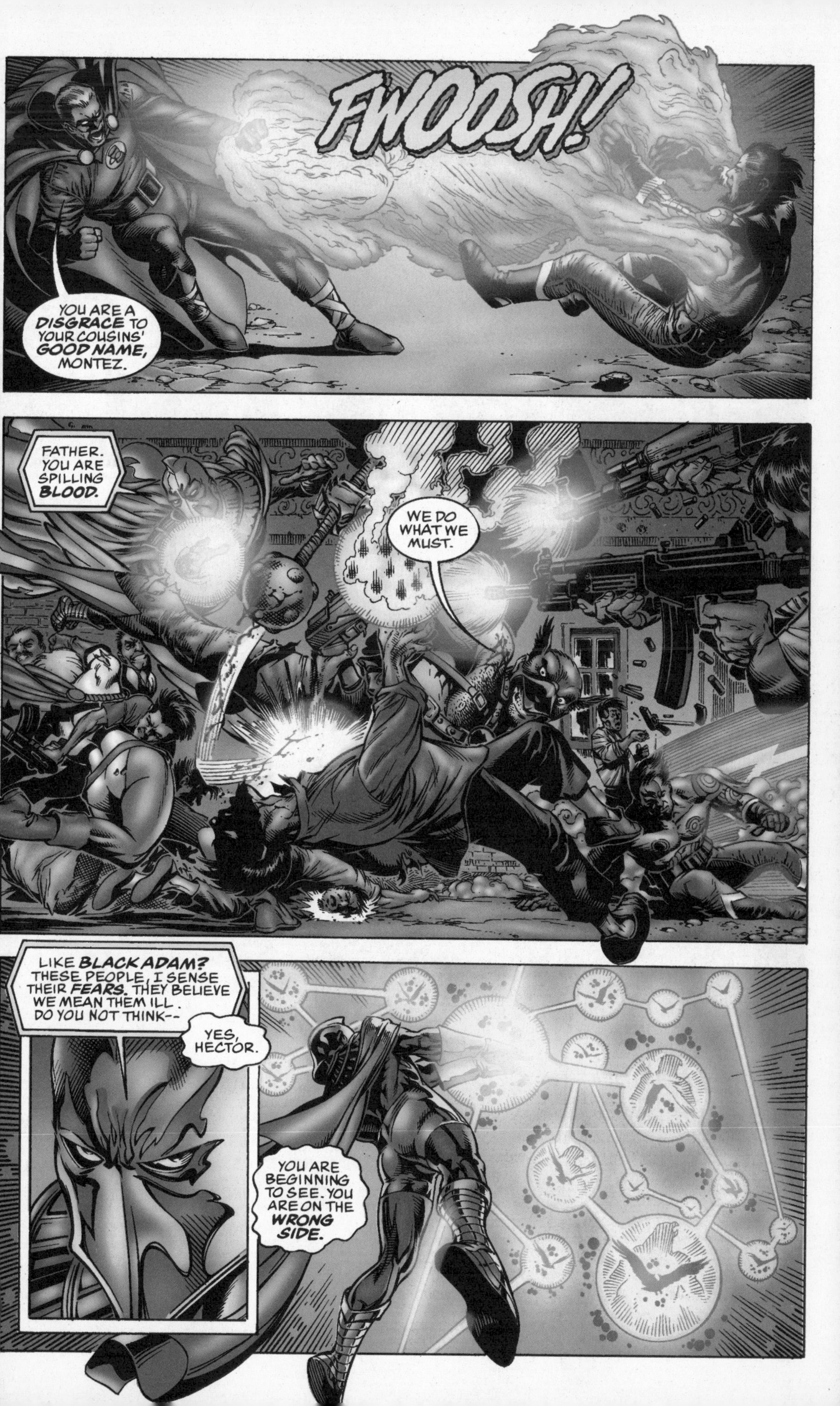
FWOOSH!
YOU ARE A DISGRACE TO YOUR COUSINS' GOOD NAME, MONTEZ.
FATHER. YOU ARE SPILLING BLOOD.
WE DO WHAT WE MUST.
LIKE BLACK ADAM? THESE PEOPLE, I SENSE THEIR FEARS. THEY BELIEVE WE MEAN THEM ILL. DO YOU NOT THINK--
YES, HECTOR.
YOU ARE BEGINNING TO SEE. YOU ARE ON THE WRONG SIDE.

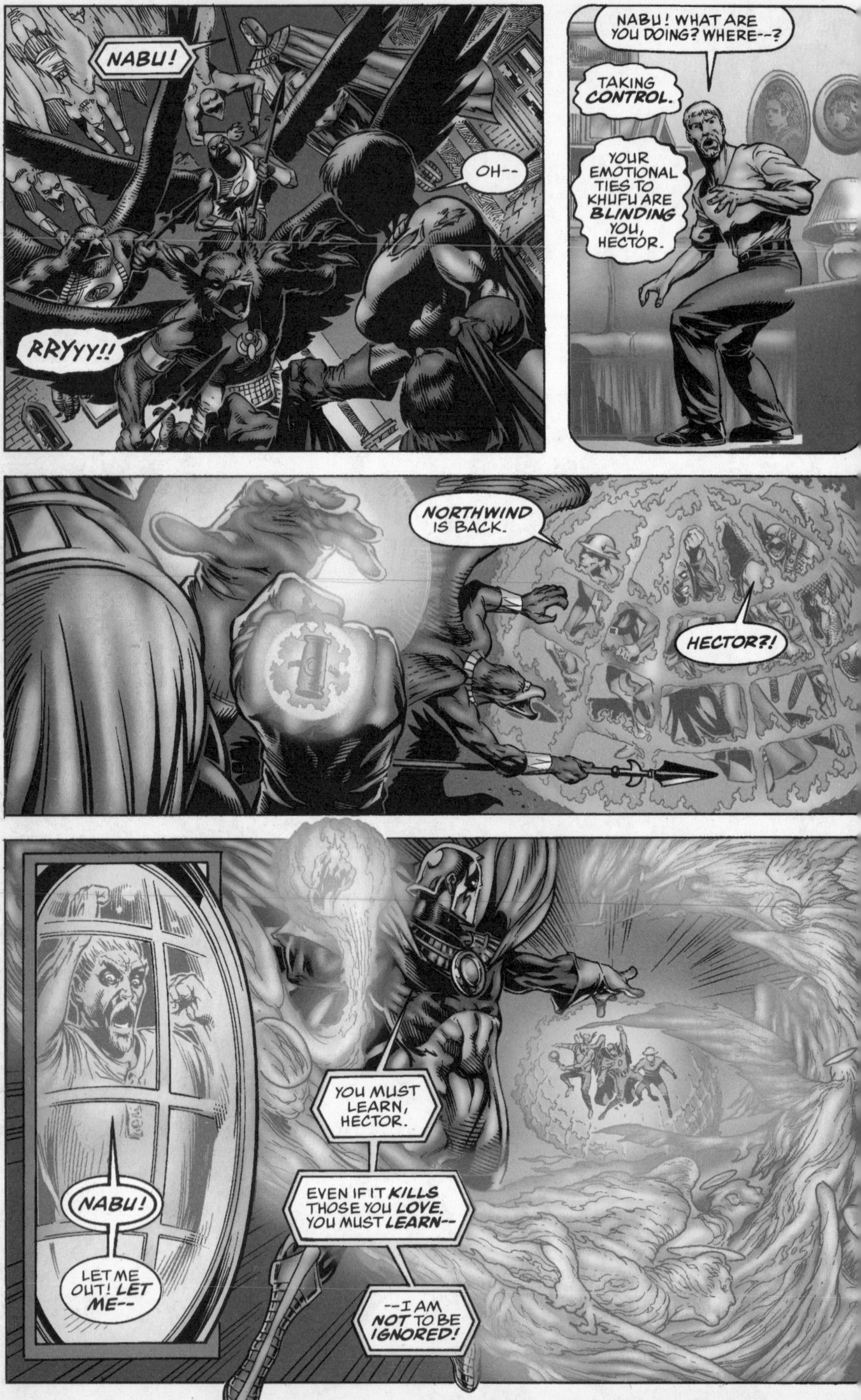
NABU!
OH--
RRYYY!!
NABU! WHAT ARE YOU DOING? WHERE--?
TAKING CONTROL.
YOUR EMOTIONAL TIES TO KHUFU ARE BLINDING YOU, HECTOR.
NORTHWIND IS BACK.
HECTOR?!
YOU MUST LEARN, HECTOR.
EVEN IF IT KILLS THOSE YOU LOVE. YOU MUST LEARN--
--I AM NOT TO BE IGNORED!
NABU!
LET ME OUT! LET ME--

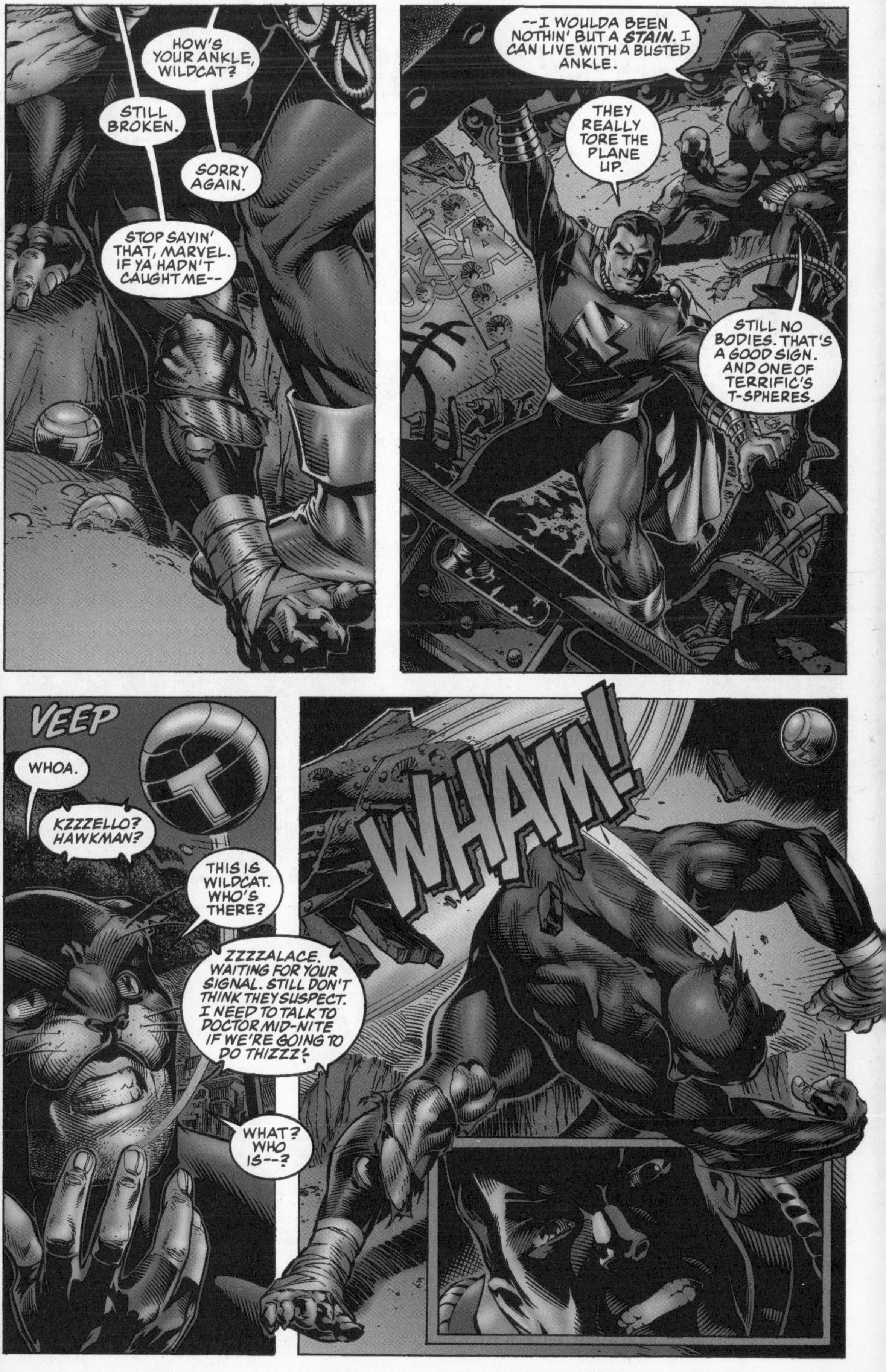
HOW'S YOUR ANKLE, WILDCAT?
STILL BROKEN.
SORRY AGAIN.
STOP SAYIN' THAT, MARVEL. IF YA HADN'T CAUGHT ME--
--I WOULDA BEEN NOTHIN' BUT A STAIN. I CAN LIVE WITH A BUSTED ANKLE.
THEY REALLY TORE THE PLANE UP.
STILL NO BODIES. THAT'S A GOOD SIGN. AND ONE OF TERRIFIC'S T-SPHERES.
VEEP
WHOA.
KZZZELLO? HAWKMAN?
THIS IS WILDCAT. WHO'S THERE?
ZZZZALACE. WAITING FOR YOUR SIGNAL. STILL DON'T THINK THEY SUSPECT. I NEED TO TALK TO DOCTOR MID-NITE IF WE'RE GOING TO DO THIZZZ
WHAT? WHO IS--?
WHAM!

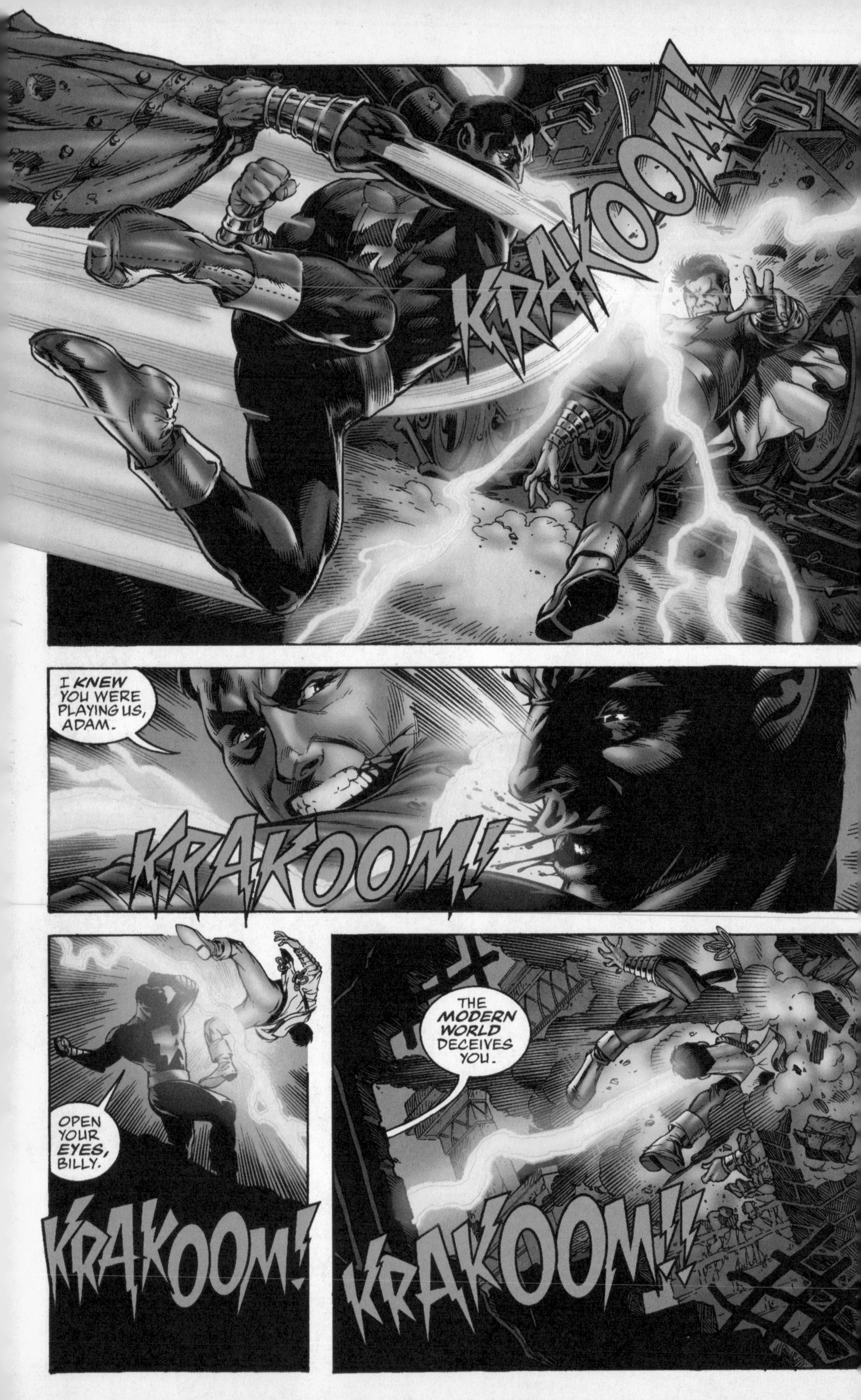
KRAKOOM!
I KNEW YOU WERE PLAYING US, ADAM.
KRAKOOM!
OPEN YOUR EYES, BILLY.
KRAKOOM!
THE MODERN WORLD DECEIVES YOU.
KRAKOOM!!

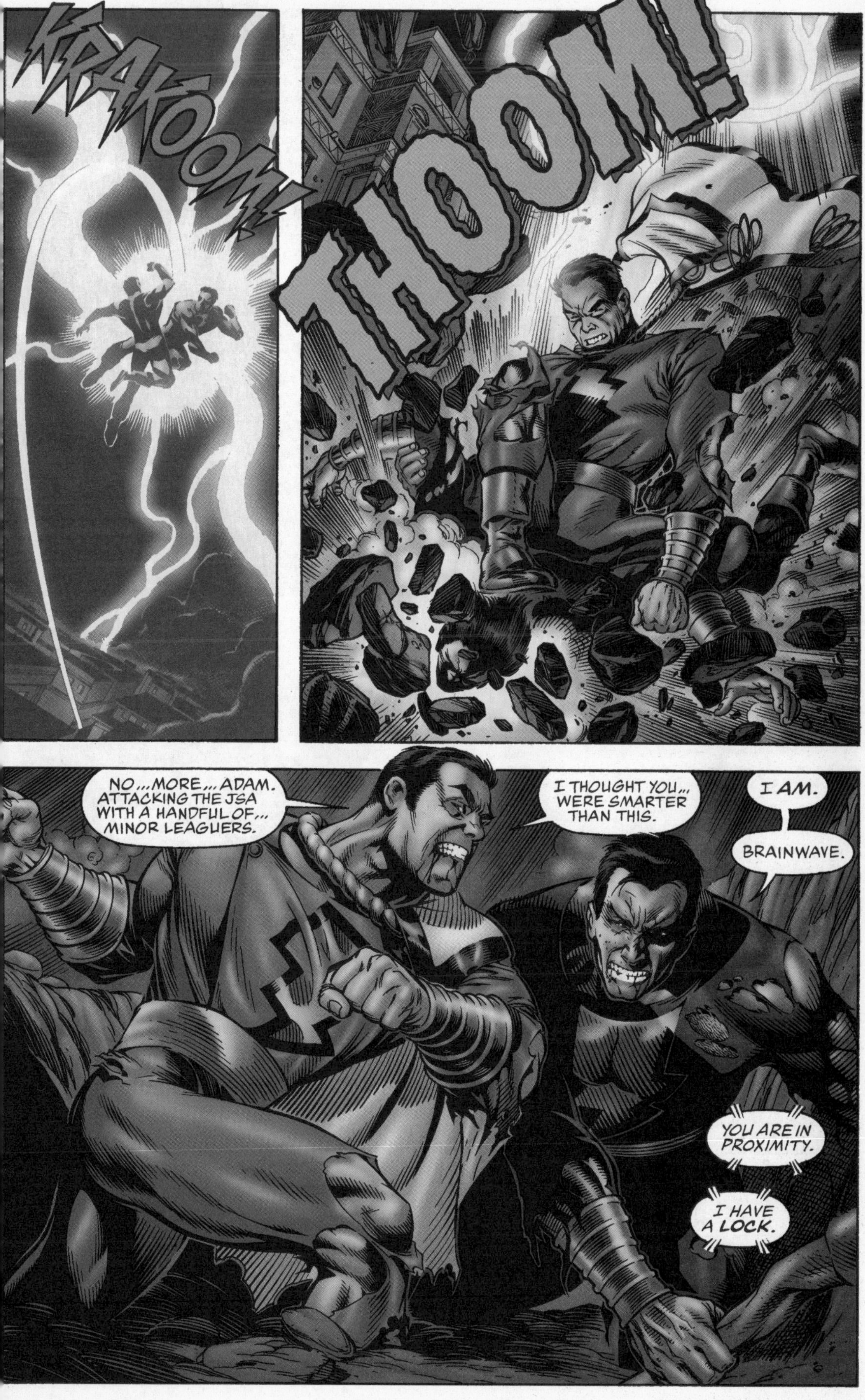
KRAKOOM!
THOOM!
NO... MORE... ADAM. ATTACKING THE JSA WITH A HANDFUL OF... MINOR LEAGUERS.
I THOUGHT YOU... WERE SMARTER THAN THIS.
I AM.
BRAINWAVE.
YOU ARE IN PROXIMITY.
I HAVE A LOCK.

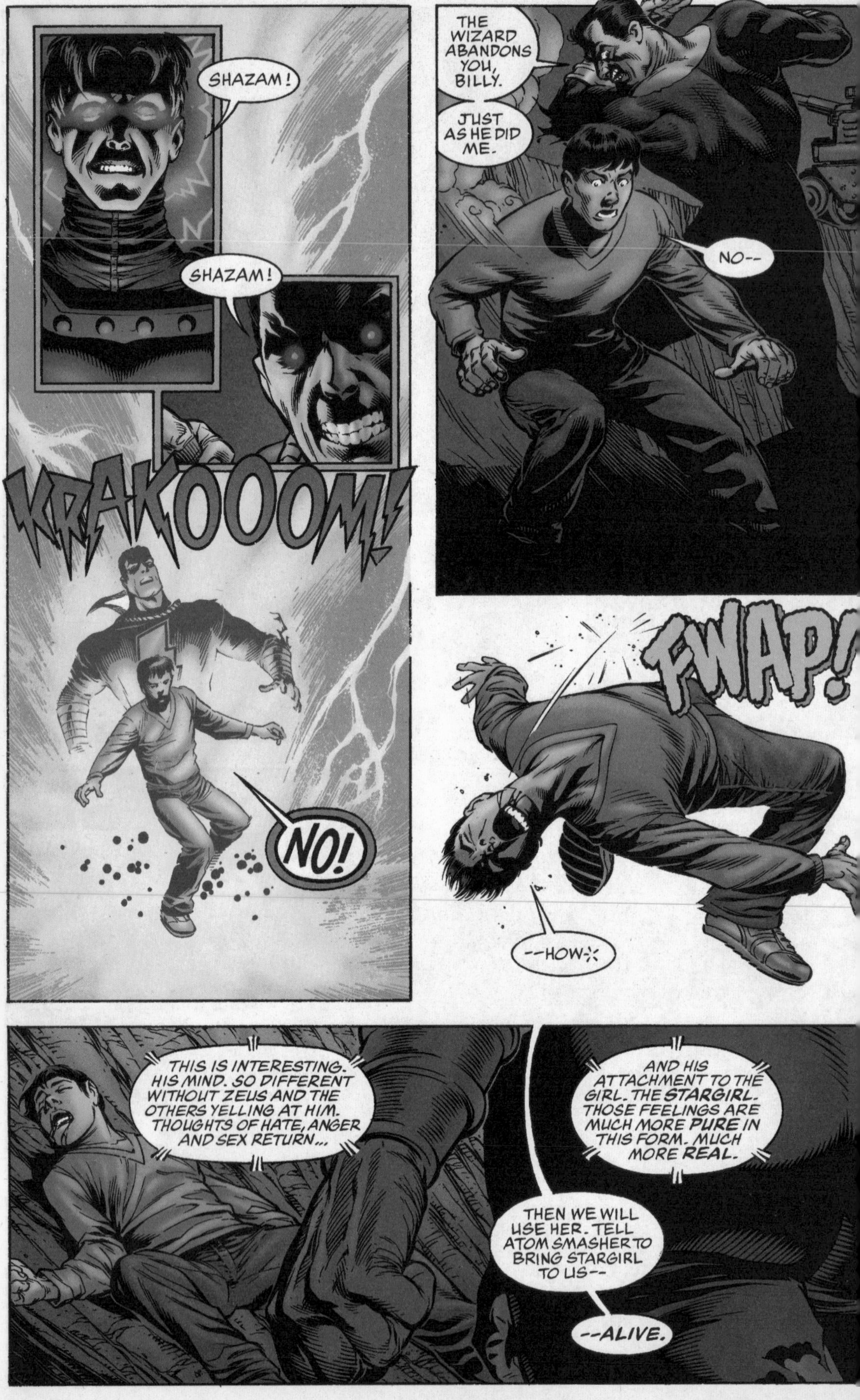
SHAZAM!
SHAZAM!
KRAKOOOM!
NO!
THE WIZARD ABANDONS YOU, BILLY.
JUST AS HE DID ME.
NO--
FWAP!
--HOW⁘
THIS IS INTERESTING. HIS MIND. SO DIFFERENT WITHOUT ZEUS AND THE OTHERS YELLING AT HIM. THOUGHTS OF HATE, ANGER AND SEX RETURN...
AND HIS ATTACHMENT TO THE GIRL. THE STARGIRL. THOSE FEELINGS ARE MUCH MORE PURE IN THIS FORM. MUCH MORE REAL.
THEN WE WILL USE HER. TELL ATOM SMASHER TO BRING STARGIRL TO US--
--ALIVE.

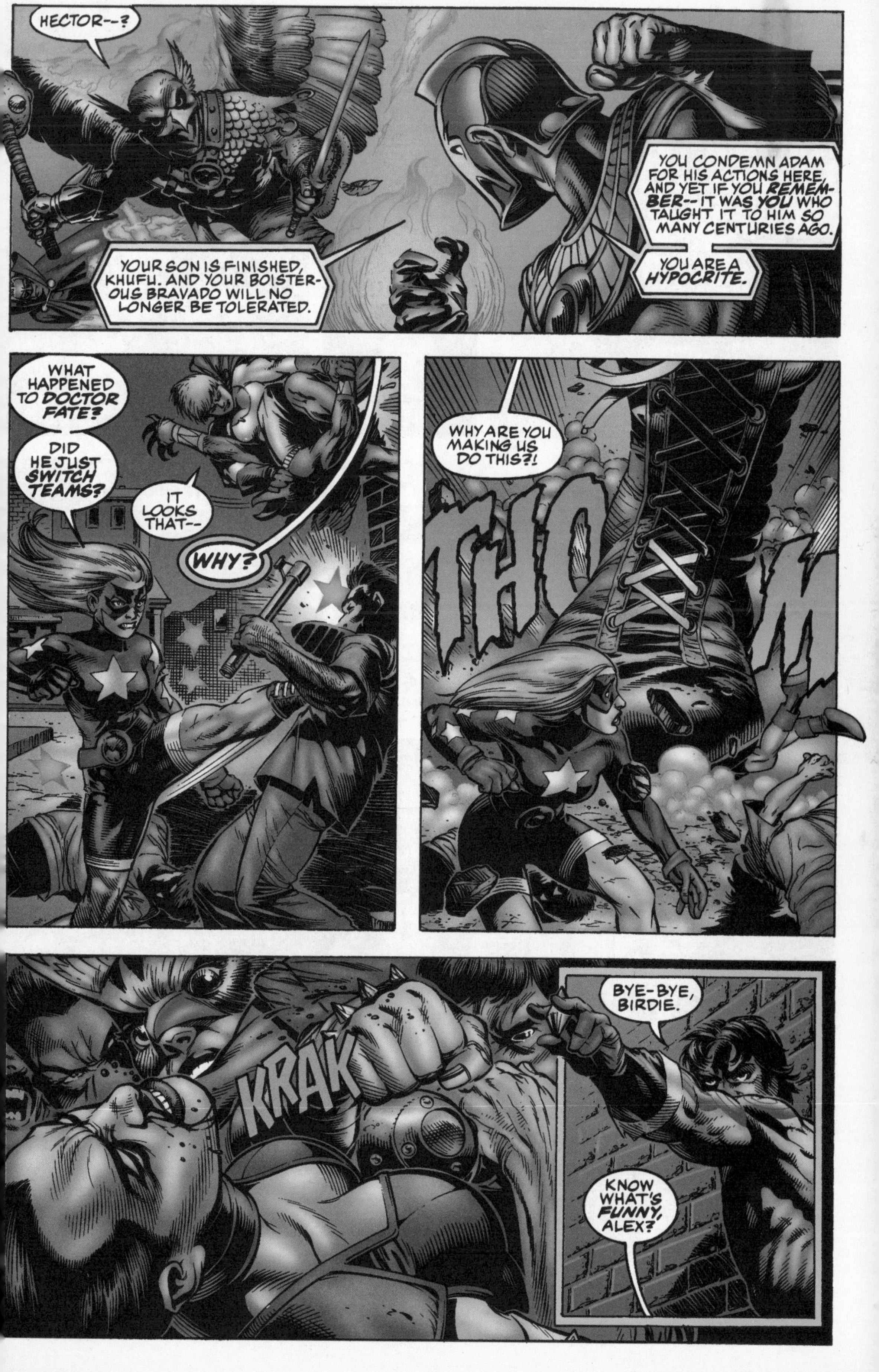
HECTOR--?
YOUR SON IS FINISHED, KHUFU. AND YOUR BOISTEROUS BRAVADO WILL NO LONGER BE TOLERATED.
YOU CONDEMN ADAM FOR HIS ACTIONS HERE, AND YET IF YOU REMEMBER-- IT WAS YOU WHO TAUGHT IT TO HIM SO MANY CENTURIES AGO.
YOU ARE A HYPOCRITE.
WHAT HAPPENED TO DOCTOR FATE?
DID HE JUST SWITCH TEAMS?
IT LOOKS THAT--
WHY?
WHY ARE YOU MAKING US DO THIS?!
THOOM
KRAK
BYE-BYE, BIRDIE.
KNOW WHAT'S FUNNY, ALEX?

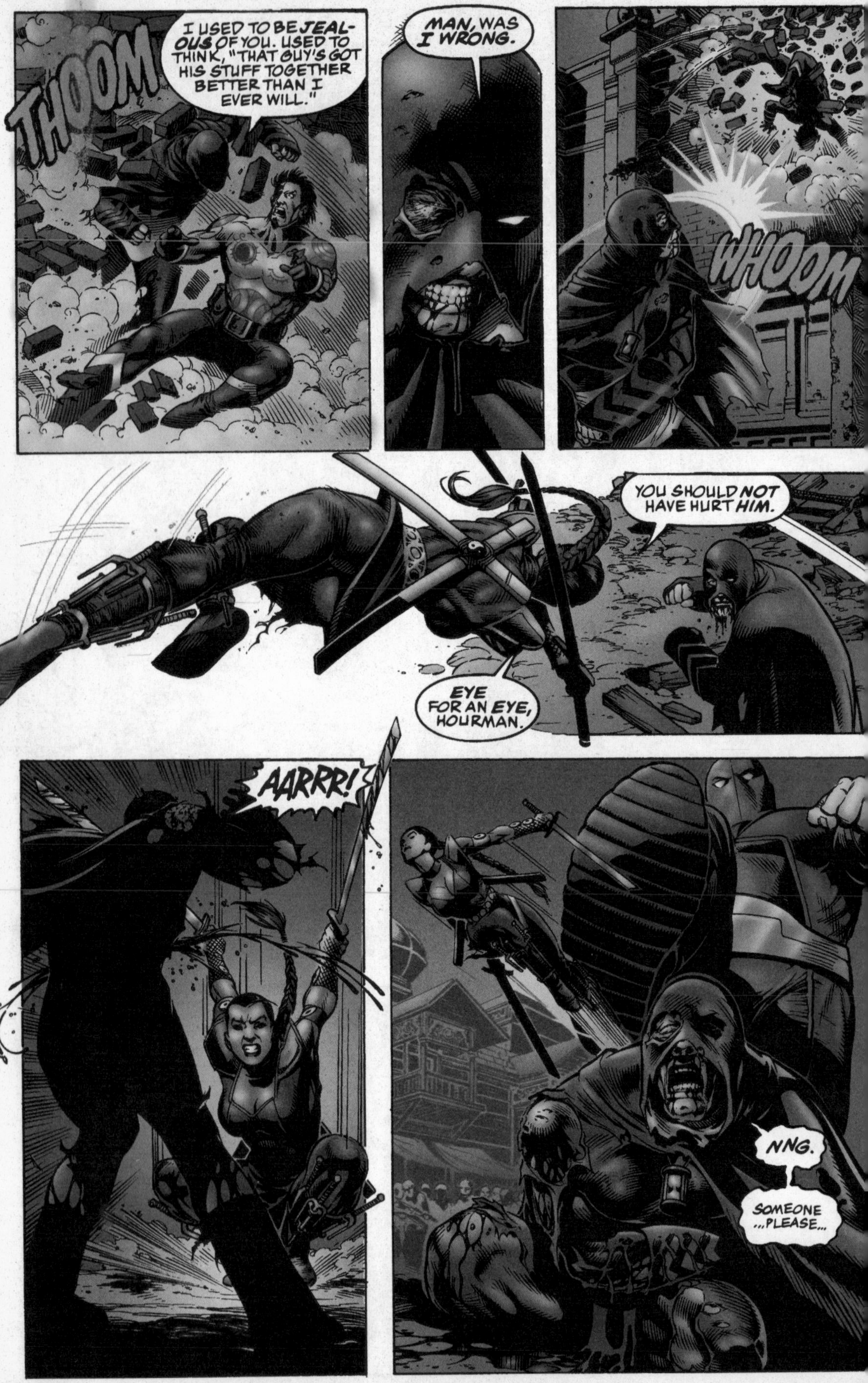
THOOM
I USED TO BE JEALOUS OF YOU. USED TO THINK, "THAT GUY'S GOT HIS STUFF TOGETHER BETTER THAN I EVER WILL."
MAN, WAS I WRONG.
WHOOM
YOU SHOULD NOT HAVE HURT HIM.
EYE FOR AN EYE, HOURMAN.
AARRR!
NNG.
SOMEONE ...PLEASE...

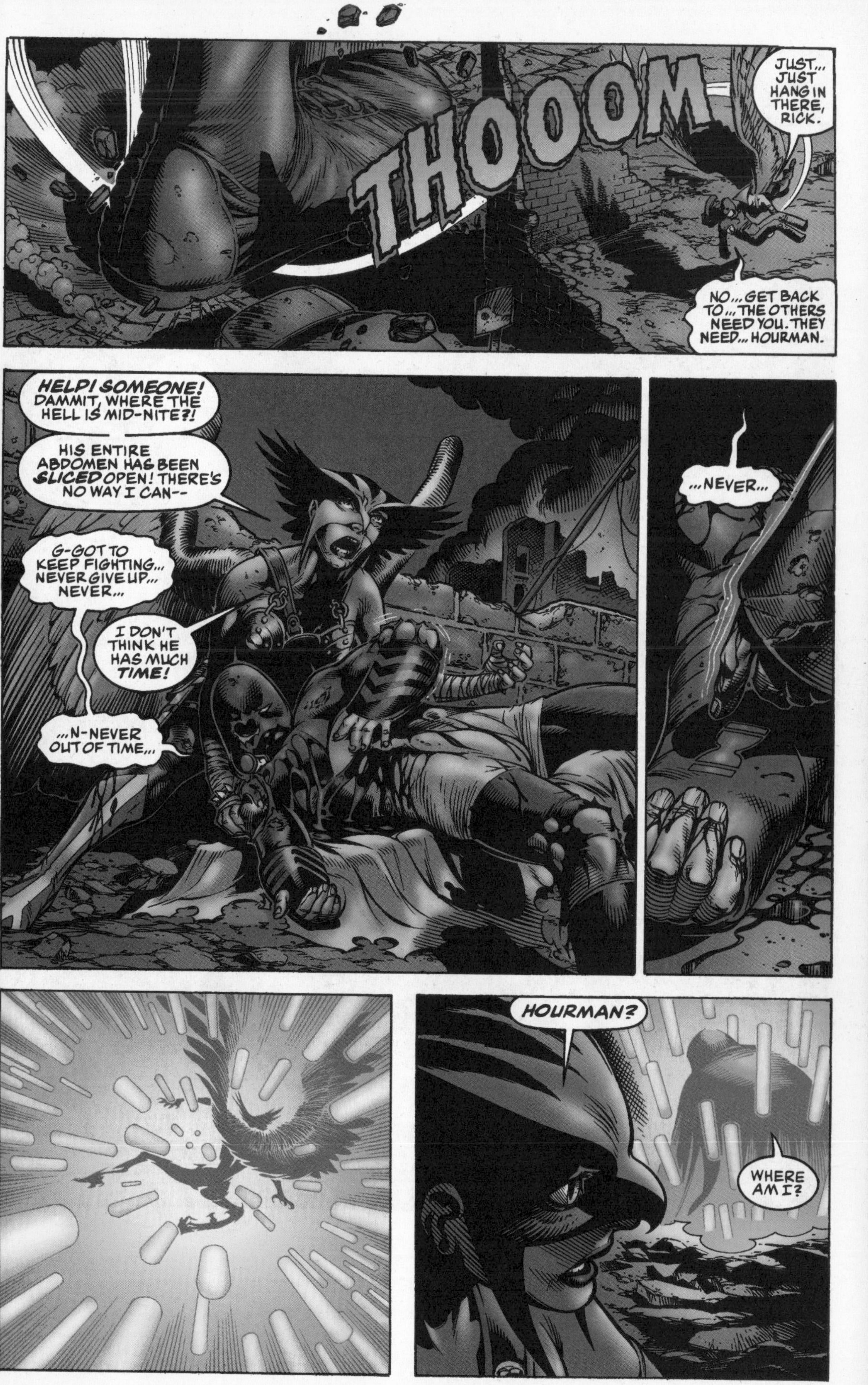
THOOOM
JUST... JUST HANG IN THERE, RICK.
NO... GET BACK TO... THE OTHERS NEED YOU. THEY NEED... HOURMAN.
HELP! SOMEONE! DAMMIT, WHERE THE HELL IS MID-NITE?!
HIS ENTIRE ABDOMEN HAS BEEN SLICED OPEN! THERE'S NO WAY I CAN--
G-GOT TO KEEP FIGHTING... NEVER GIVE UP... NEVER...
I DON'T THINK HE HAS MUCH TIME!
...N-NEVER OUT OF TIME...
...NEVER...
HOURMAN?
WHERE AM I?

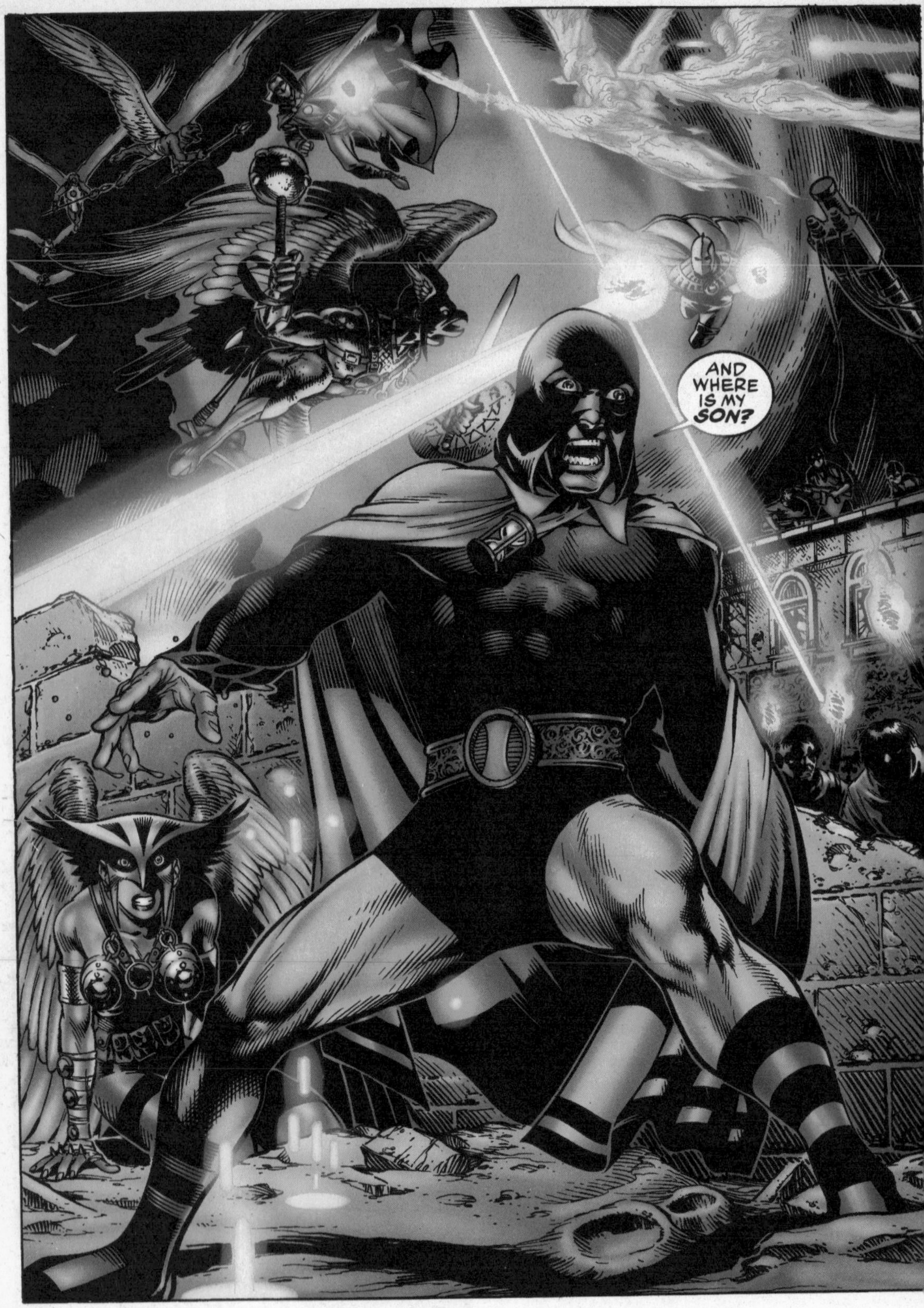
AND WHERE IS MY SON?

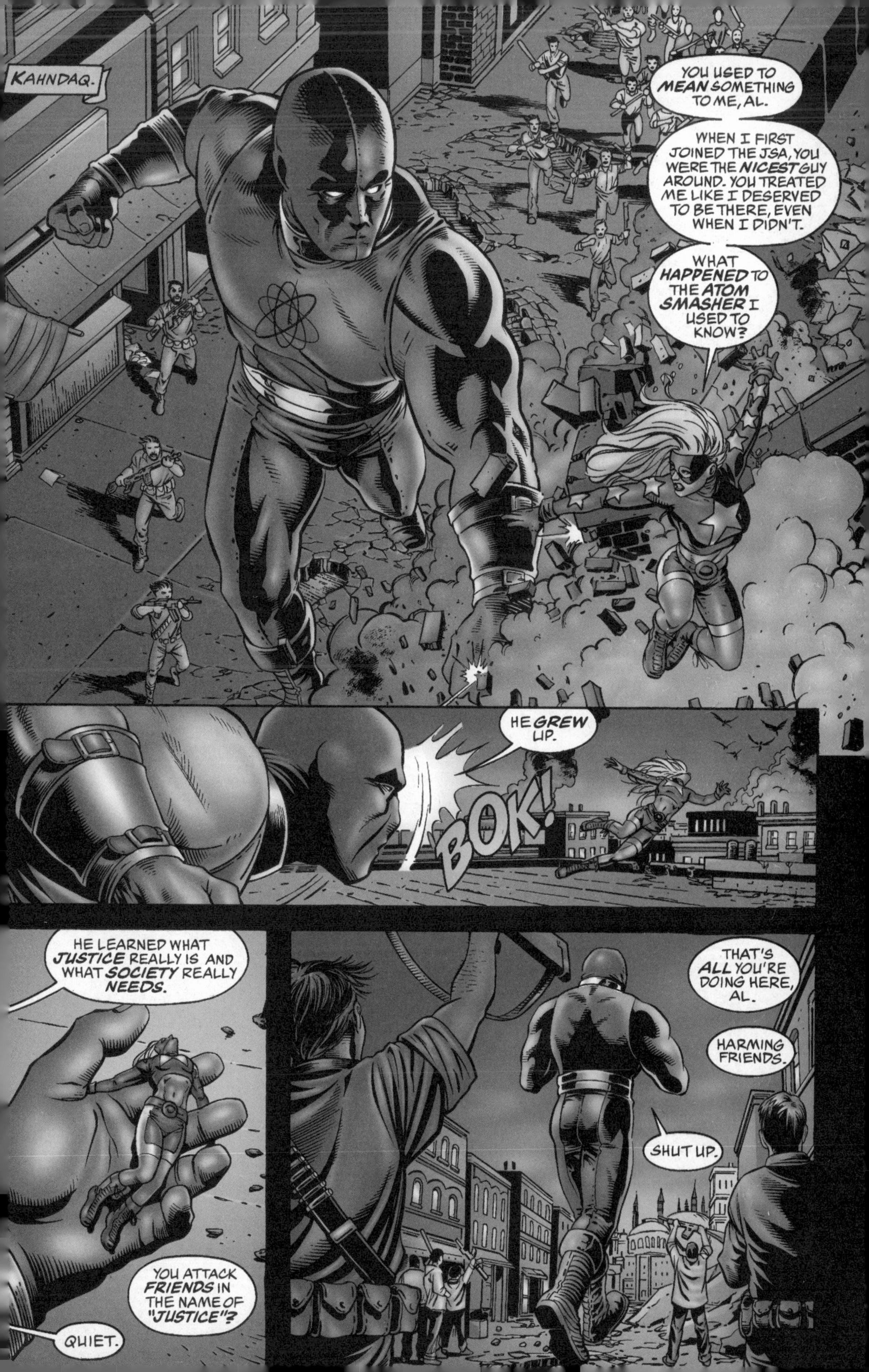
KAHNDAQ.
YOU USED TO MEAN SOMETHING TO ME, AL.
WHEN I FIRST JOINED THE JSA, YOU WERE THE NICEST GUY AROUND. YOU TREATED ME LIKE I DESERVED TO BE THERE, EVEN WHEN I DIDN'T.
WHAT HAPPENED TO THE ATOM SMASHER I USED TO KNOW?
HE GREW UP.
BOK!
HE LEARNED WHAT JUSTICE REALLY IS AND WHAT SOCIETY REALLY NEEDS.
YOU ATTACK FRIENDS IN THE NAME OF "JUSTICE"?
QUIET.
THAT'S ALL YOU'RE DOING HERE, AL.
HARMING FRIENDS.
SHUT UP.

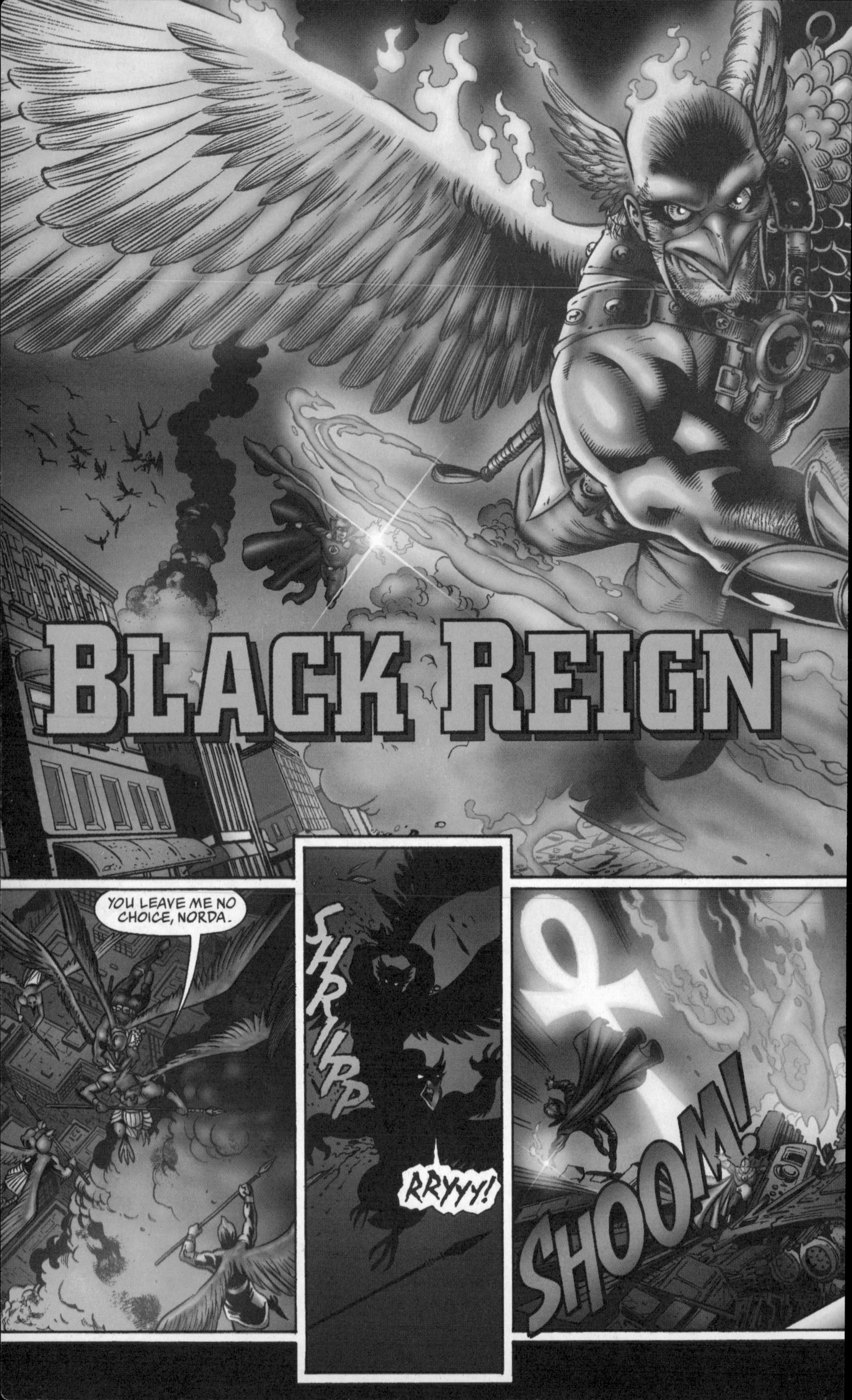
BLACK REIGN
YOU LEAVE ME NO CHOICE, NORDA.
SHRIPP
RRYYY!
SHOOM!

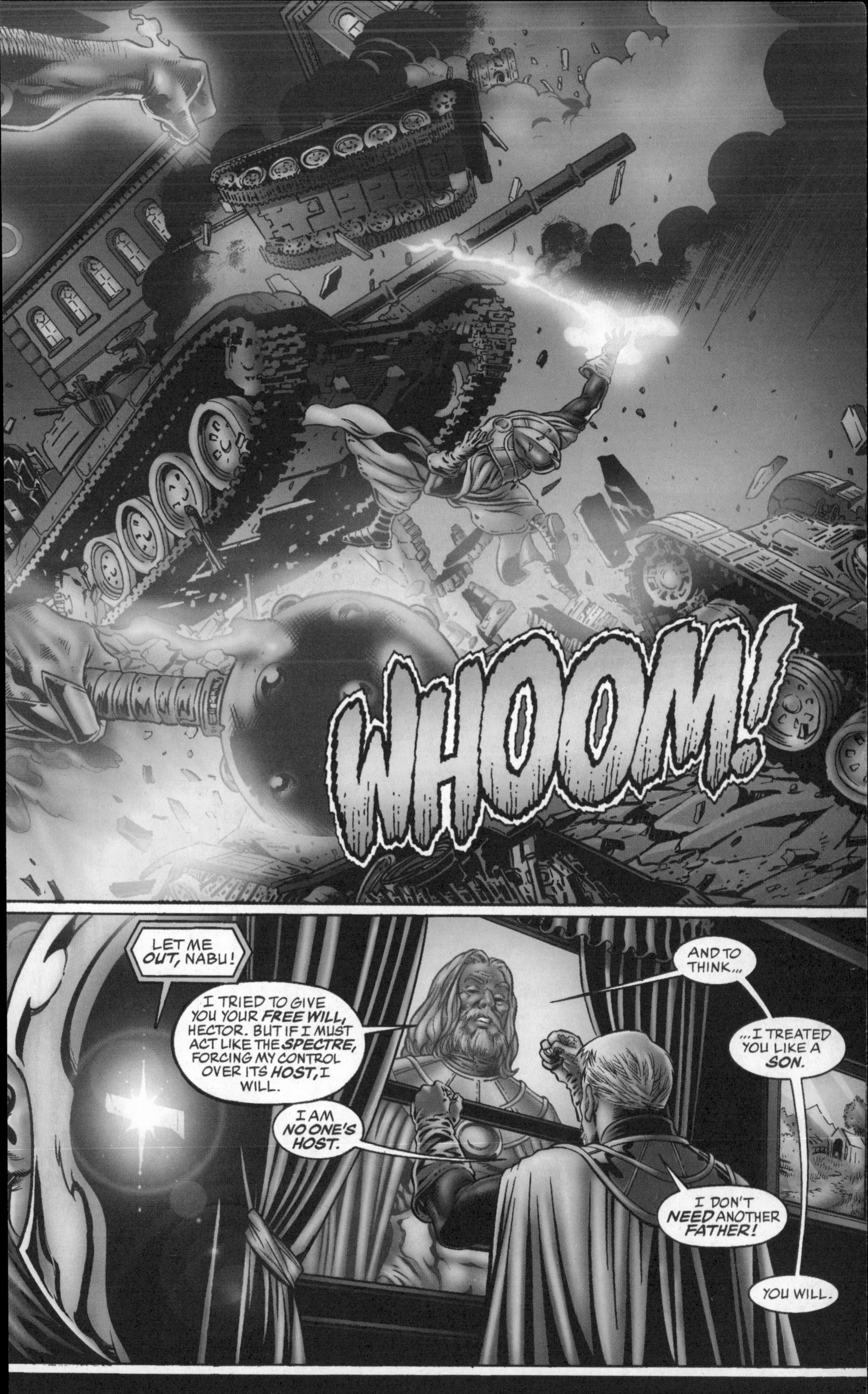
WHOOM!
LET ME OUT, NABU!
I TRIED TO GIVE YOU YOUR FREE WILL, HECTOR. BUT IF I MUST ACT LIKE THE SPECTRE, FORCING MY CONTROL OVER ITS HOST, I WILL.
I AM NO ONE'S HOST.
AND TO THINK...
...I TREATED YOU LIKE A SON.
I DON'T NEED ANOTHER FATHER!
YOU WILL.

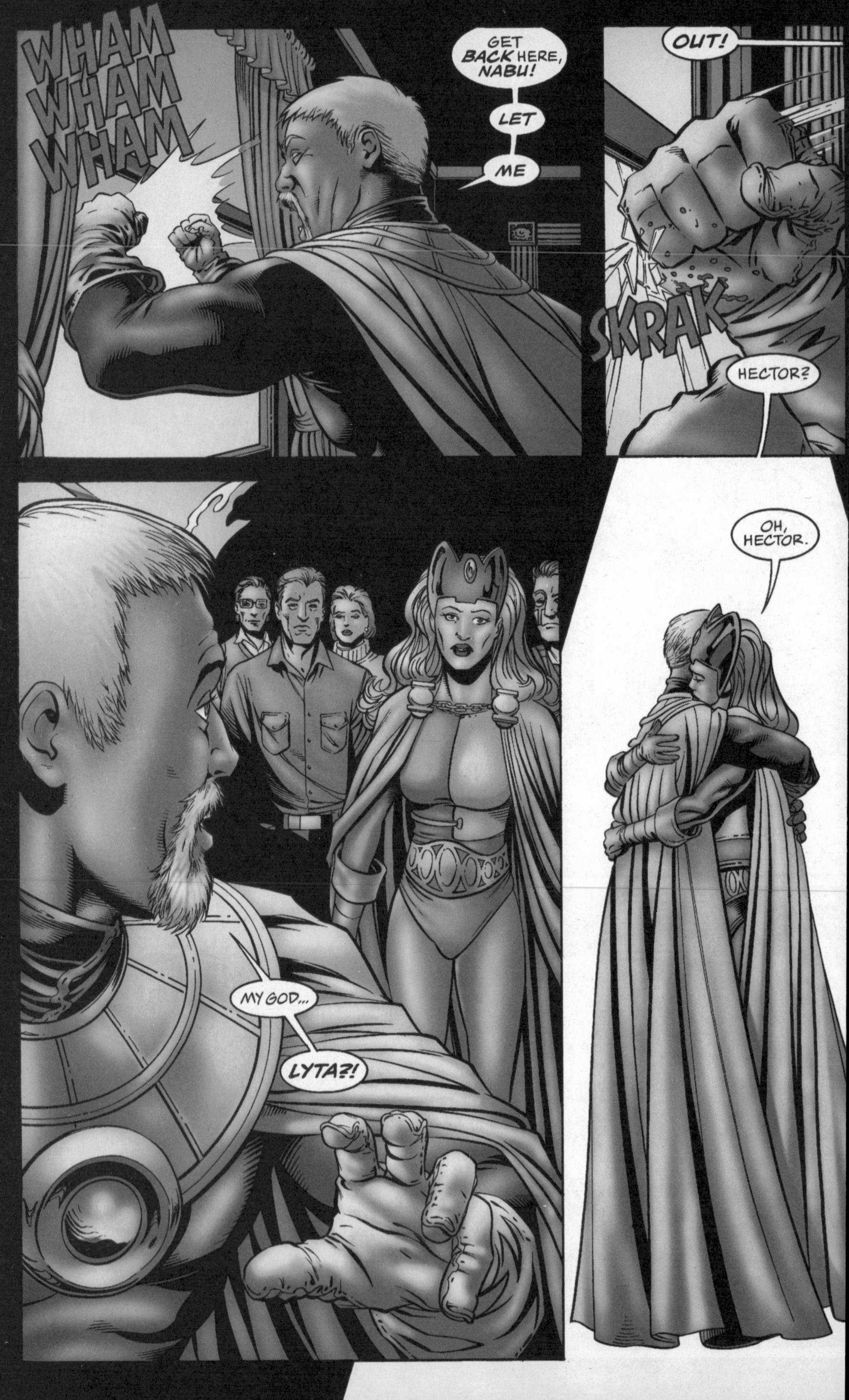
WHAM WHAM WHAM
GET BACK HERE, NABU!
LET
ME
OUT!
SKRAK
HECTOR?
MY GOD...
LYTA?!
OH, HECTOR.

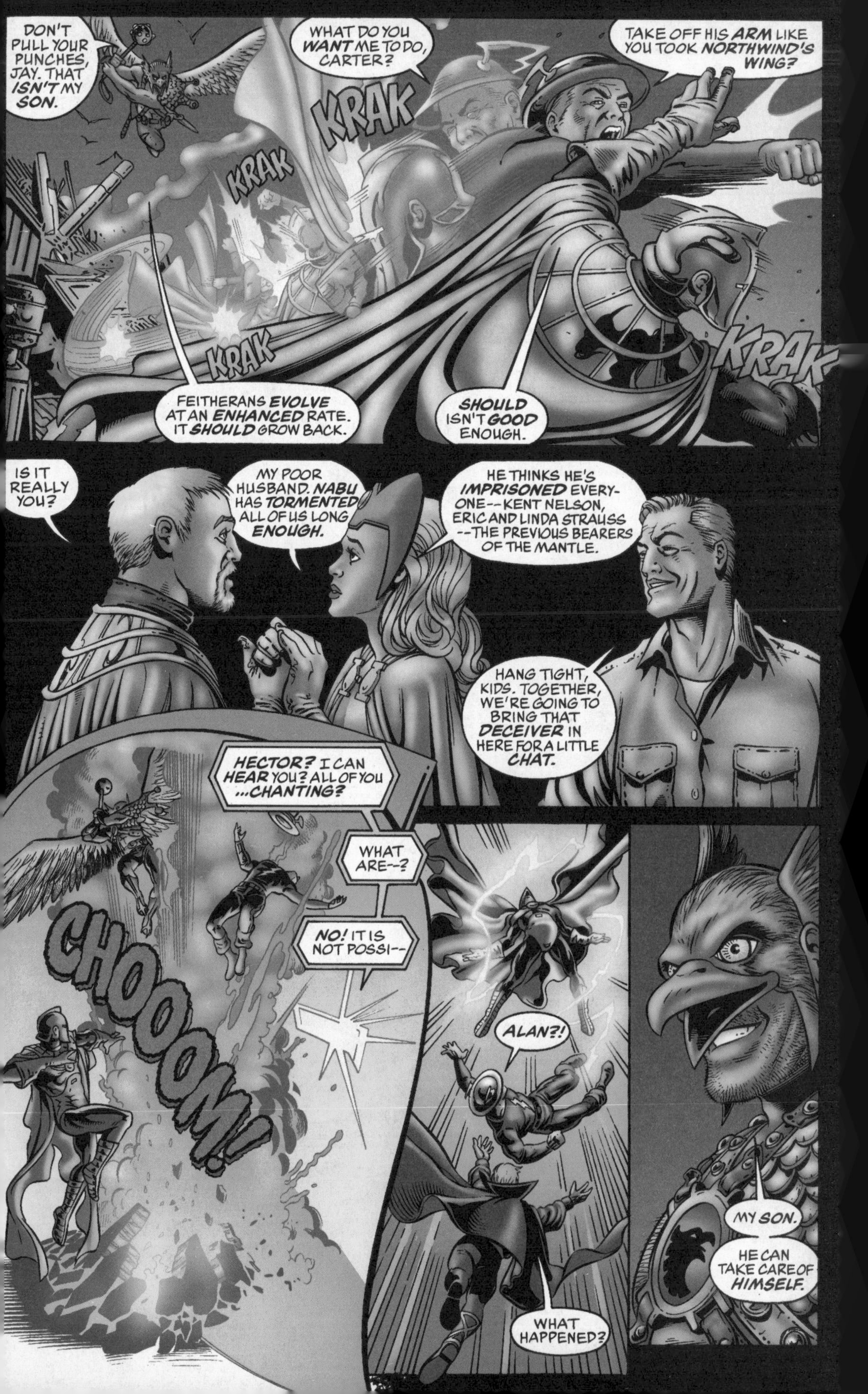
DON'T PULL YOUR PUNCHES, JAY. THAT ISN'T MY SON.
WHAT DO YOU WANT ME TO DO, CARTER?
TAKE OFF HIS ARM LIKE YOU TOOK NORTHWIND'S WING?
KRAK
KRAK
KRAK
KRAK
FEITHERANS EVOLVE AT AN ENHANCED RATE. IT SHOULD GROW BACK.
SHOULD ISN'T GOOD ENOUGH.
IS IT REALLY YOU?
MY POOR HUSBAND. NABU HAS TORMENTED ALL OF US LONG ENOUGH.
HE THINKS HE'S IMPRISONED EVERY-ONE--KENT NELSON, ERIC AND LINDA STRAUSS --THE PREVIOUS BEARERS OF THE MANTLE.
HANG TIGHT, KIDS. TOGETHER, WE'RE GOING TO BRING THAT DECEIVER IN HERE FOR A LITTLE CHAT.
HECTOR? I CAN HEAR YOU? ALL OF YOU ...CHANTING?
WHAT ARE--?
NO! IT IS NOT POSSI--
CHOOOM!
ALAN?!
WHAT HAPPENED?
MY SON.
HE CAN TAKE CARE OF HIMSELF.

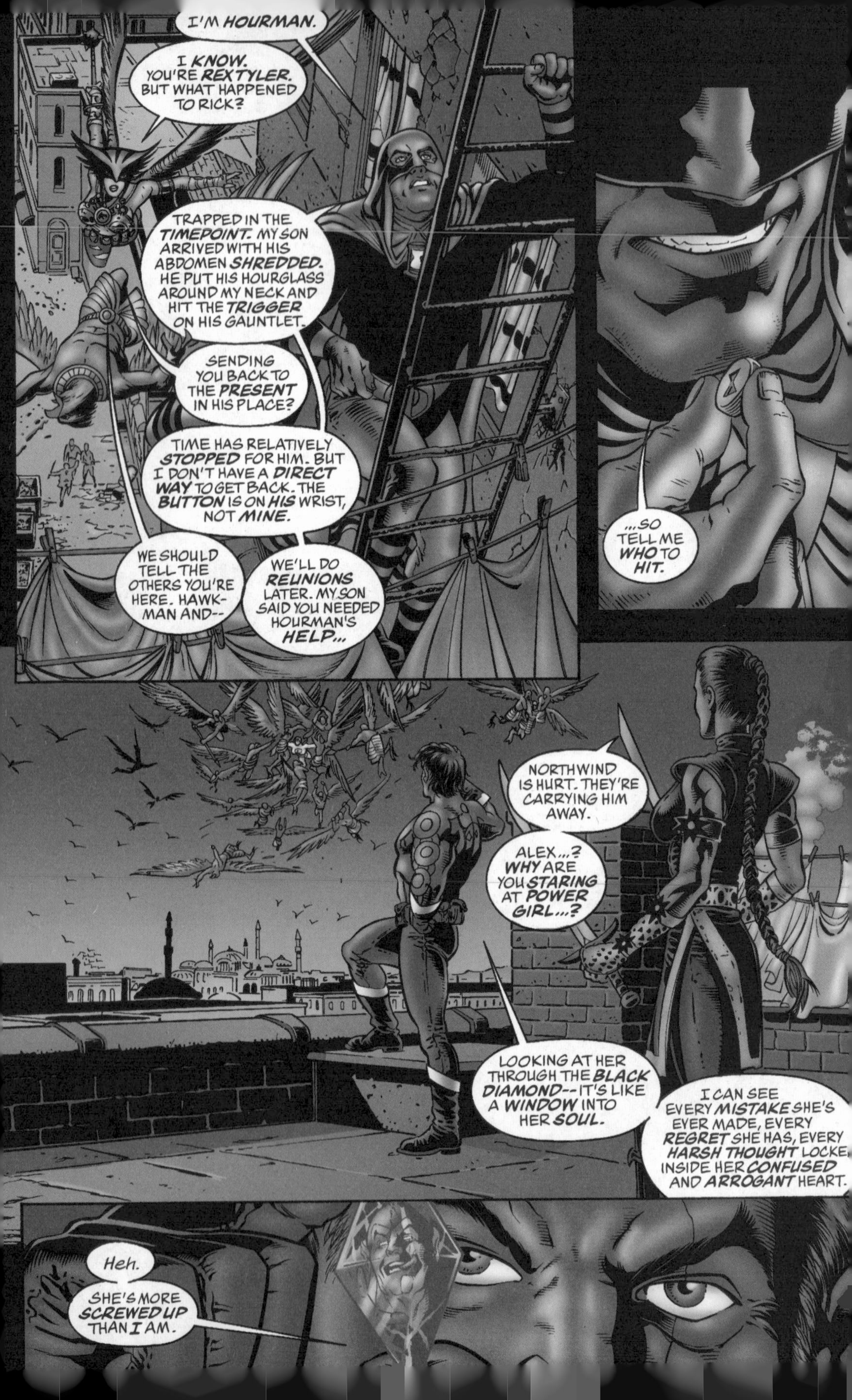
I'M HOURMAN.
I KNOW. YOU'RE REX TYLER. BUT WHAT HAPPENED TO RICK?
TRAPPED IN THE TIMEPOINT. MY SON ARRIVED WITH HIS ABDOMEN SHREDDED. HE PUT HIS HOURGLASS AROUND MY NECK AND HIT THE TRIGGER ON HIS GAUNTLET.
SENDING YOU BACK TO THE PRESENT IN HIS PLACE?
TIME HAS RELATIVELY STOPPED FOR HIM. BUT I DON'T HAVE A DIRECT WAY TO GET BACK. THE BUTTON IS ON HIS WRIST, NOT MINE.
WE SHOULD TELL THE OTHERS YOU'RE HERE. HAWK-MAN AND--
WE'LL DO REUNIONS LATER. MY SON SAID YOU NEEDED HOURMAN'S HELP...
...SO TELL ME WHO TO HIT.
NORTHWIND IS HURT. THEY'RE CARRYING HIM AWAY.
ALEX...? WHY ARE YOU STARING AT POWER GIRL...?
LOOKING AT HER THROUGH THE BLACK DIAMOND--IT'S LIKE A WINDOW INTO HER SOUL.
I CAN SEE EVERY MISTAKE SHE'S EVER MADE, EVERY REGRET SHE HAS, EVERY HARSH THOUGHT LOCKE INSIDE HER CONFUSED AND ARROGANT HEART.
Heh.
SHE'S MORE SCREWED UP THAN I AM.

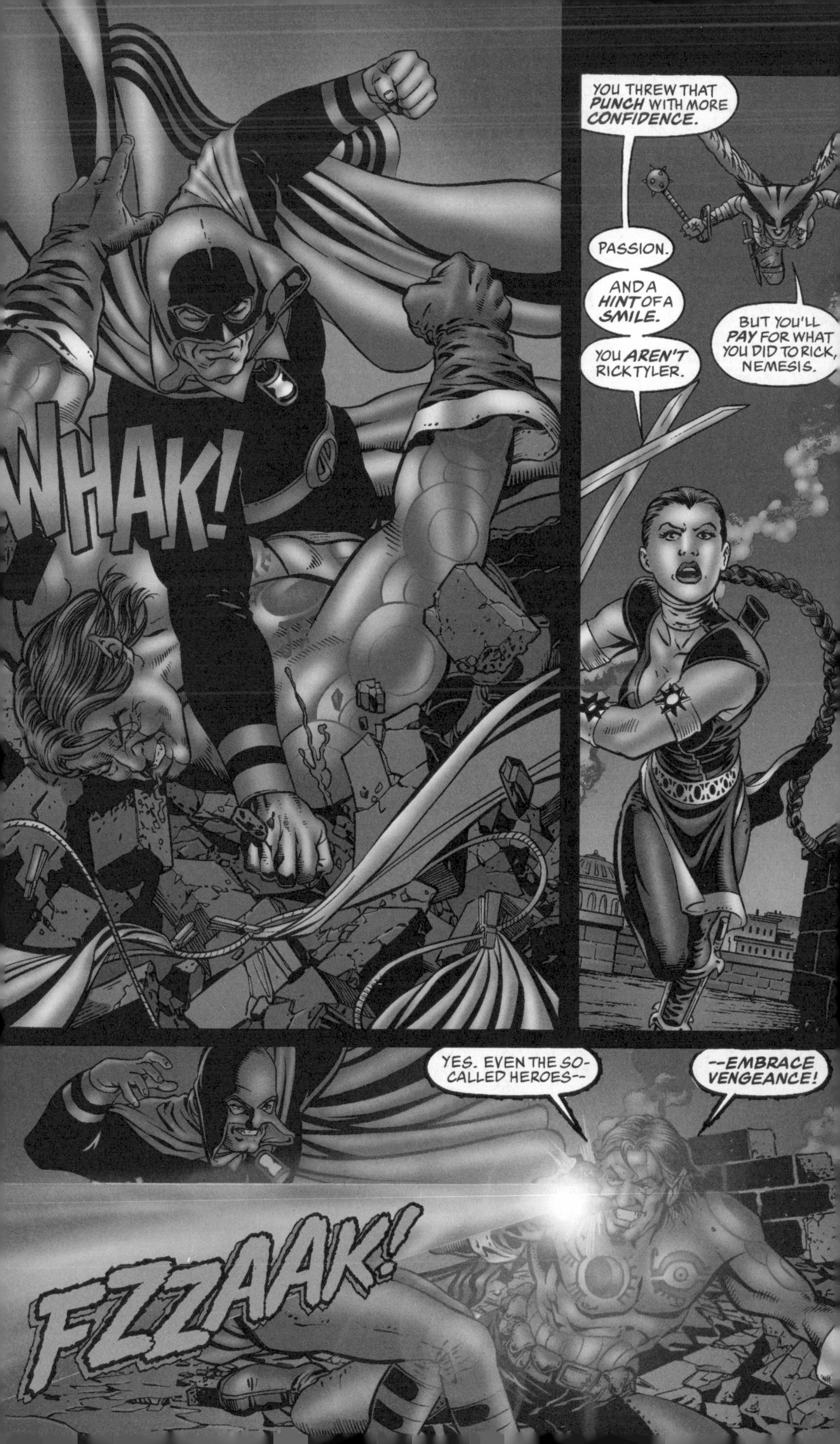
WHAK!
YOU THREW THAT PUNCH WITH MORE CONFIDENCE.
PASSION.
AND A HINT OF A SMILE.
YOU AREN'T RICK TYLER.
BUT YOU'LL PAY FOR WHAT YOU DID TO RICK, NEMESIS.
YES. EVEN THE SO-CALLED HEROES--
--EMBRACE VENGEANCE!
FZZAAK!

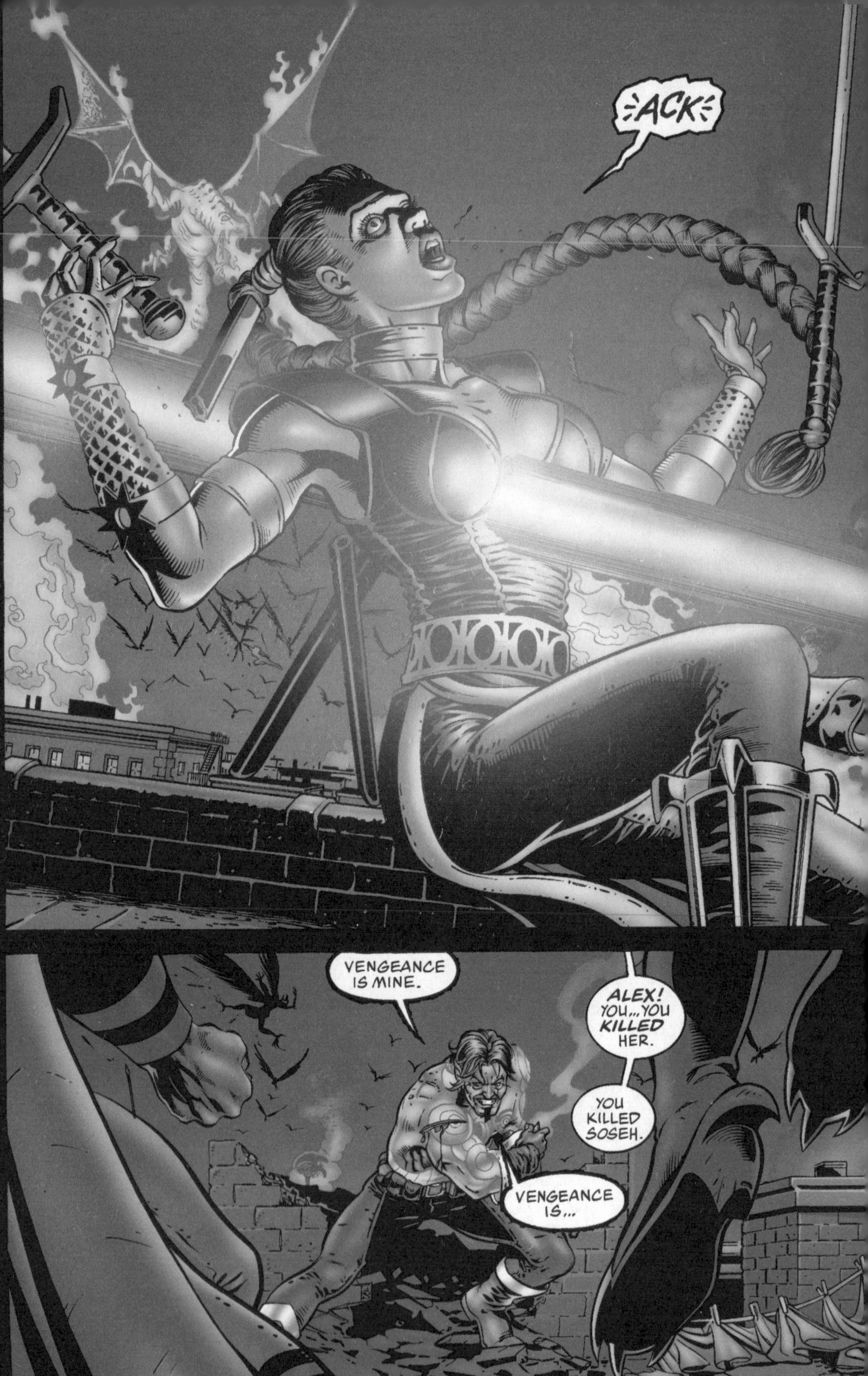
ACK
VENGEANCE IS MINE.
ALEX! YOU... YOU KILLED HER.
YOU KILLED SOSEH.
VENGEANCE IS...

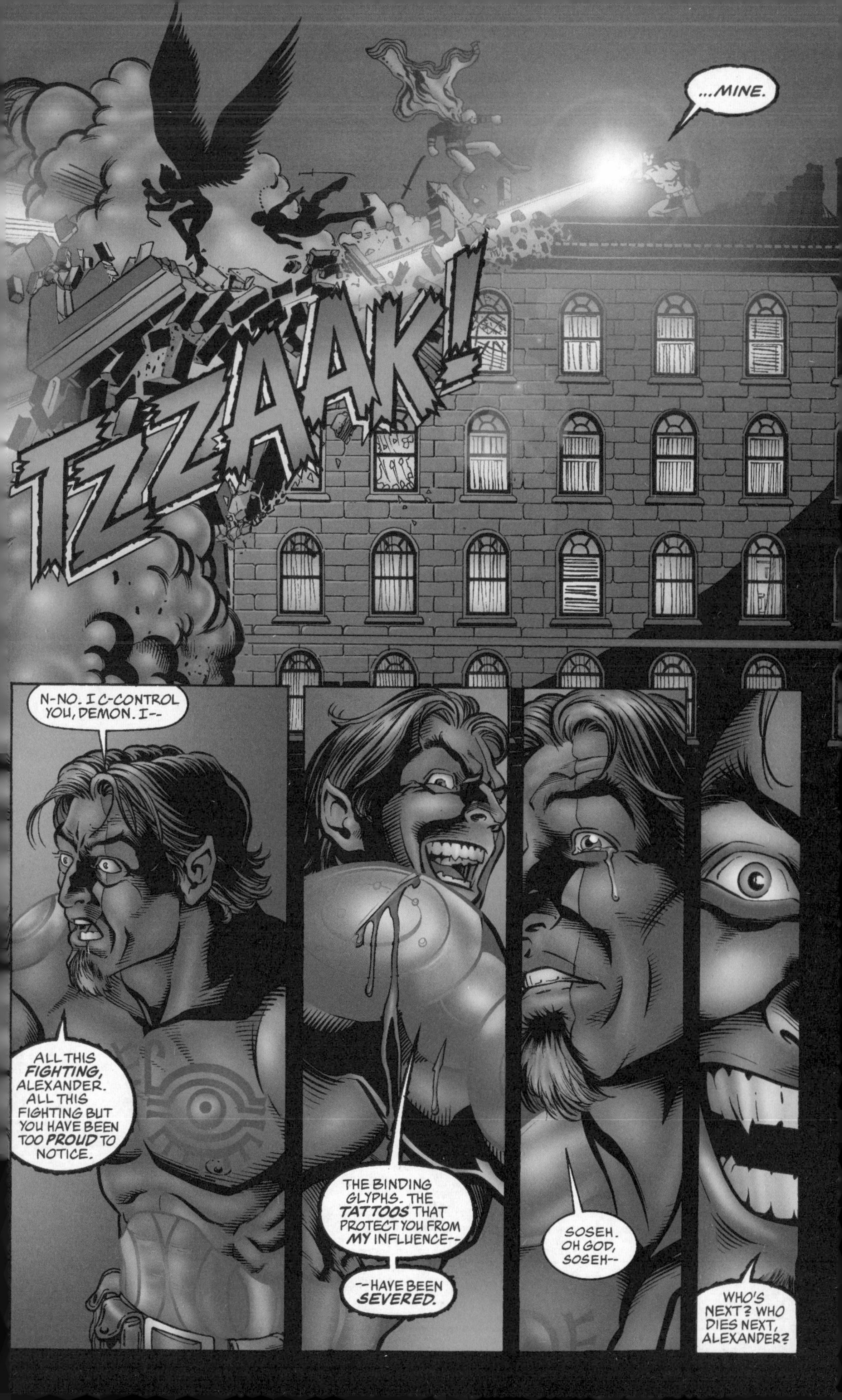

...MINE.
TZZAAK!
N-NO. I C-CONTROL YOU, DEMON. I--
ALL THIS FIGHTING, ALEXANDER. ALL THIS FIGHTING BUT YOU HAVE BEEN TOO PROUD TO NOTICE.
THE BINDING GLYPHS. THE TATTOOS THAT PROTECT YOU FROM MY INFLUENCE--
--HAVE BEEN SEVERED.
SOSEH. OH GOD, SOSEH--
WHO'S NEXT? WHO DIES NEXT, ALEXANDER?

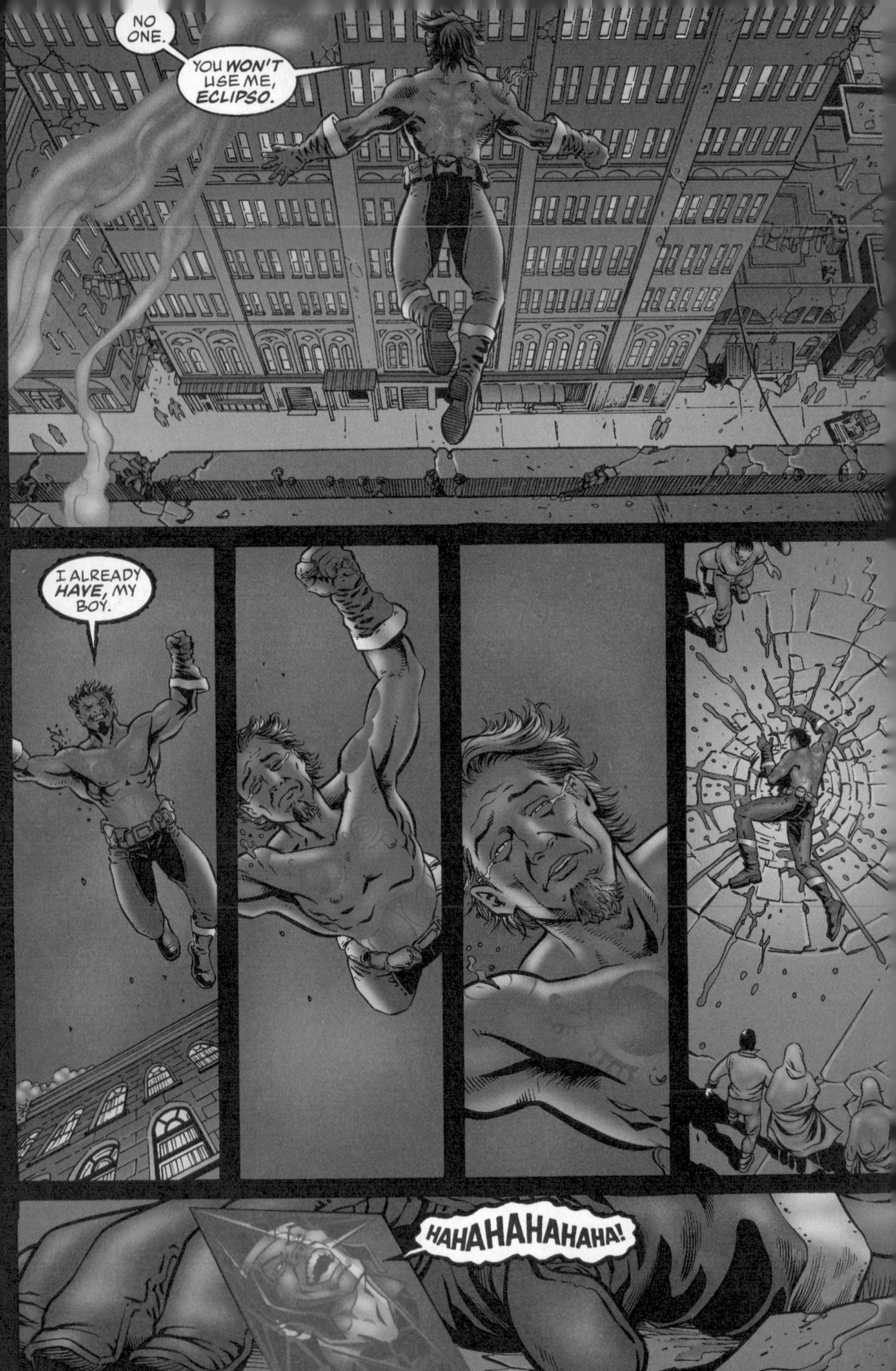

NO ONE.
YOU WON'T USE ME, ECLIPSO.
I ALREADY HAVE, MY BOY.
HAHAHAHAHAHA!

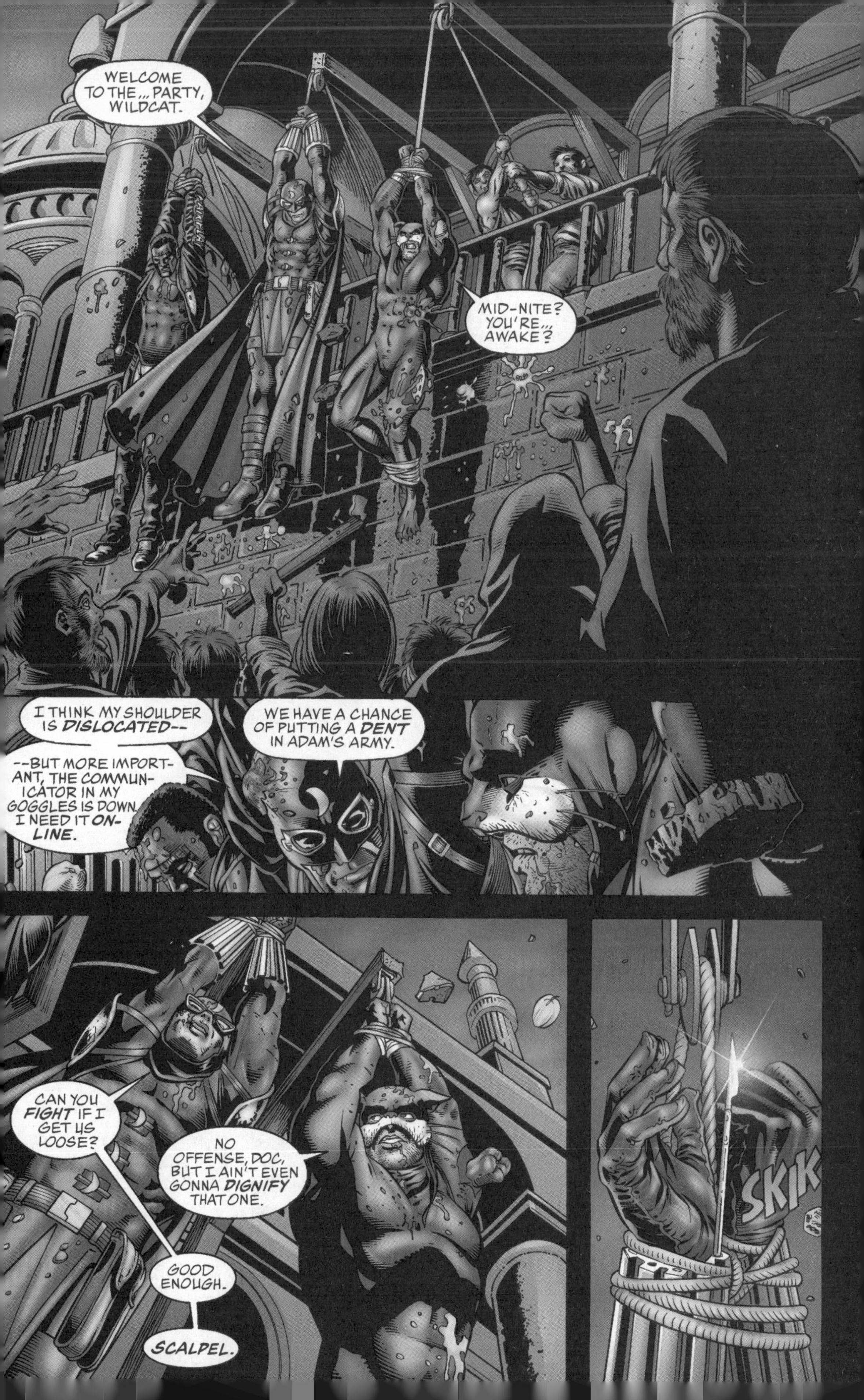
WELCOME TO THE... PARTY, WILDCAT.
MID-NITE? YOU'RE... AWAKE?
I THINK MY SHOULDER IS DISLOCATED--
--BUT MORE IMPORTANT, THE COMMUNICATOR IN MY GOGGLES IS DOWN. I NEED IT ON-LINE.
WE HAVE A CHANCE OF PUTTING A DENT IN ADAM'S ARMY.
CAN YOU FIGHT IF I GET US LOOSE?
NO OFFENSE, DOC, BUT I AIN'T EVEN GONNA DIGNIFY THAT ONE.
GOOD ENOUGH.
SCALPEL.
SKIK

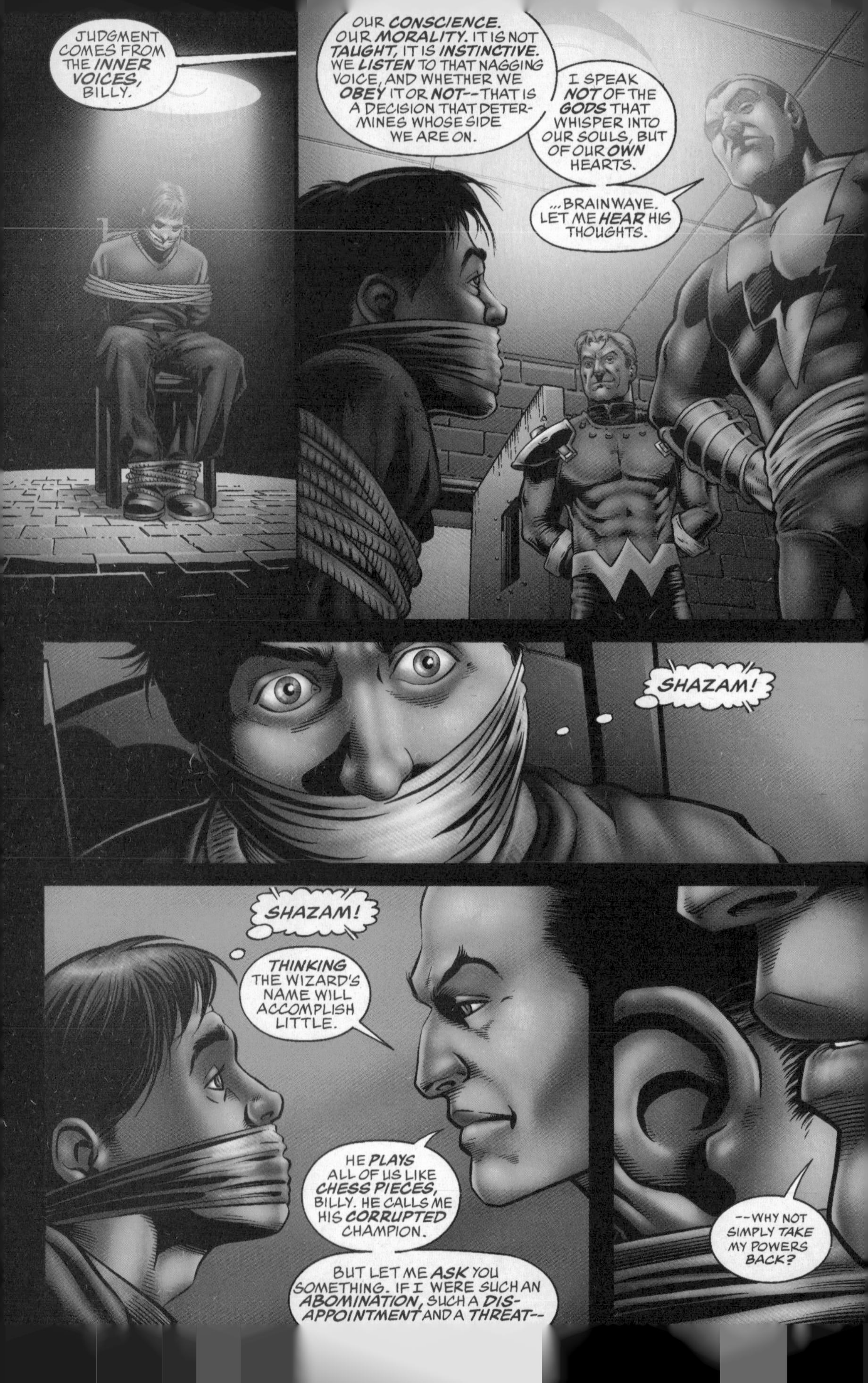

JUDGMENT COMES FROM THE *INNER VOICES*, BILLY.
OUR *CONSCIENCE*. OUR *MORALITY*. IT IS NOT *TAUGHT*, IT IS *INSTINCTIVE*. WE *LISTEN* TO THAT NAGGING VOICE, AND WHETHER WE *OBEY* IT OR *NOT*--THAT IS A DECISION THAT DETERMINES WHOSE SIDE WE ARE ON.
I SPEAK *NOT* OF THE *GODS* THAT WHISPER INTO OUR SOULS, BUT OF OUR *OWN* HEARTS.
...BRAINWAVE. LET ME *HEAR* HIS THOUGHTS.
SHAZAM!
SHAZAM!
*THINKING* THE WIZARD'S NAME WILL ACCOMPLISH LITTLE.
HE *PLAYS* ALL OF US LIKE *CHESS PIECES*, BILLY. HE CALLS ME HIS *CORRUPTED* CHAMPION.
BUT LET ME *ASK* YOU SOMETHING. IF I WERE SUCH AN *ABOMINATION*, SUCH A *DISAPPOINTMENT* AND A *THREAT*--
--WHY NOT SIMPLY *TAKE* MY POWERS BACK?

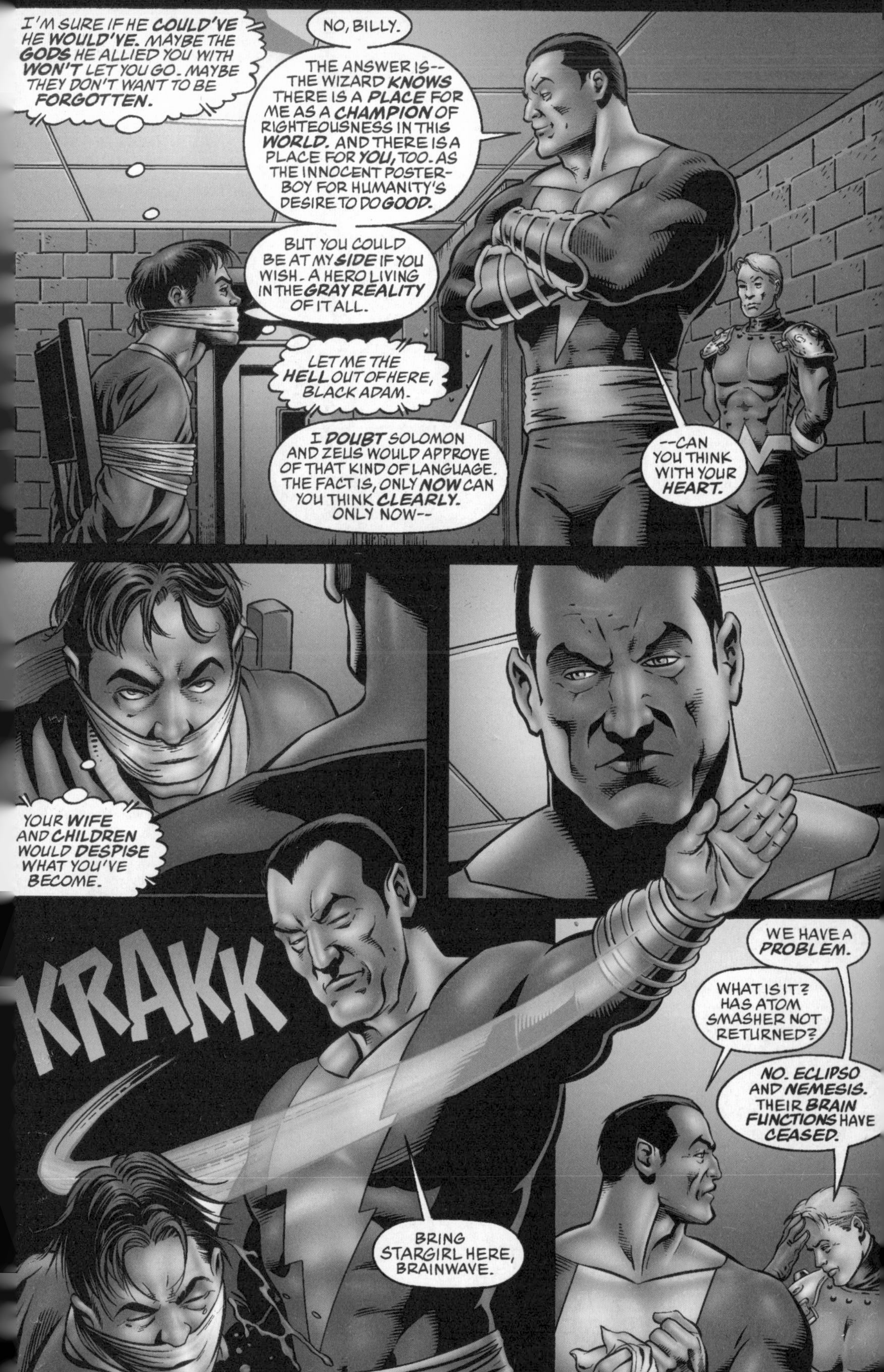

I'M SURE IF HE COULD'VE HE WOULD'VE. MAYBE THE GODS HE ALLIED YOU WITH WON'T LET YOU GO. MAYBE THEY DON'T WANT TO BE FORGOTTEN.
NO, BILLY.
THE ANSWER IS-- THE WIZARD KNOWS THERE IS A PLACE FOR ME AS A CHAMPION OF RIGHTEOUSNESS IN THIS WORLD. AND THERE IS A PLACE FOR YOU, TOO. AS THE INNOCENT POSTER-BOY FOR HUMANITY'S DESIRE TO DO GOOD.
BUT YOU COULD BE AT MY SIDE IF YOU WISH. A HERO LIVING IN THE GRAY REALITY OF IT ALL.
LET ME THE HELL OUT OF HERE, BLACK ADAM.
I DOUBT SOLOMON AND ZEUS WOULD APPROVE OF THAT KIND OF LANGUAGE. THE FACT IS, ONLY NOW CAN YOU THINK CLEARLY. ONLY NOW--
--CAN YOU THINK WITH YOUR HEART.
YOUR WIFE AND CHILDREN WOULD DESPISE WHAT YOU'VE BECOME.
KRAKK
BRING STARGIRL HERE, BRAINWAVE.
WE HAVE A PROBLEM.
WHAT IS IT? HAS ATOM SMASHER NOT RETURNED?
NO. ECLIPSO AND NEMESIS. THEIR BRAIN FUNCTIONS HAVE CEASED.

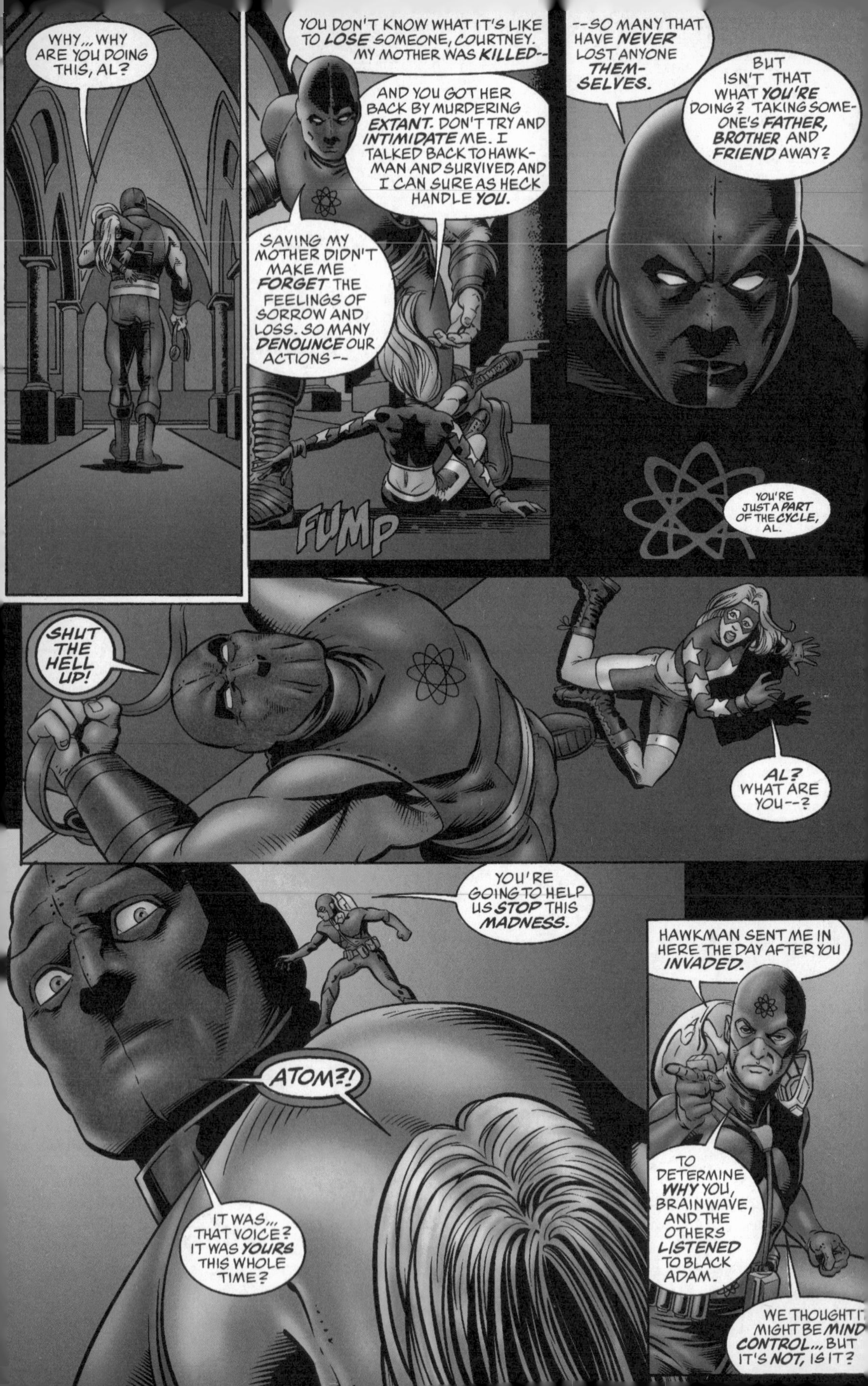
WHY,,, WHY ARE YOU DOING THIS, AL?
YOU DON'T KNOW WHAT IT'S LIKE TO LOSE SOMEONE, COURTNEY. MY MOTHER WAS KILLED--
AND YOU GOT HER BACK BY MURDERING EXTANT. DON'T TRY AND INTIMIDATE ME. I TALKED BACK TO HAWK-MAN AND SURVIVED, AND I CAN SURE AS HECK HANDLE YOU.
SAVING MY MOTHER DIDN'T MAKE ME FORGET THE FEELINGS OF SORROW AND LOSS. SO MANY DENOUNCE OUR ACTIONS --
FUMP
--SO MANY THAT HAVE NEVER LOST ANYONE THEM-SELVES.
BUT ISN'T THAT WHAT YOU'RE DOING? TAKING SOME-ONE'S FATHER, BROTHER AND FRIEND AWAY?
YOU'RE JUST A PART OF THE CYCLE, AL.
SHUT THE HELL UP!
AL? WHAT ARE YOU--?
YOU'RE GOING TO HELP US STOP THIS MADNESS.
ATOM?!
IT WAS,,, THAT VOICE? IT WAS YOURS THIS WHOLE TIME?
HAWKMAN SENT ME IN HERE THE DAY AFTER YOU INVADED.
TO DETERMINE WHY YOU, BRAINWAVE, AND THE OTHERS LISTENED TO BLACK ADAM.
WE THOUGHT IT MIGHT BE MIND CONTROL... BUT IT'S NOT, IS IT?

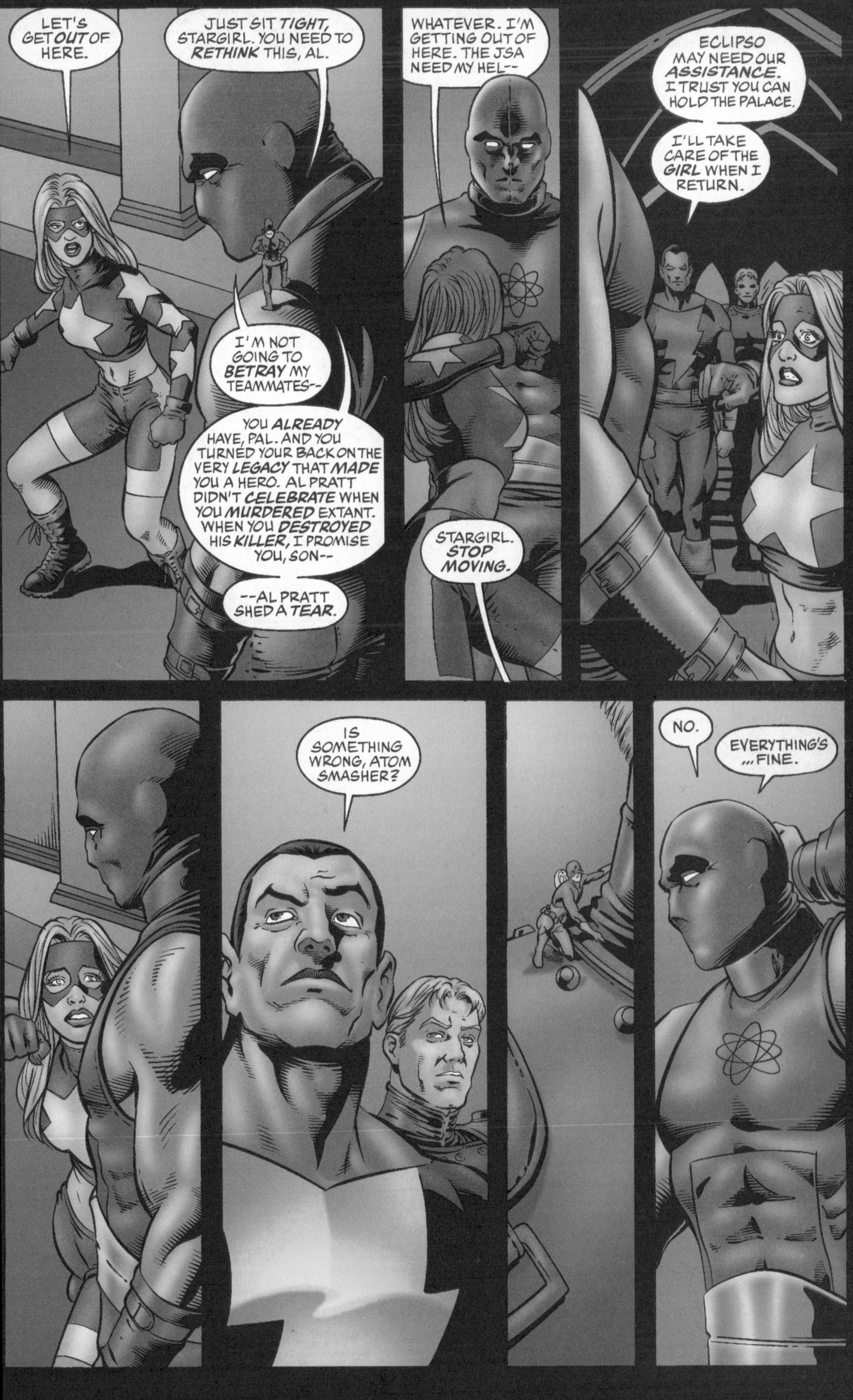
LET'S GET OUT OF HERE.
JUST SIT TIGHT, STARGIRL. YOU NEED TO RETHINK THIS, AL.
I'M NOT GOING TO BETRAY MY TEAMMATES--
YOU ALREADY HAVE, PAL. AND YOU TURNED YOUR BACK ON THE VERY LEGACY THAT MADE YOU A HERO. AL PRATT DIDN'T CELEBRATE WHEN YOU MURDERED EXTANT. WHEN YOU DESTROYED HIS KILLER, I PROMISE YOU, SON--
--AL PRATT SHED A TEAR.
WHATEVER. I'M GETTING OUT OF HERE. THE JSA NEED MY HEL--
STARGIRL. STOP MOVING.
ECLIPSO MAY NEED OUR ASSISTANCE. I TRUST YOU CAN HOLD THE PALACE.
I'LL TAKE CARE OF THE GIRL WHEN I RETURN.
IS SOMETHING WRONG, ATOM SMASHER?
NO.
EVERYTHING'S ...FINE.

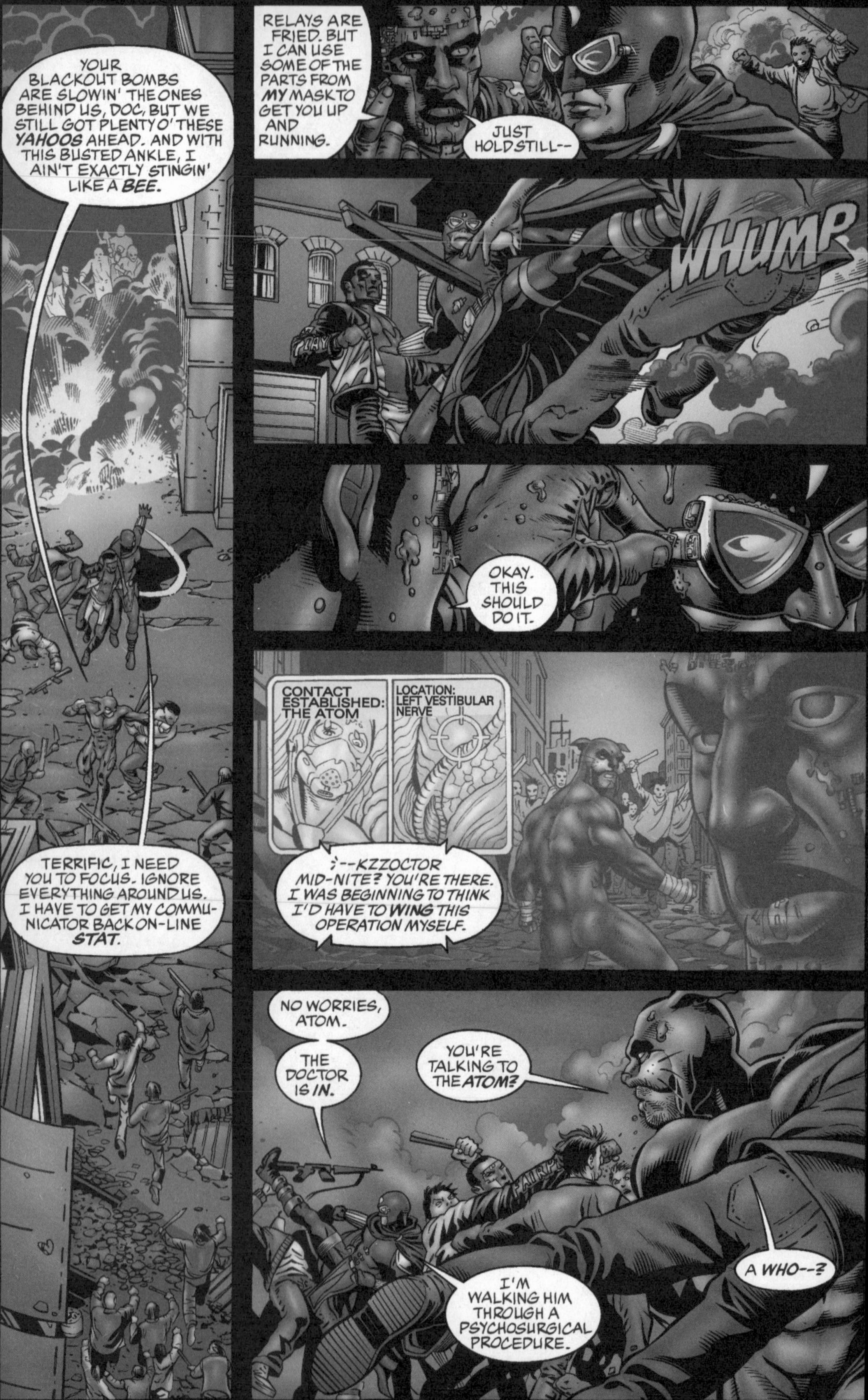
YOUR BLACKOUT BOMBS ARE SLOWIN' THE ONES BEHIND US, DOC, BUT WE STILL GOT PLENTY O' THESE YAHOOS AHEAD. AND WITH THIS BUSTED ANKLE, I AIN'T EXACTLY STINGIN' LIKE A BEE.
TERRIFIC, I NEED YOU TO FOCUS. IGNORE EVERYTHING AROUND US. I HAVE TO GET MY COMMUNICATOR BACK ON-LINE STAT.
RELAYS ARE FRIED. BUT I CAN USE SOME OF THE PARTS FROM MY MASK TO GET YOU UP AND RUNNING.
JUST HOLD STILL--
WHUMP
OKAY. THIS SHOULD DO IT.
CONTACT ESTABLISHED: THE ATOM
LOCATION: LEFT VESTIBULAR NERVE
--KZZOCTOR MID-NITE? YOU'RE THERE. I WAS BEGINNING TO THINK I'D HAVE TO WING THIS OPERATION MYSELF.
NO WORRIES, ATOM.
THE DOCTOR IS IN.
YOU'RE TALKING TO THE ATOM?
A WHO--?
I'M WALKING HIM THROUGH A PSYCHOSURGICAL PROCEDURE.

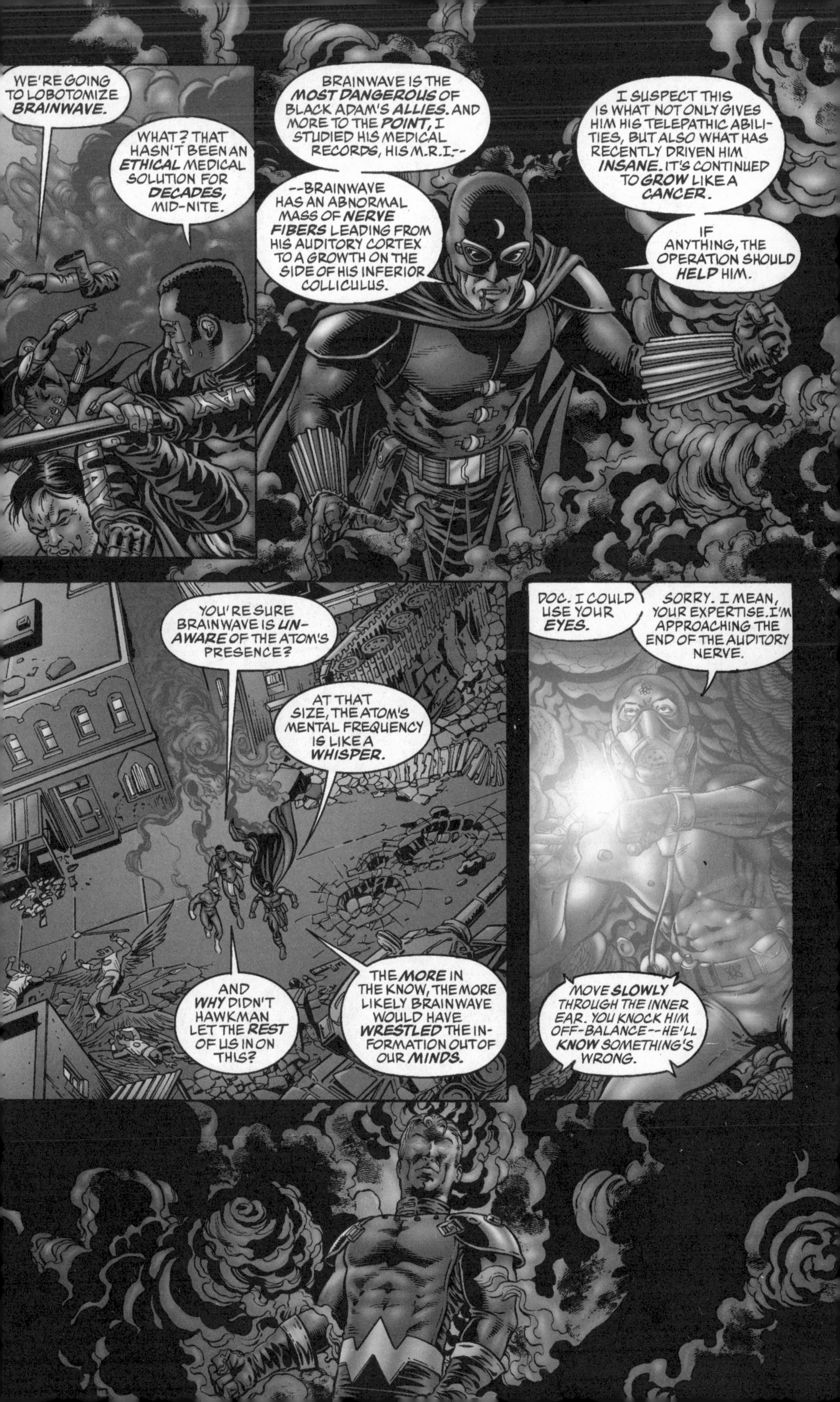

WE'RE GOING TO LOBOTOMIZE BRAINWAVE.
WHAT? THAT HASN'T BEEN AN ETHICAL MEDICAL SOLUTION FOR DECADES, MID-NITE.
BRAINWAVE IS THE MOST DANGEROUS OF BLACK ADAM'S ALLIES. AND MORE TO THE POINT, I STUDIED HIS MEDICAL RECORDS, HIS M.R.I.--
--BRAINWAVE HAS AN ABNORMAL MASS OF NERVE FIBERS LEADING FROM HIS AUDITORY CORTEX TO A GROWTH ON THE SIDE OF HIS INFERIOR COLLICULUS.
I SUSPECT THIS IS WHAT NOT ONLY GIVES HIM HIS TELEPATHIC ABILITIES, BUT ALSO WHAT HAS RECENTLY DRIVEN HIM INSANE. IT'S CONTINUED TO GROW LIKE A CANCER.
IF ANYTHING, THE OPERATION SHOULD HELP HIM.
YOU'RE SURE BRAINWAVE IS UNAWARE OF THE ATOM'S PRESENCE?
AT THAT SIZE, THE ATOM'S MENTAL FREQUENCY IS LIKE A WHISPER.
AND WHY DIDN'T HAWKMAN LET THE REST OF US IN ON THIS?
THE MORE IN THE KNOW, THE MORE LIKELY BRAINWAVE WOULD HAVE WRESTLED THE INFORMATION OUT OF OUR MINDS.
DOC. I COULD USE YOUR EYES.
SORRY. I MEAN, YOUR EXPERTISE. I'M APPROACHING THE END OF THE AUDITORY NERVE.
MOVE SLOWLY THROUGH THE INNER EAR. YOU KNOCK HIM OFF-BALANCE--HE'LL KNOW SOMETHING'S WRONG.

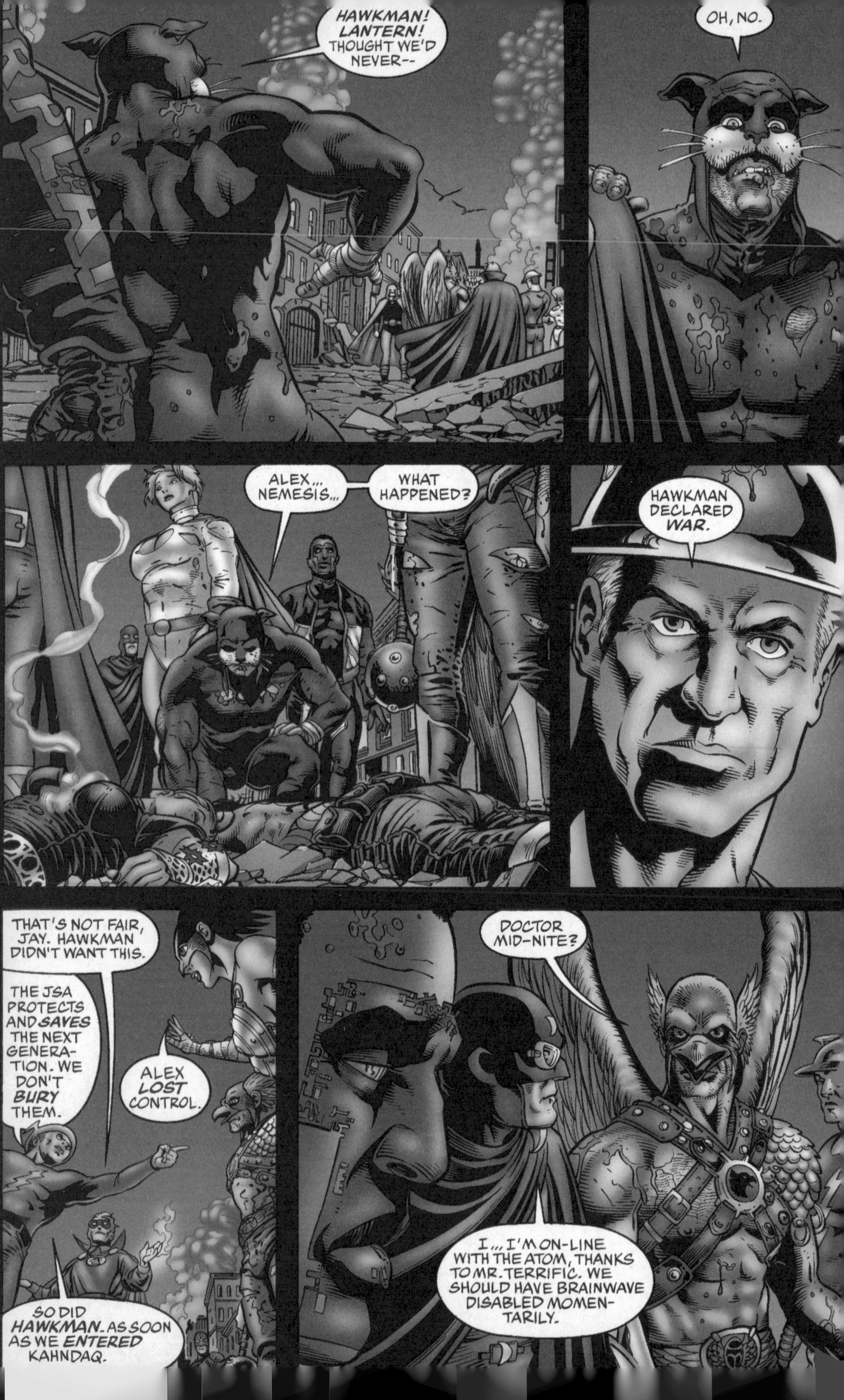

HAWKMAN! LANTERN! THOUGHT WE'D NEVER--
OH, NO.
ALEX... NEMESIS...
WHAT HAPPENED?
HAWKMAN DECLARED WAR.
THAT'S NOT FAIR, JAY. HAWKMAN DIDN'T WANT THIS.
THE JSA PROTECTS AND SAVES THE NEXT GENERATION. WE DON'T BURY THEM.
ALEX LOST CONTROL.
SO DID HAWKMAN. AS SOON AS WE ENTERED KAHNDAQ.
DOCTOR MID-NITE?
I... I'M ON-LINE WITH THE ATOM, THANKS TO MR. TERRIFIC. WE SHOULD HAVE BRAINWAVE DISABLED MOMENTARILY.

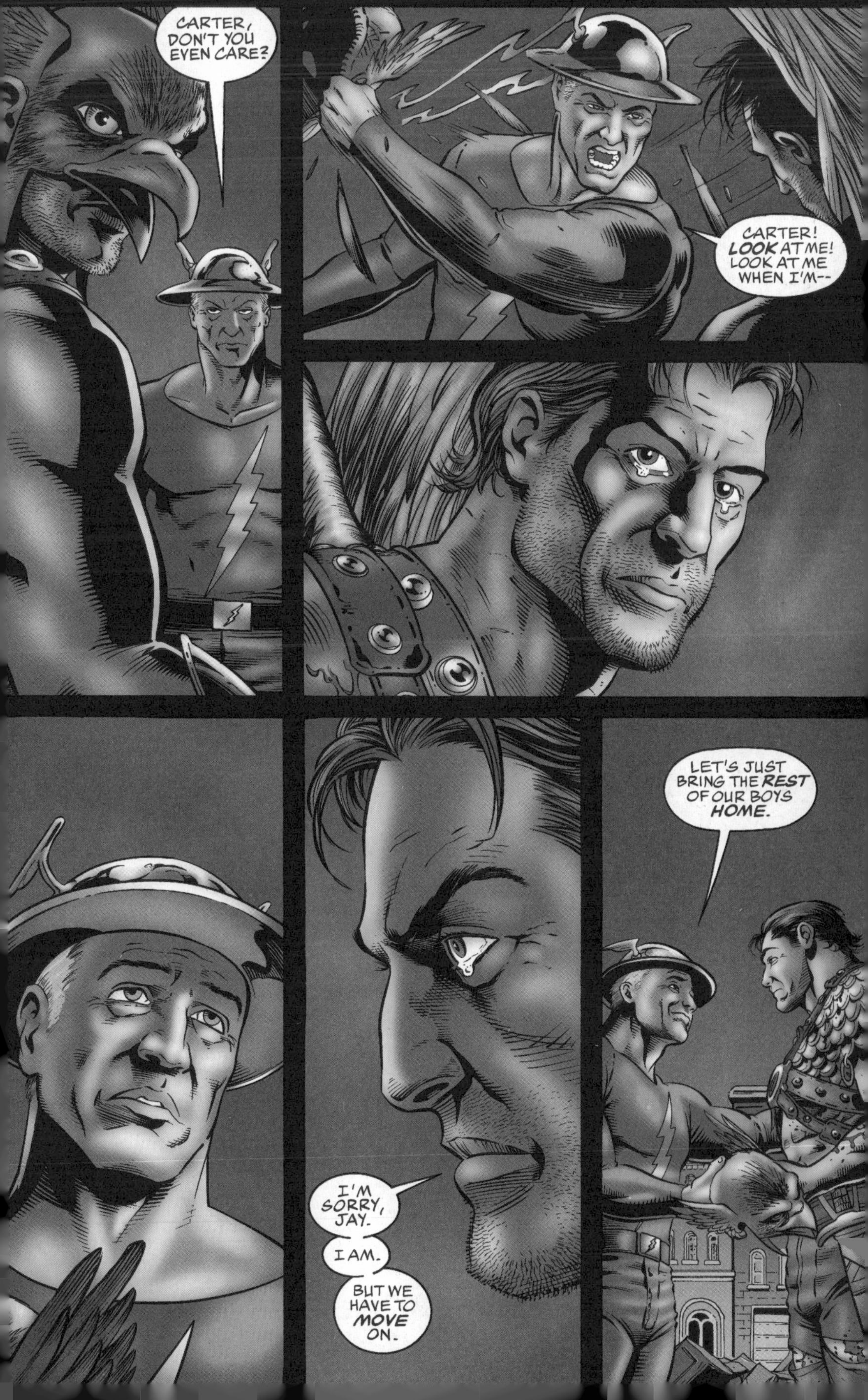
CARTER, DON'T YOU EVEN CARE?
CARTER! LOOK AT ME! LOOK AT ME WHEN I'M--
I'M SORRY, JAY.
I AM.
BUT WE HAVE TO MOVE ON.
LET'S JUST BRING THE REST OF OUR BOYS HOME.

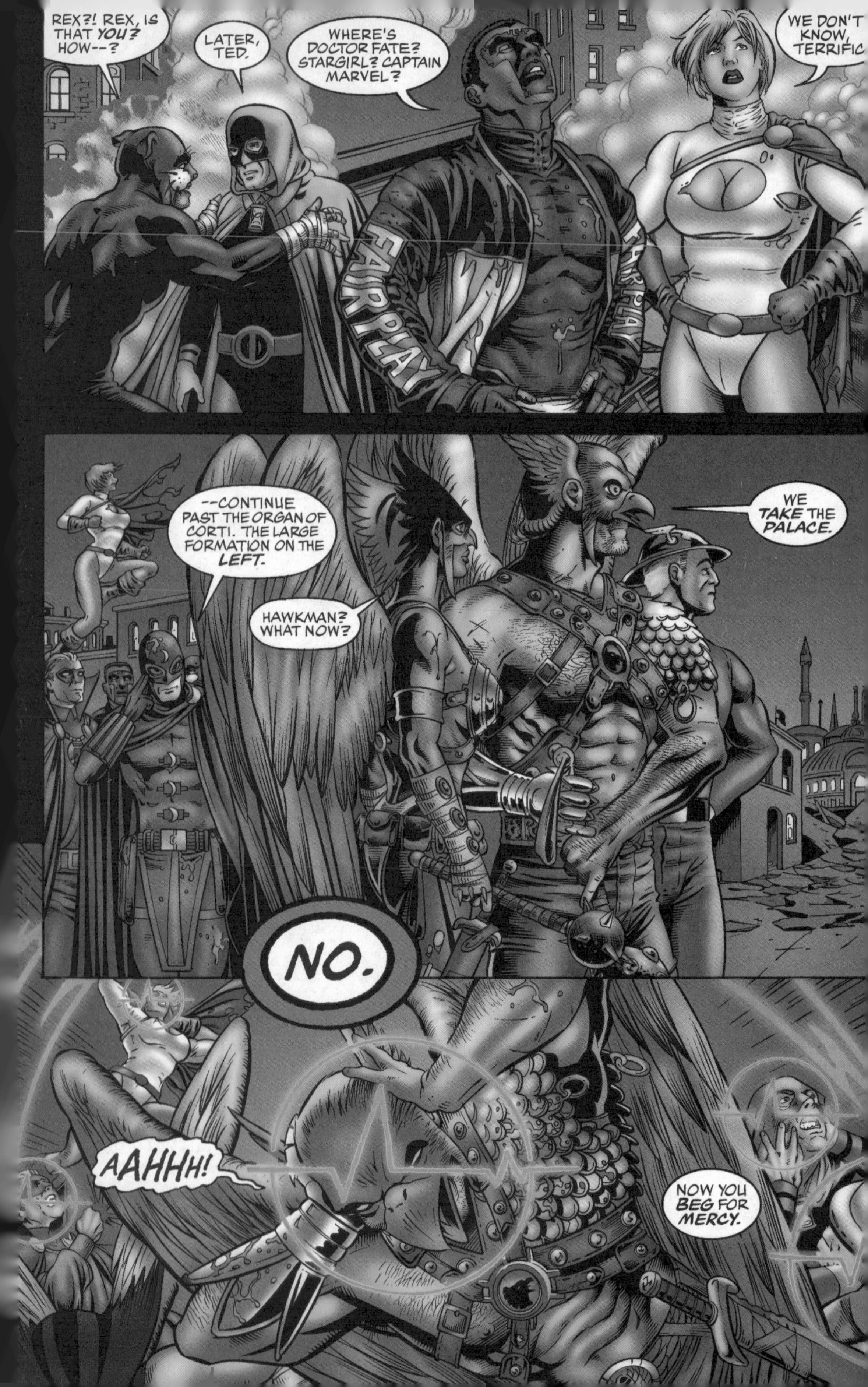
REX?! REX, IS THAT YOU? HOW--?
LATER, TED.
WHERE'S DOCTOR FATE? STARGIRL? CAPTAIN MARVEL?
WE DON'T KNOW, TERRIFIC
--CONTINUE PAST THE ORGAN OF CORTI. THE LARGE FORMATION ON THE LEFT.
HAWKMAN? WHAT NOW?
WE TAKE THE PALACE.
NO.
AAHHH!
NOW YOU BEG FOR MERCY.

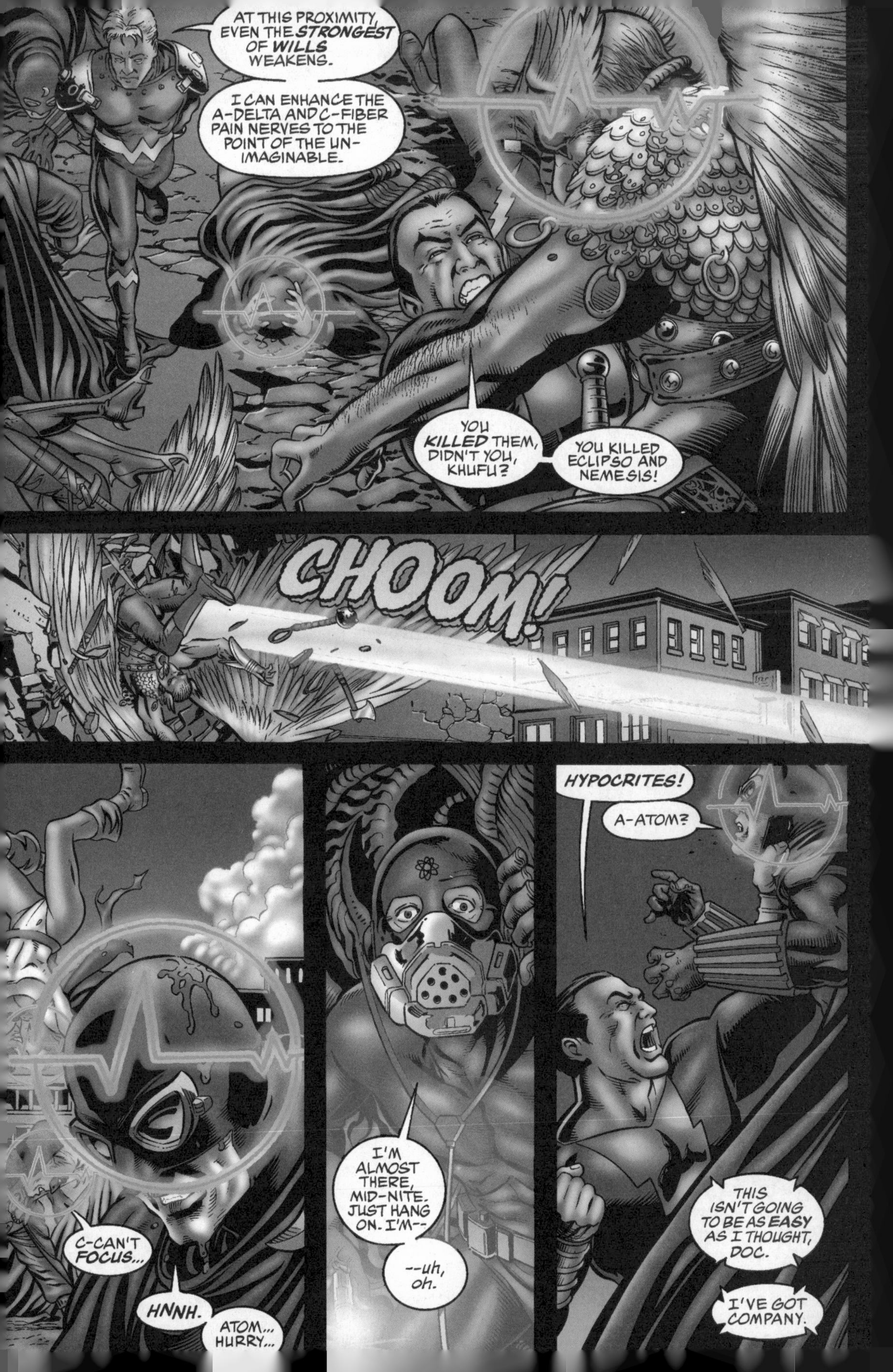

AT THIS PROXIMITY, EVEN THE STRONGEST OF WILLS WEAKENS.
I CAN ENHANCE THE A-DELTA AND C-FIBER PAIN NERVES TO THE POINT OF THE UN-IMAGINABLE.
YOU KILLED THEM, DIDN'T YOU, KHUFU?
YOU KILLED ECLIPSO AND NEMESIS!
CHOOM!
C-CAN'T FOCUS...
HNNH.
ATOM... HURRY...
I'M ALMOST THERE, MID-NITE. JUST HANG ON. I'M--
--uh, oh.
HYPOCRITES!
A-ATOM?
THIS ISN'T GOING TO BE AS EASY AS I THOUGHT, DOC.
I'VE GOT COMPANY.

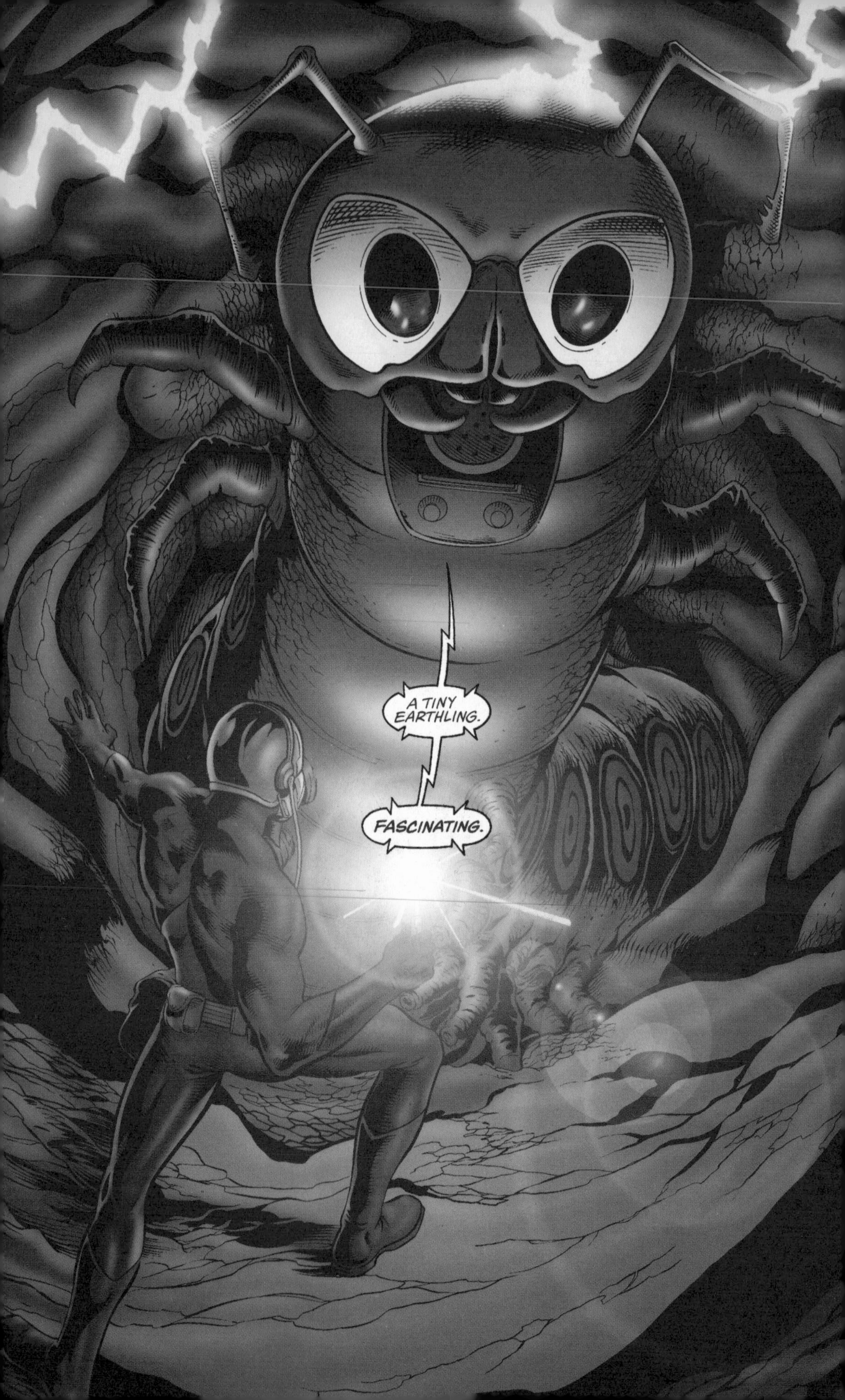
A TINY EARTHLING.
FASCINATING.

KAHNDAQ.

BRRAATT

THIS IS IT?

YES.

KRANNKKAA

HOW THEY *IMPRISONED* CAPTAIN MARVEL, I DON'T--

WAIT HERE.

WHY?

PLEASE, AL. JUST WAIT...

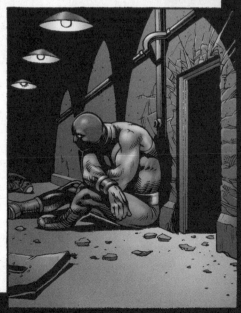

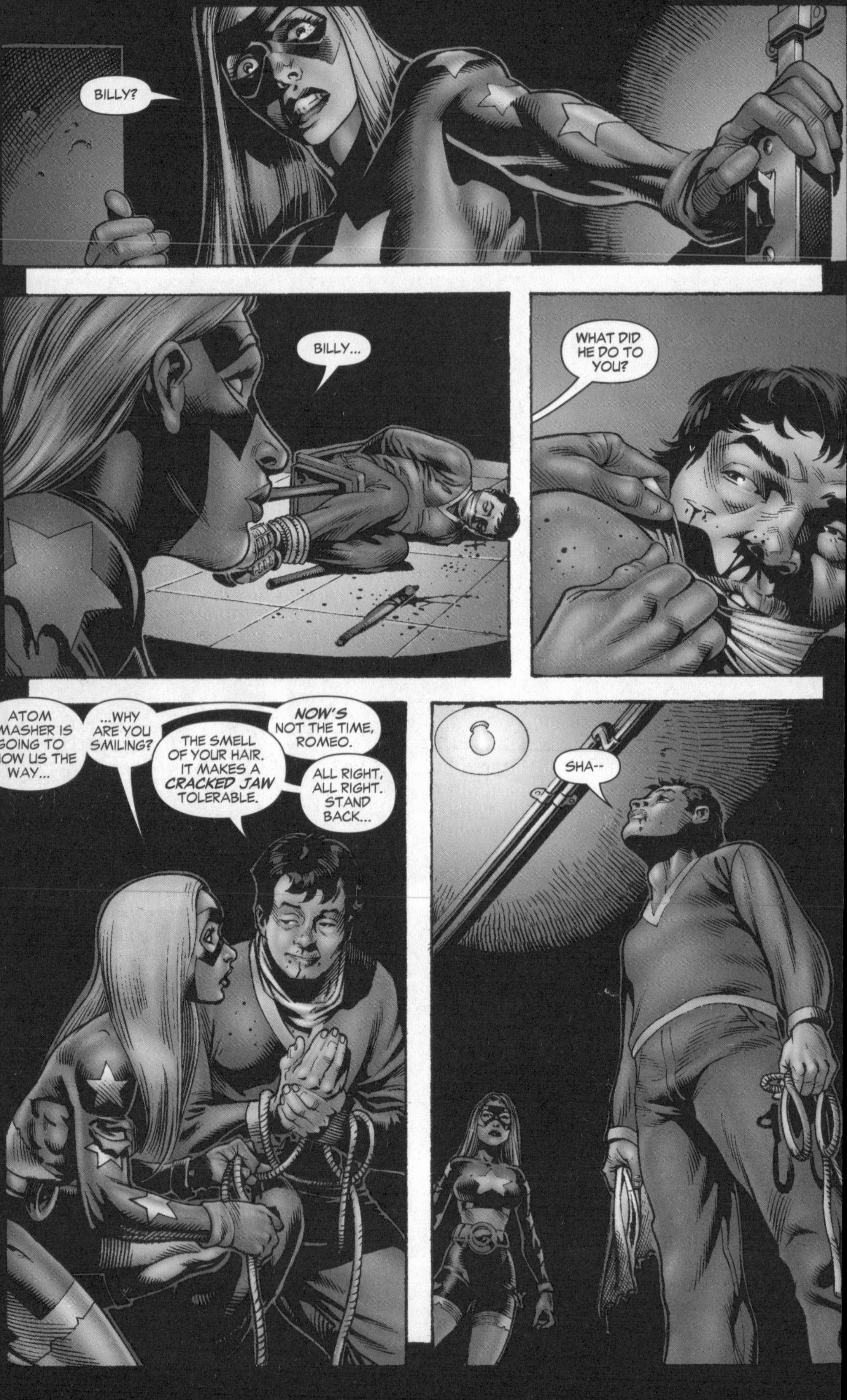

BILLY?
BILLY...
WHAT DID HE DO TO YOU?
ATOM SMASHER IS GOING TO SHOW US THE WAY...
...WHY ARE YOU SMILING?
THE SMELL OF YOUR HAIR. IT MAKES A CRACKED JAW TOLERABLE.
NOW'S NOT THE TIME, ROMEO.
ALL RIGHT, ALL RIGHT. STAND BACK...
SHA--

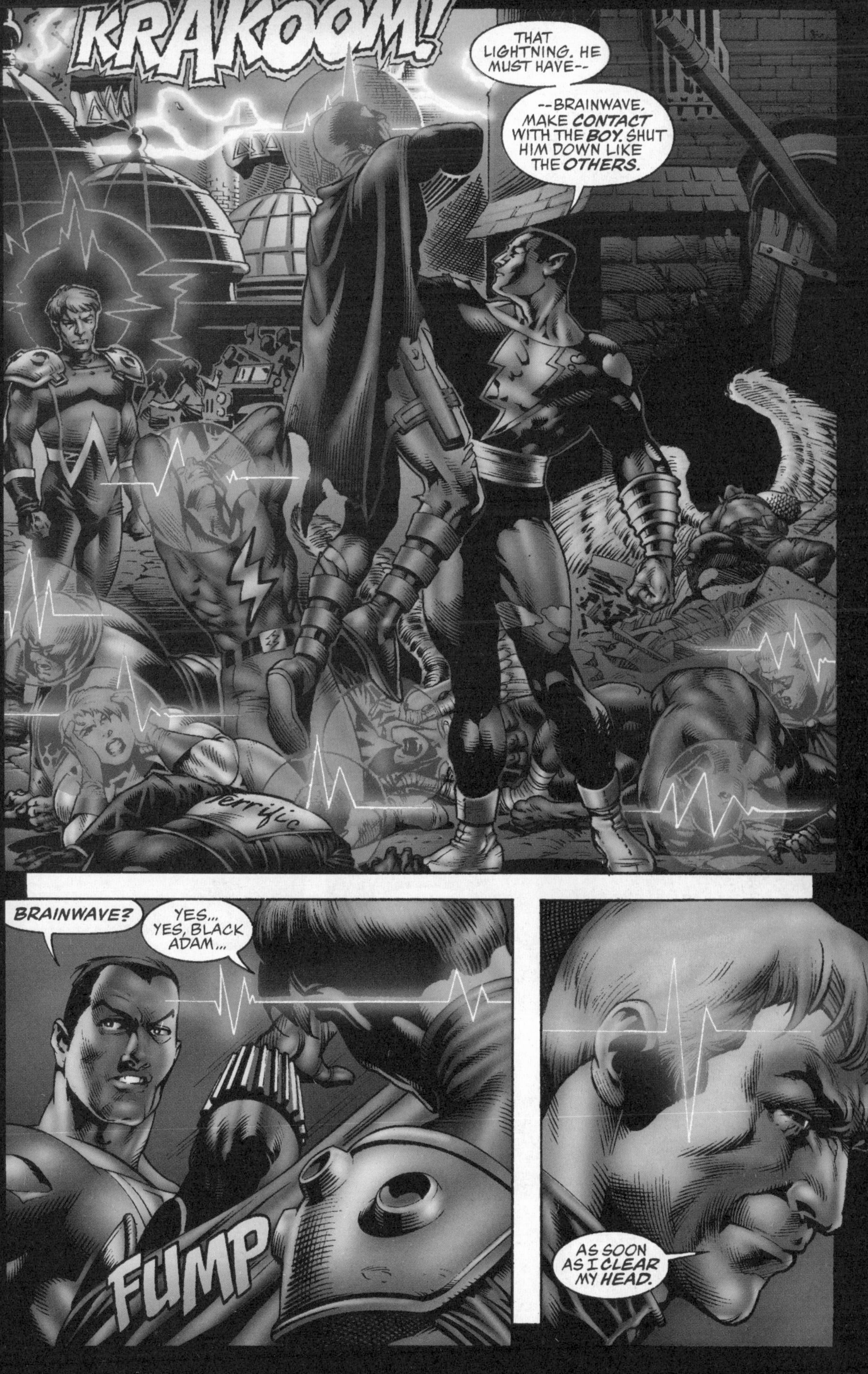
KRAKOOM!
THAT LIGHTNING. HE MUST HAVE--
--BRAINWAVE, MAKE CONTACT WITH THE BOY. SHUT HIM DOWN LIKE THE OTHERS.
Terrific
BRAINWAVE?
YES... YES, BLACK ADAM...
FUMP
AS SOON AS I CLEAR MY HEAD.

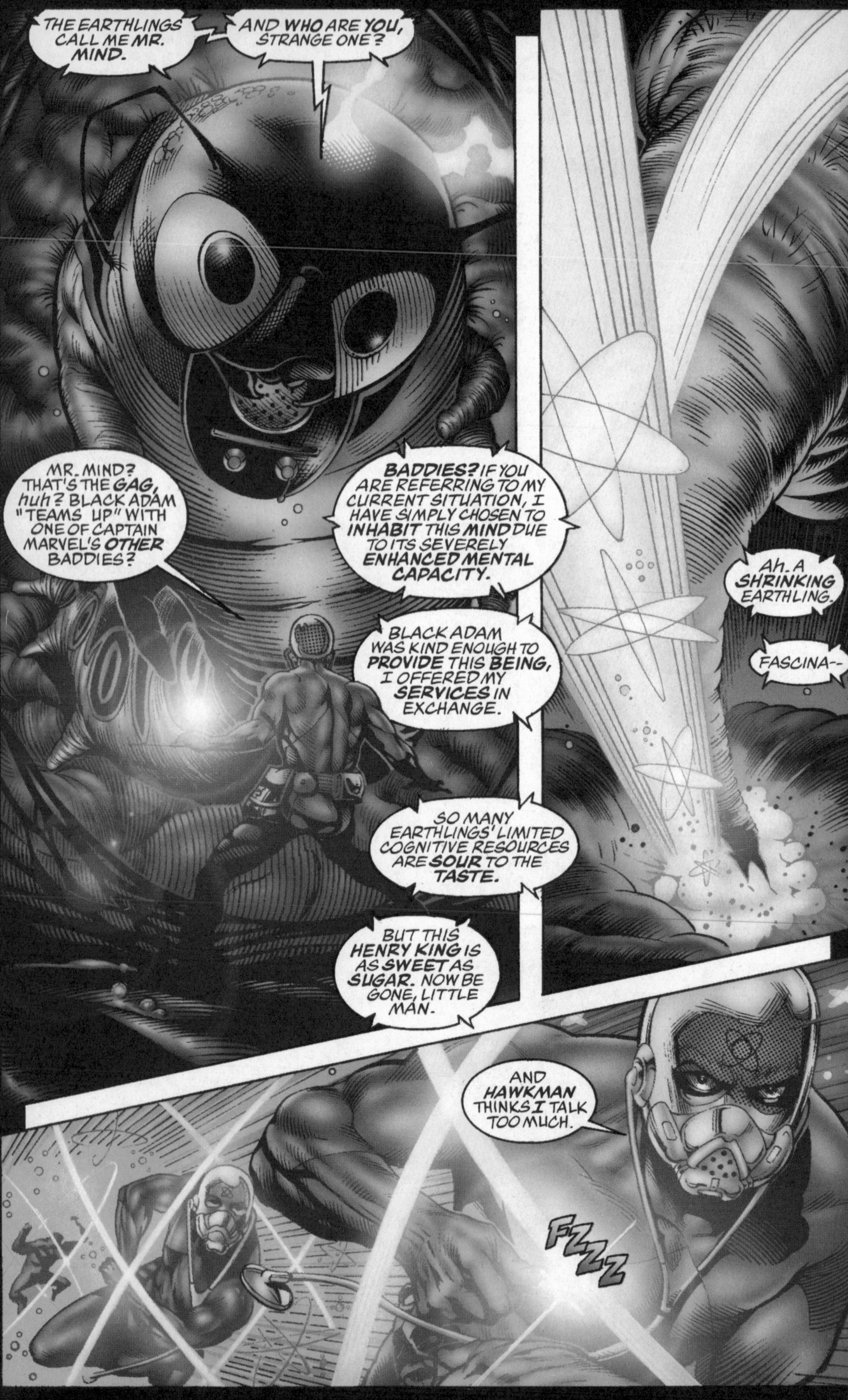
THE EARTHLINGS CALL ME MR. MIND.
AND WHO ARE YOU, STRANGE ONE?
MR. MIND? THAT'S THE GAG, huh? BLACK ADAM "TEAMS UP" WITH ONE OF CAPTAIN MARVEL'S OTHER BADDIES?
BADDIES? IF YOU ARE REFERRING TO MY CURRENT SITUATION, I HAVE SIMPLY CHOSEN TO INHABIT THIS MIND DUE TO ITS SEVERELY ENHANCED MENTAL CAPACITY.
BLACK ADAM WAS KIND ENOUGH TO PROVIDE THIS BEING, I OFFERED MY SERVICES IN EXCHANGE.
SO MANY EARTHLINGS' LIMITED COGNITIVE RESOURCES ARE SOUR TO THE TASTE.
BUT THIS HENRY KING IS AS SWEET AS SUGAR. NOW BE GONE, LITTLE MAN.
Ah. A SHRINKING EARTHLING.
FASCINA--
AND HAWKMAN THINKS I TALK TOO MUCH.
FZZZ

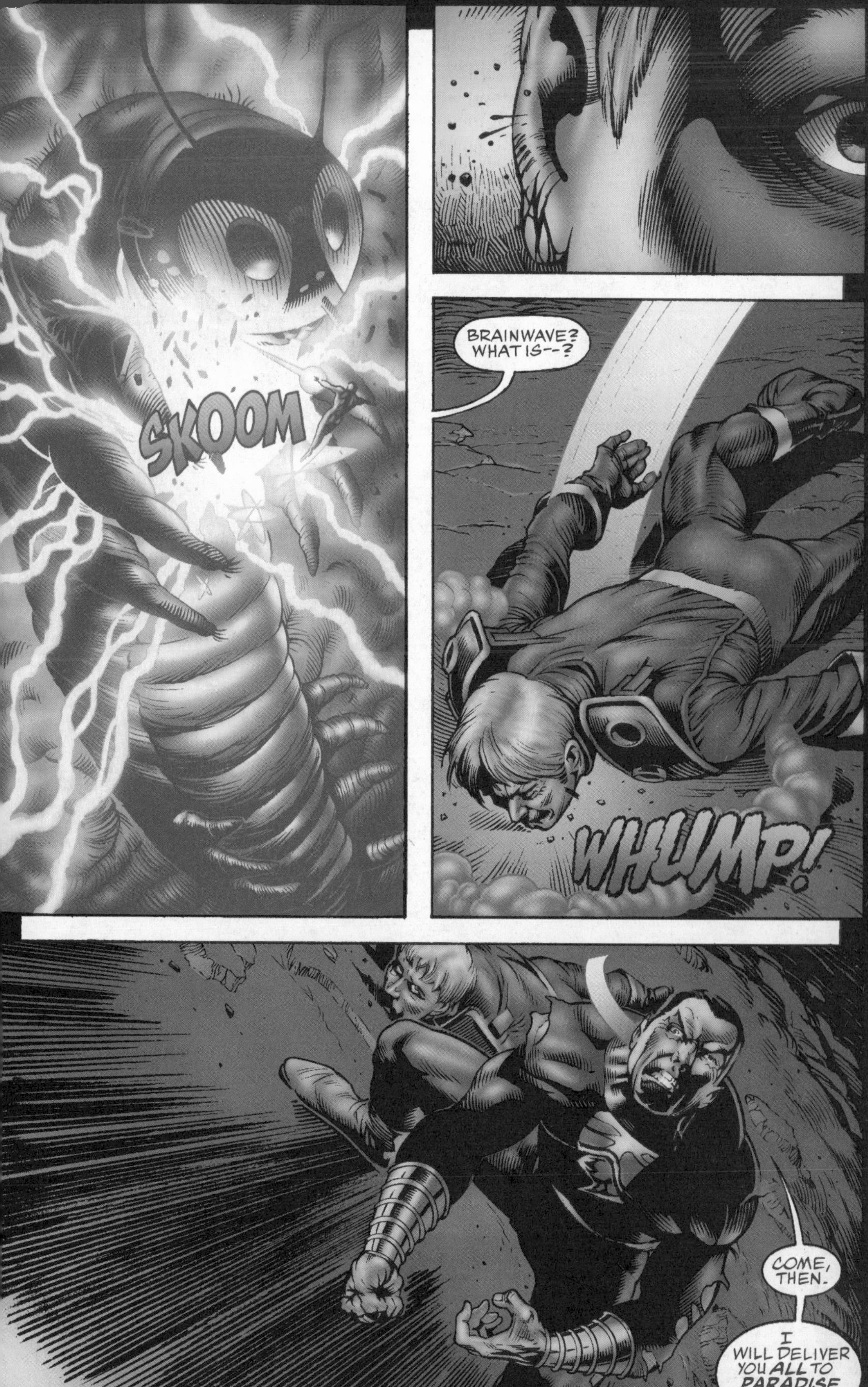

SKOOM
BRAINWAVE? WHAT IS--?
WHUMP!
COME, THEN.
I WILL DELIVER YOU ALL TO PARADISE MYSELF.

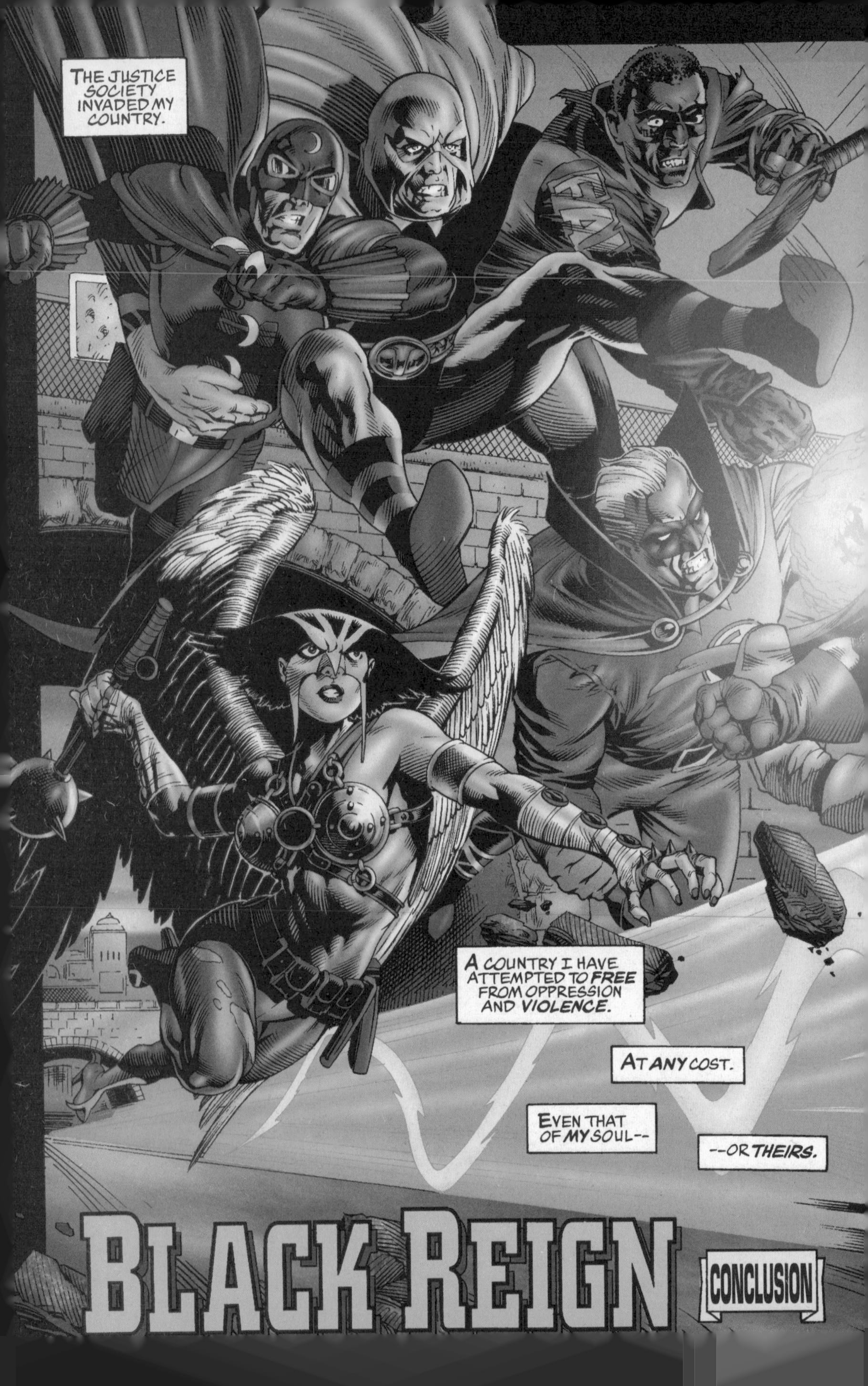
THE JUSTICE SOCIETY INVADED MY COUNTRY.
A COUNTRY I HAVE ATTEMPTED TO FREE FROM OPPRESSION AND VIOLENCE.
AT ANY COST.
EVEN THAT OF MY SOUL--
--OR THEIRS.
BLACK REIGN
CONCLUSION

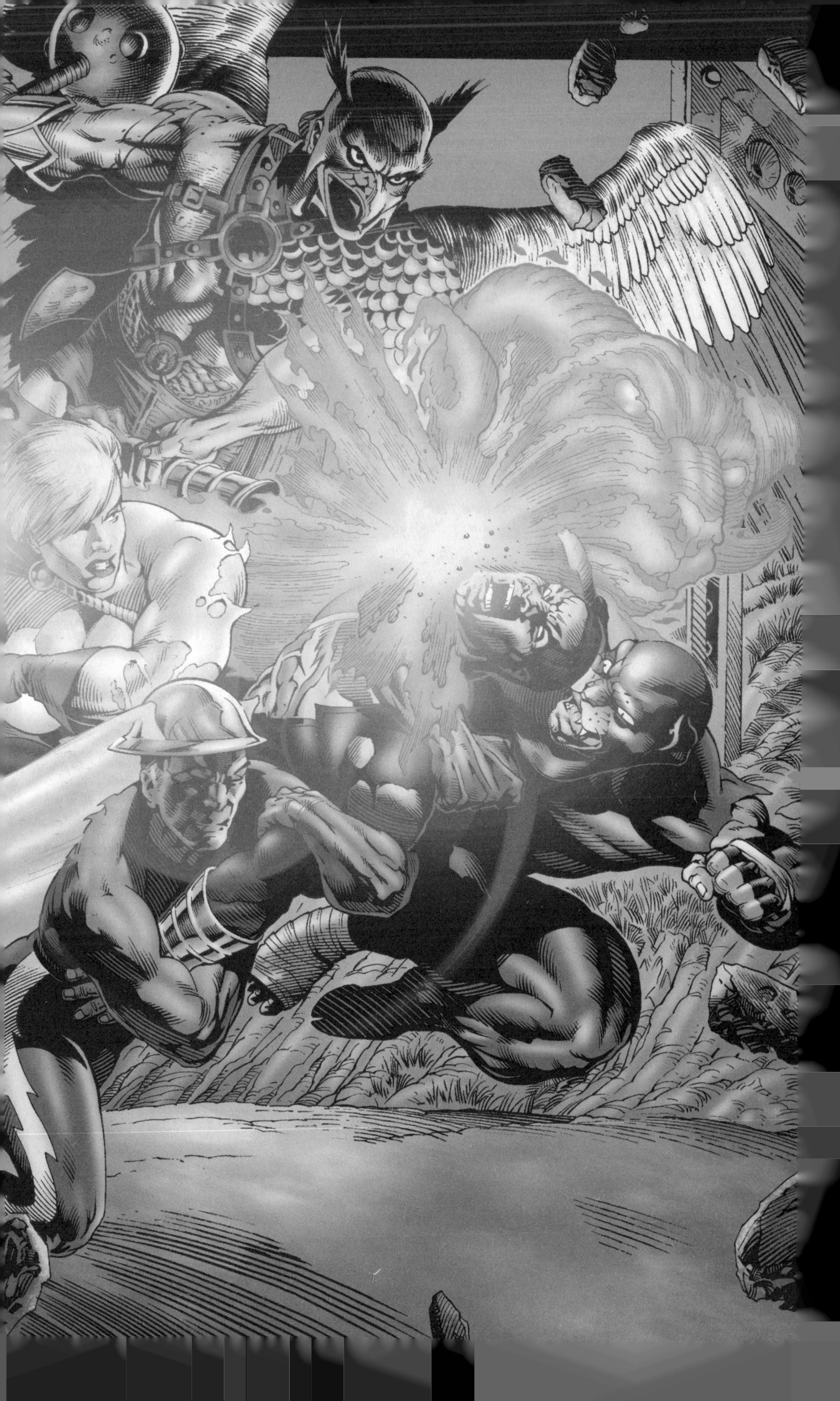

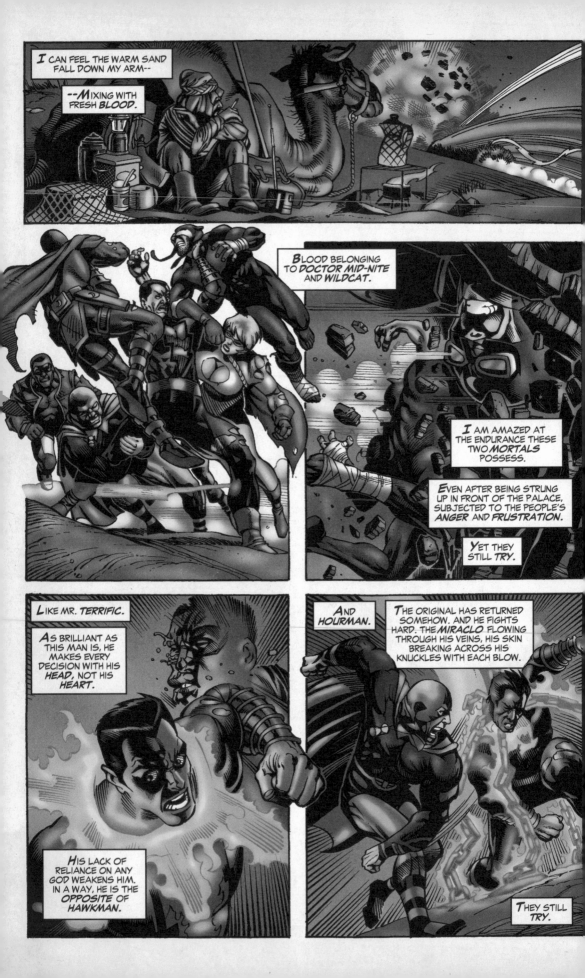

I CAN FEEL THE WARM SAND FALL DOWN MY ARM--

--MIXING WITH FRESH BLOOD.

BLOOD BELONGING TO DOCTOR MID-NITE AND WILDCAT.

I AM AMAZED AT THE ENDURANCE THESE TWO MORTALS POSSESS.

EVEN AFTER BEING STRUNG UP IN FRONT OF THE PALACE, SUBJECTED TO THE PEOPLE'S ANGER AND FRUSTRATION.

YET THEY STILL TRY.

LIKE MR. TERRIFIC.

AS BRILLIANT AS THIS MAN IS, HE MAKES EVERY DECISION WITH HIS HEAD, NOT HIS HEART.

HIS LACK OF RELIANCE ON ANY GOD WEAKENS HIM. IN A WAY, HE IS THE OPPOSITE OF HAWKMAN.

AND HOURMAN.

THE ORIGINAL HAS RETURNED SOMEHOW. AND HE FIGHTS HARD. THE MIRACLO FLOWING THROUGH HIS VEINS, HIS SKIN BREAKING ACROSS HIS KNUCKLES WITH EACH BLOW.

THEY STILL TRY.

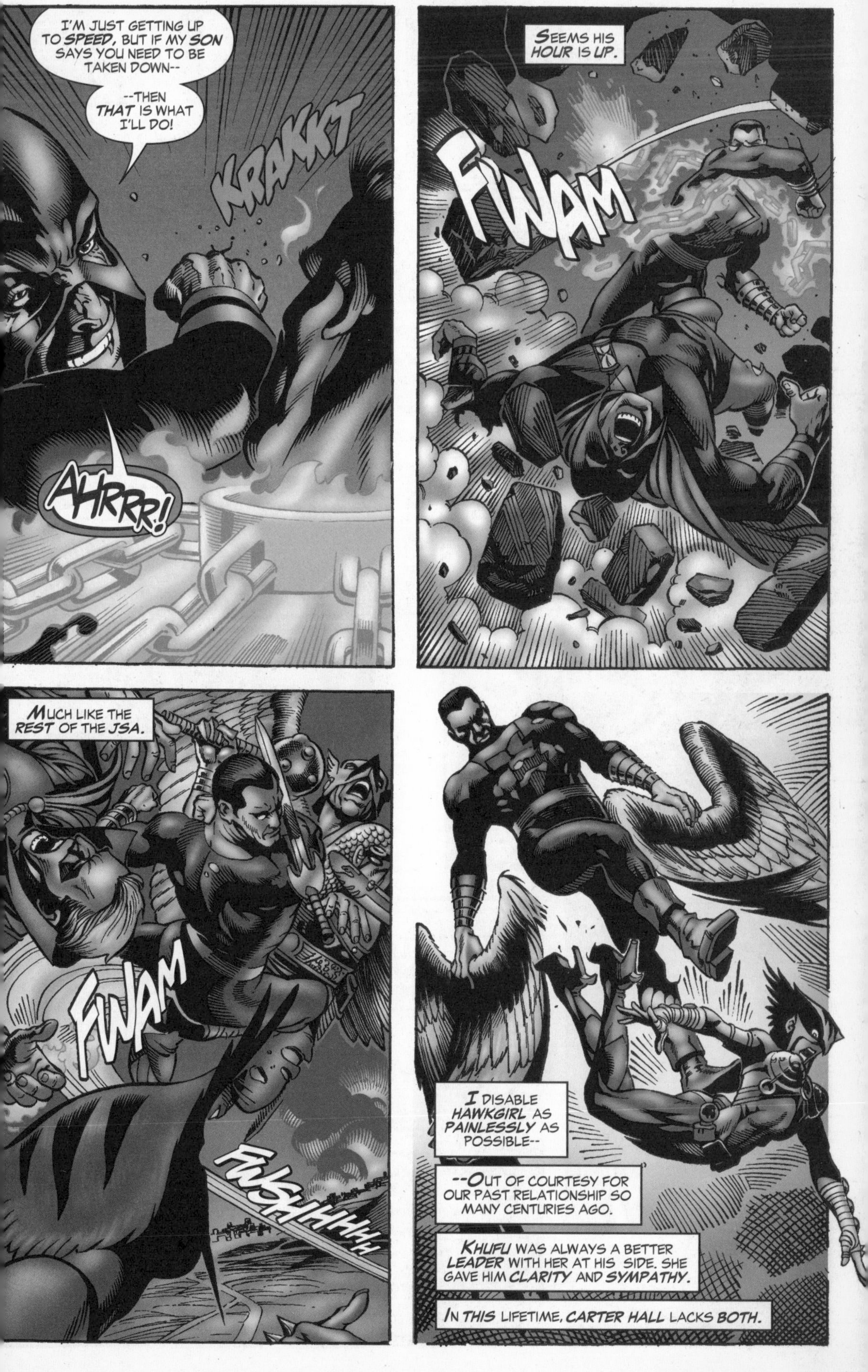

I'M JUST GETTING UP TO SPEED, BUT IF MY SON SAYS YOU NEED TO BE TAKEN DOWN--
--THEN THAT IS WHAT I'LL DO!
KRAKKT
AHRRR!
SEEMS HIS HOUR IS UP.
FWAM
MUCH LIKE THE REST OF THE JSA.
FWAM
FWSHHHHH
I DISABLE HAWKGIRL AS PAINLESSLY AS POSSIBLE--
--OUT OF COURTESY FOR OUR PAST RELATIONSHIP SO MANY CENTURIES AGO.
KHUFU WAS ALWAYS A BETTER LEADER WITH HER AT HIS SIDE. SHE GAVE HIM CLARITY AND SYMPATHY.
IN THIS LIFETIME, CARTER HALL LACKS BOTH.

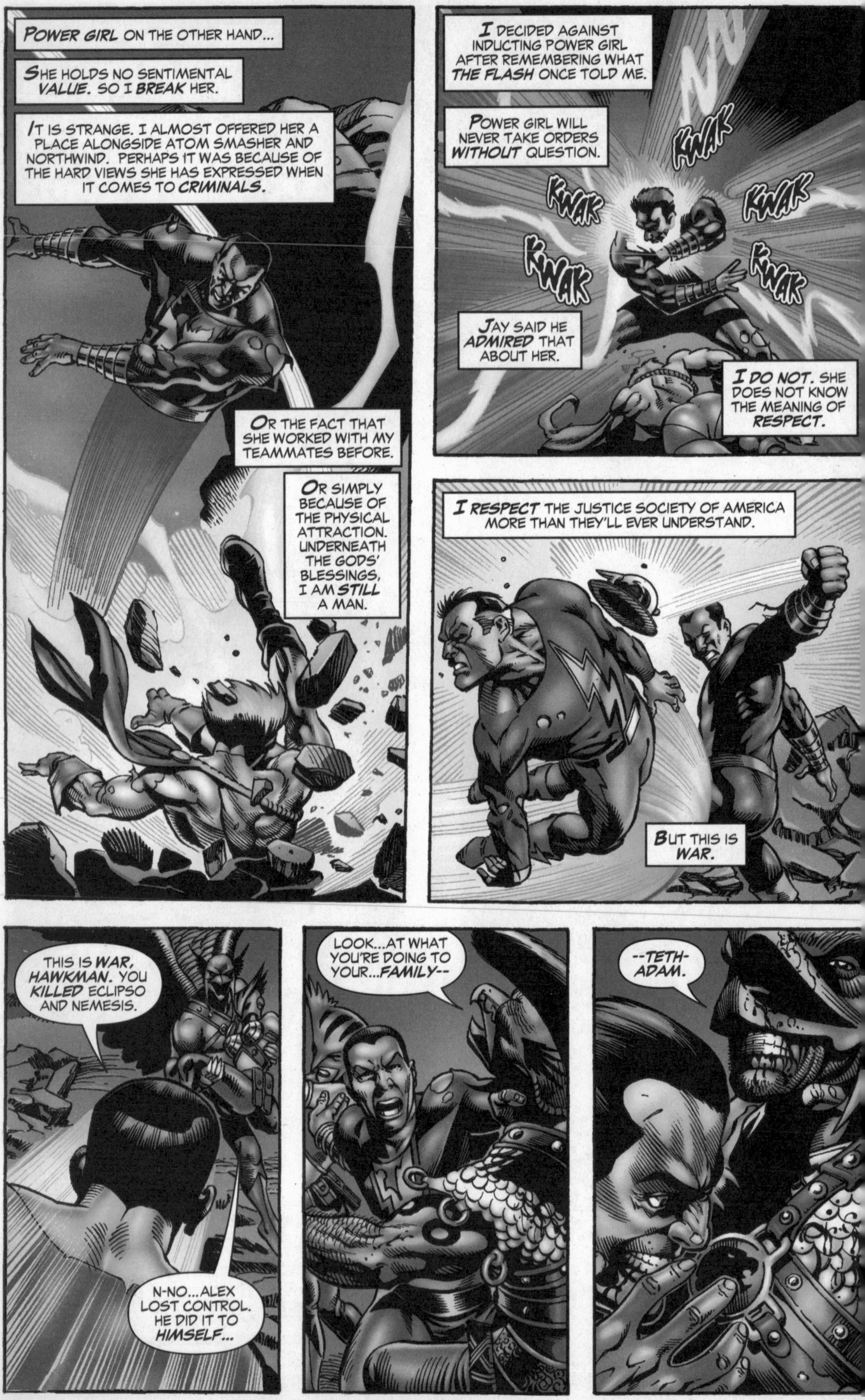
POWER GIRL ON THE OTHER HAND...
SHE HOLDS NO SENTIMENTAL VALUE. SO I BREAK HER.
IT IS STRANGE. I ALMOST OFFERED HER A PLACE ALONGSIDE ATOM SMASHER AND NORTHWIND. PERHAPS IT WAS BECAUSE OF THE HARD VIEWS SHE HAS EXPRESSED WHEN IT COMES TO CRIMINALS.
OR THE FACT THAT SHE WORKED WITH MY TEAMMATES BEFORE.
OR SIMPLY BECAUSE OF THE PHYSICAL ATTRACTION. UNDERNEATH THE GODS' BLESSINGS, I AM STILL A MAN.
I DECIDED AGAINST INDUCTING POWER GIRL AFTER REMEMBERING WHAT THE FLASH ONCE TOLD ME.
POWER GIRL WILL NEVER TAKE ORDERS WITHOUT QUESTION.
KWAK
KWAK
KWAK
KWAK
KWAK
JAY SAID HE ADMIRED THAT ABOUT HER.
I DO NOT. SHE DOES NOT KNOW THE MEANING OF RESPECT.
I RESPECT THE JUSTICE SOCIETY OF AMERICA MORE THAN THEY'LL EVER UNDERSTAND.
BUT THIS IS WAR.
THIS IS WAR, HAWKMAN. YOU KILLED ECLIPSO AND NEMESIS.
N-NO...ALEX LOST CONTROL. HE DID IT TO HIMSELF...
LOOK...AT WHAT YOU'RE DOING TO YOUR...FAMILY--
--TETH-ADAM.

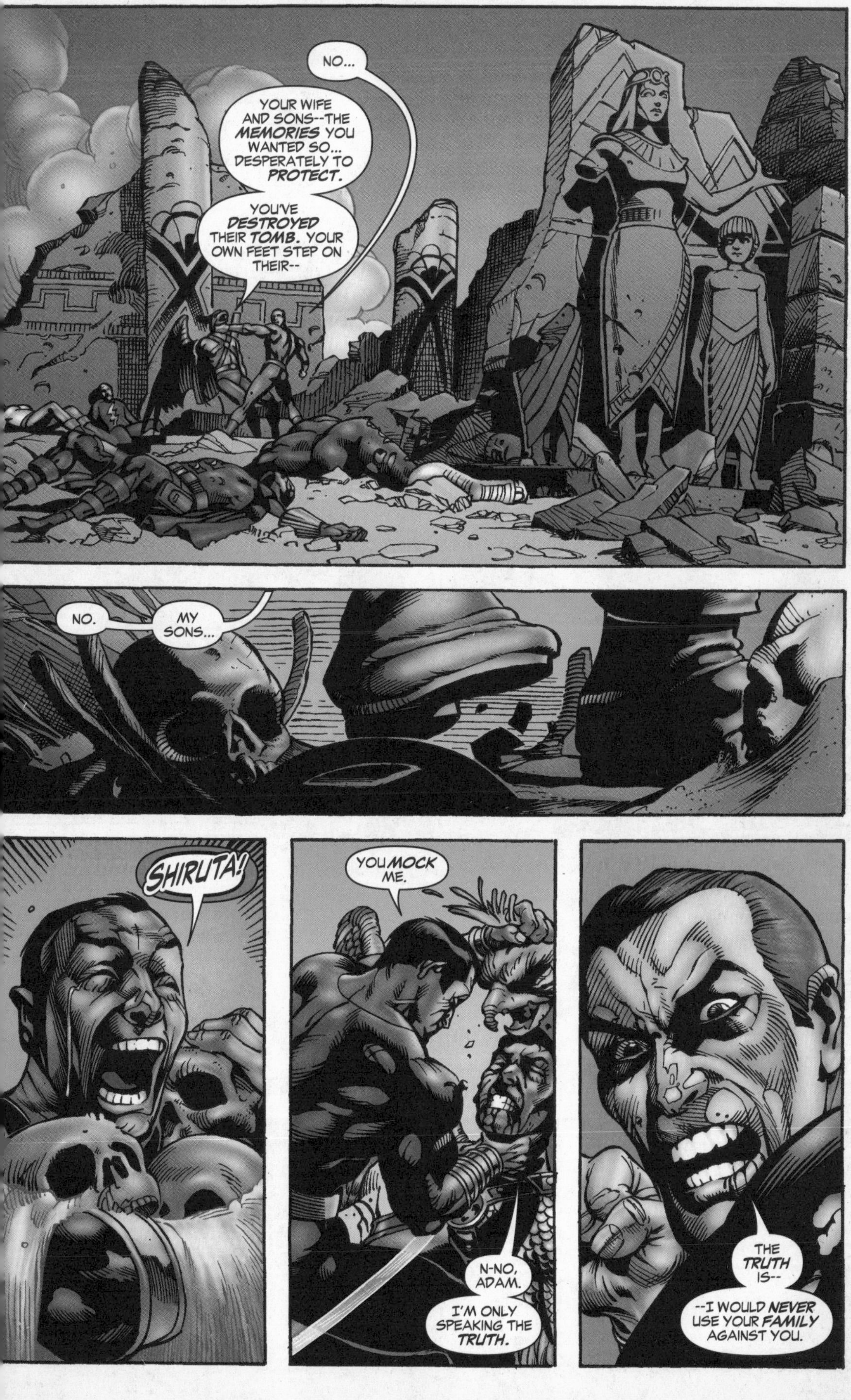
NO...
YOUR WIFE AND SONS--THE MEMORIES YOU WANTED SO... DESPERATELY TO PROTECT.
YOU'VE DESTROYED THEIR TOMB. YOUR OWN FEET STEP ON THEIR--
NO.
MY SONS...
SHIRUTA!
YOU MOCK ME.
N-NO, ADAM.
I'M ONLY SPEAKING THE TRUTH.
THE TRUTH IS--
--I WOULD NEVER USE YOUR FAMILY AGAINST YOU.

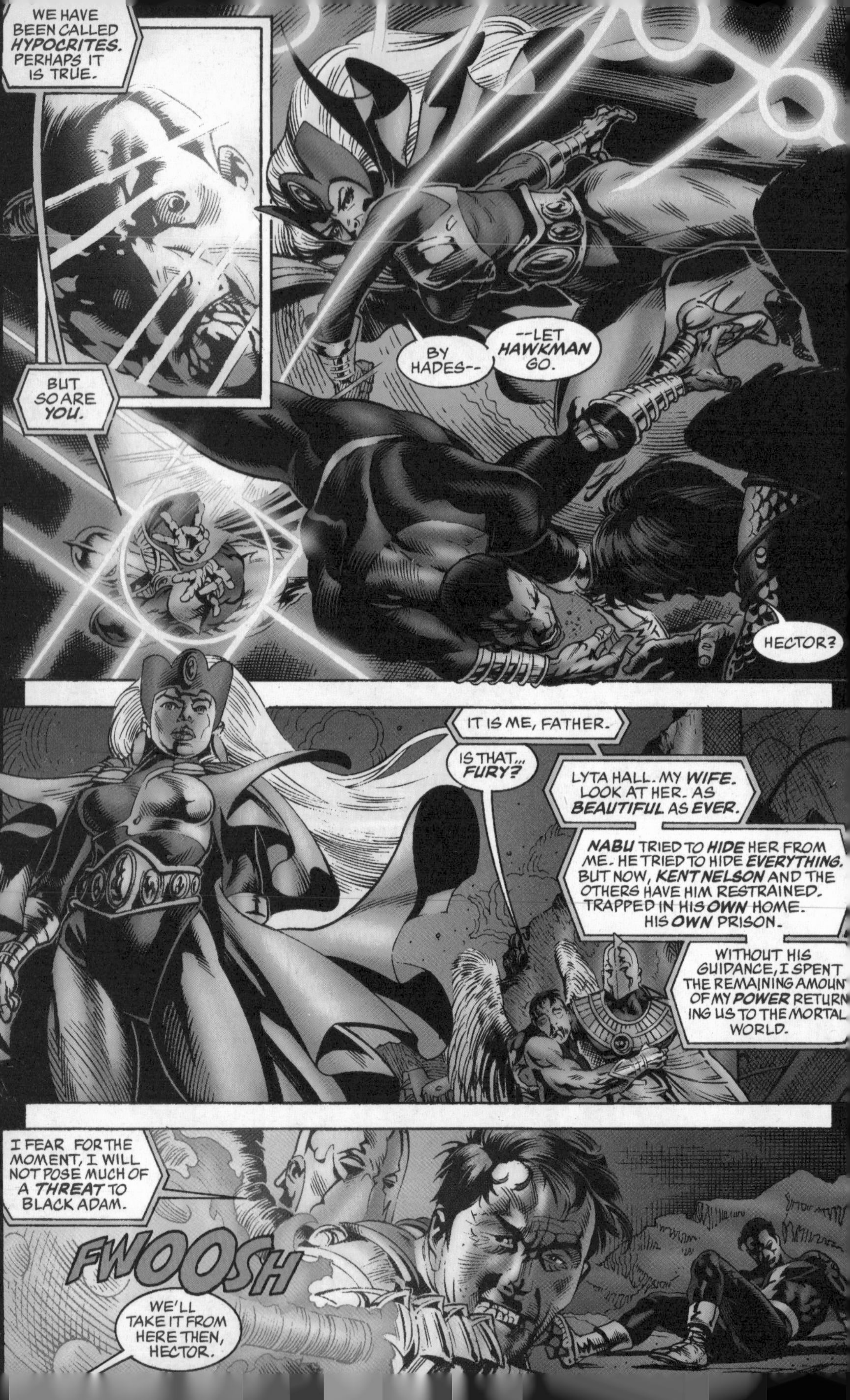
WE HAVE BEEN CALLED HYPOCRITES. PERHAPS IT IS TRUE.
BUT SO ARE YOU.
BY HADES--
--LET HAWKMAN GO.
HECTOR?
IT IS ME, FATHER.
IS THAT... FURY?
LYTA HALL. MY WIFE. LOOK AT HER. AS BEAUTIFUL AS EVER.
NABU TRIED TO HIDE HER FROM ME. HE TRIED TO HIDE EVERYTHING. BUT NOW, KENT NELSON AND THE OTHERS HAVE HIM RESTRAINED. TRAPPED IN HIS OWN HOME. HIS OWN PRISON.
WITHOUT HIS GUIDANCE, I SPENT THE REMAINING AMOUN OF MY POWER RETURN ING US TO THE MORTAL WORLD.
I FEAR FOR THE MOMENT, I WILL NOT POSE MUCH OF A THREAT TO BLACK ADAM.
FWOOSH
WE'LL TAKE IT FROM HERE THEN, HECTOR.

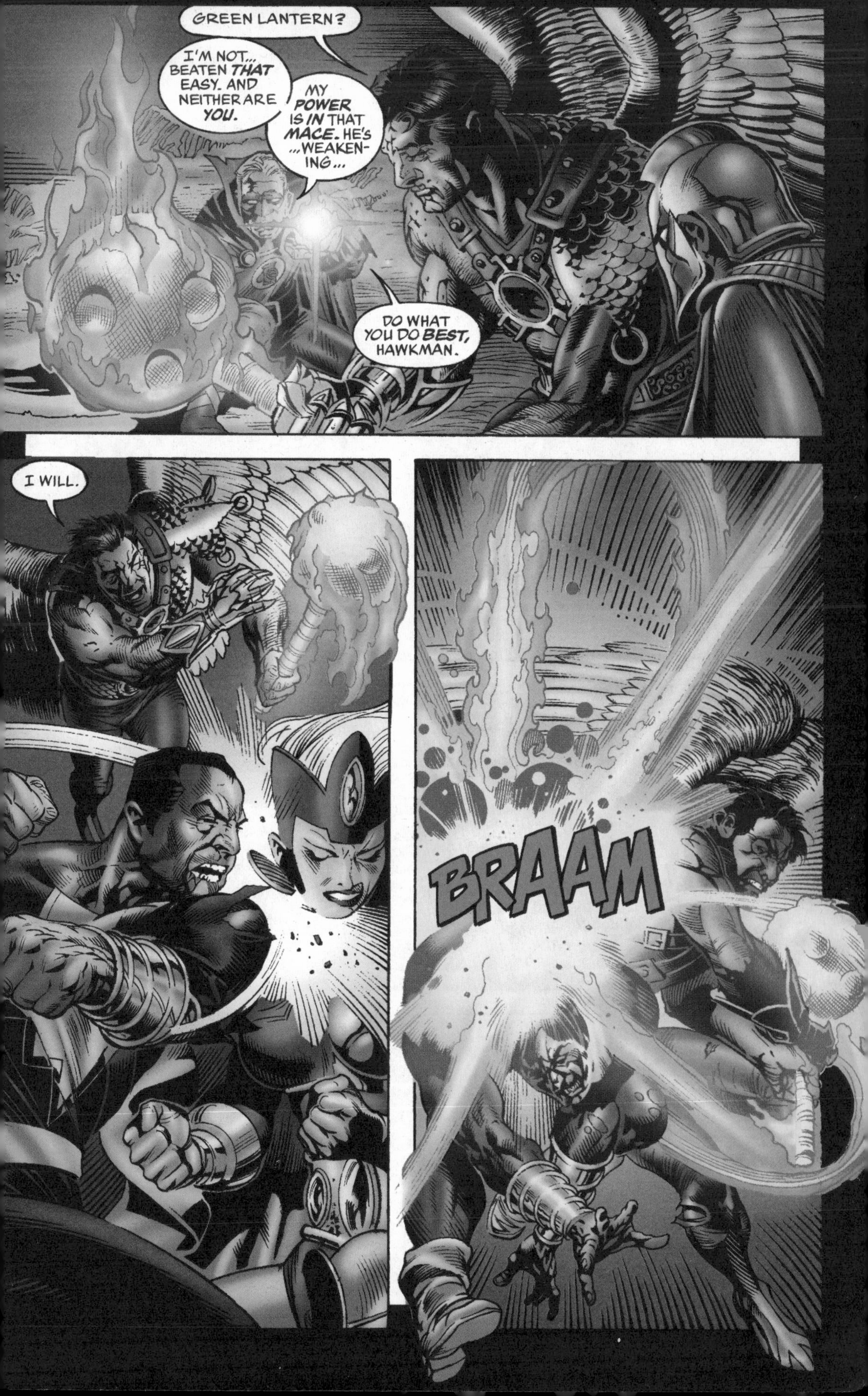
GREEN LANTERN?
I'M NOT... BEATEN THAT EASY. AND NEITHER ARE YOU.
MY POWER IS IN THAT MACE. HE'S ...WEAKENING...
DO WHAT YOU DO BEST, HAWKMAN.
I WILL.
BRAAM

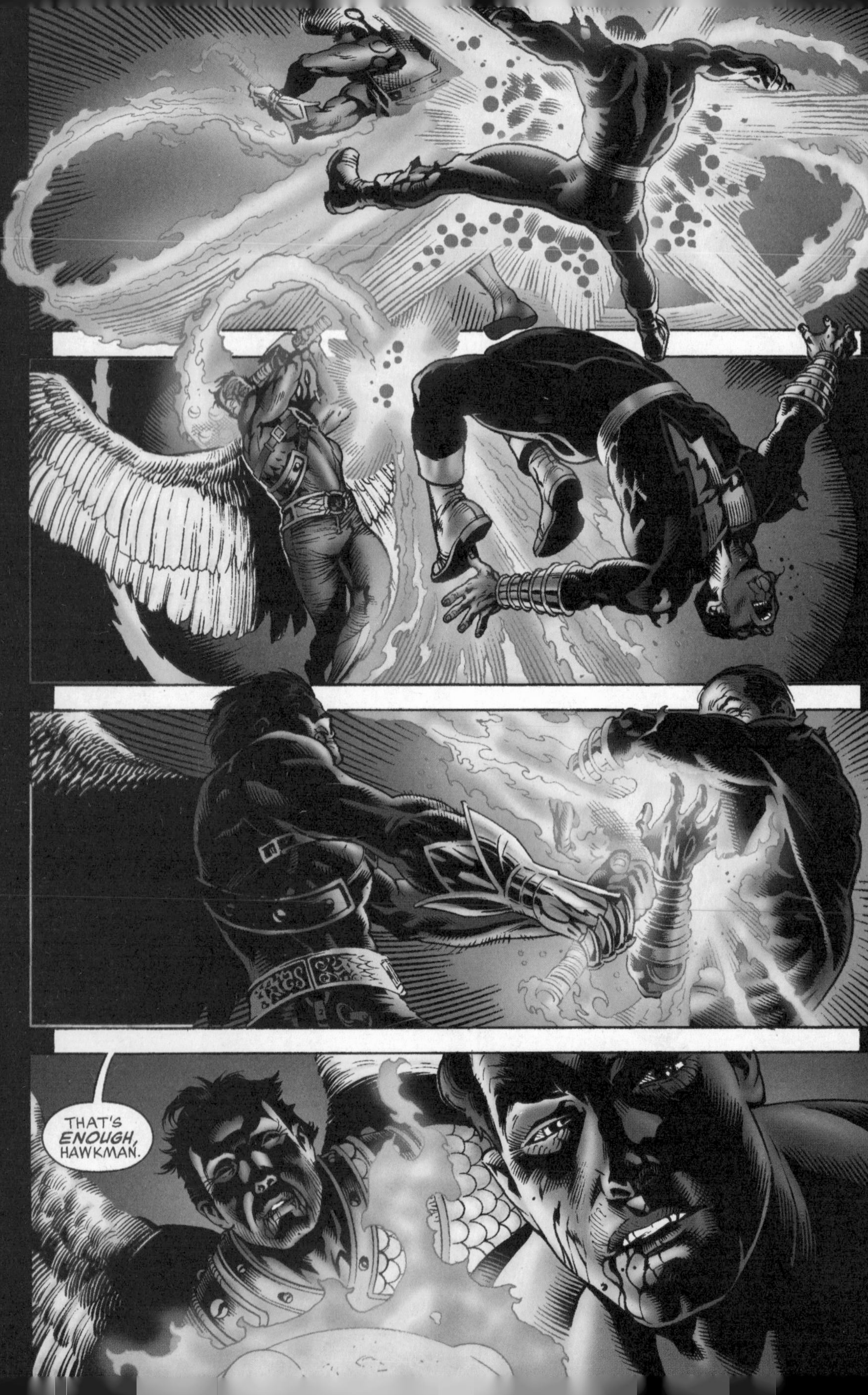
THAT'S
ENOUGH,
HAWKMAN.

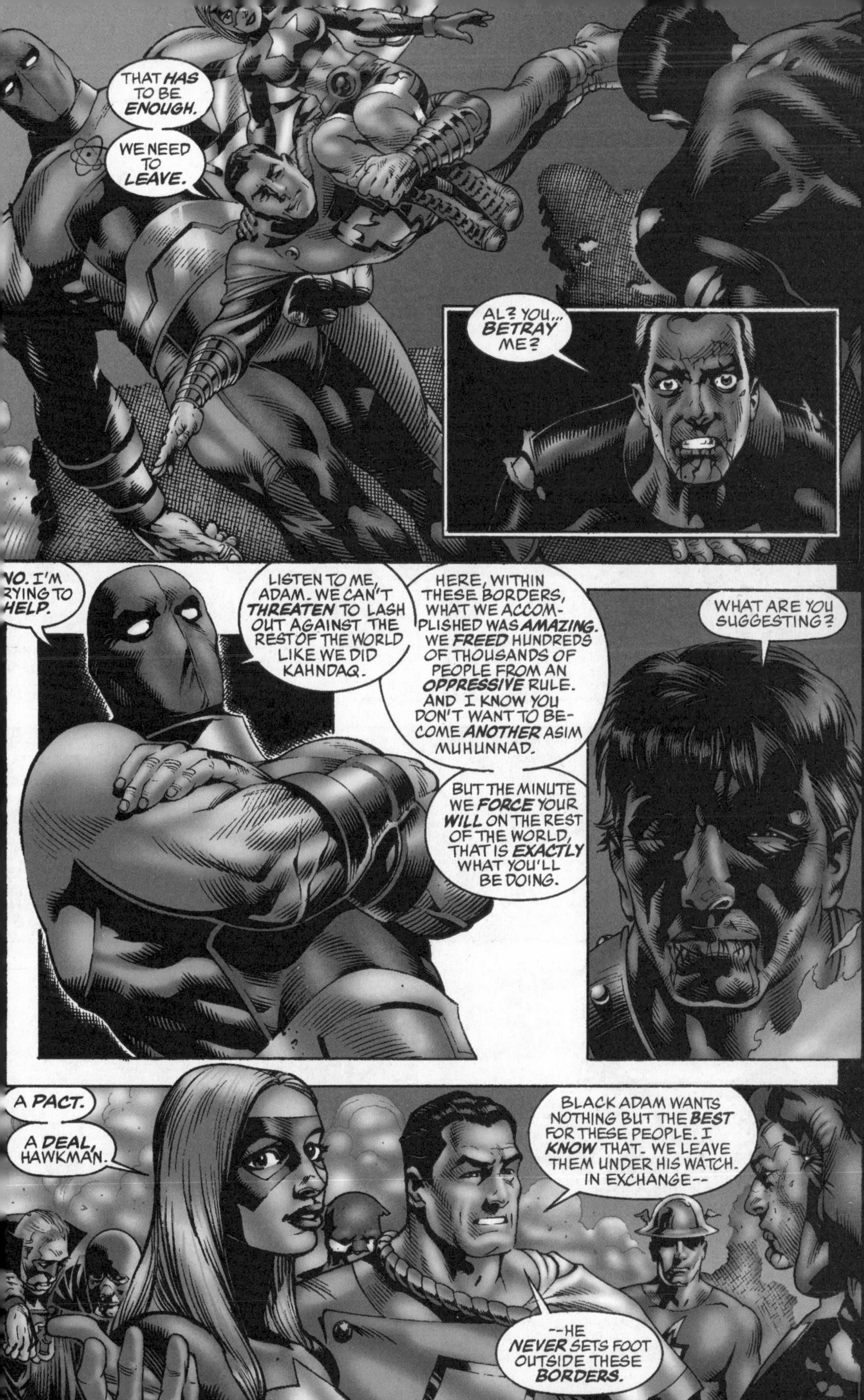

THAT HAS TO BE ENOUGH.
WE NEED TO LEAVE.
AL? YOU... BETRAY ME?
NO. I'M RYING TO HELP.
LISTEN TO ME, ADAM. WE CAN'T THREATEN TO LASH OUT AGAINST THE REST OF THE WORLD LIKE WE DID KAHNDAQ.
HERE, WITHIN THESE BORDERS, WHAT WE ACCOMPLISHED WAS AMAZING. WE FREED HUNDREDS OF THOUSANDS OF PEOPLE FROM AN OPPRESSIVE RULE. AND I KNOW YOU DON'T WANT TO BECOME ANOTHER ASIM MUHUNNAD.
BUT THE MINUTE WE FORCE YOUR WILL ON THE REST OF THE WORLD, THAT IS EXACTLY WHAT YOU'LL BE DOING.
WHAT ARE YOU SUGGESTING?
A PACT.
A DEAL, HAWKMAN.
BLACK ADAM WANTS NOTHING BUT THE BEST FOR THESE PEOPLE. I KNOW THAT. WE LEAVE THEM UNDER HIS WATCH. IN EXCHANGE--
--HE NEVER SETS FOOT OUTSIDE THESE BORDERS.

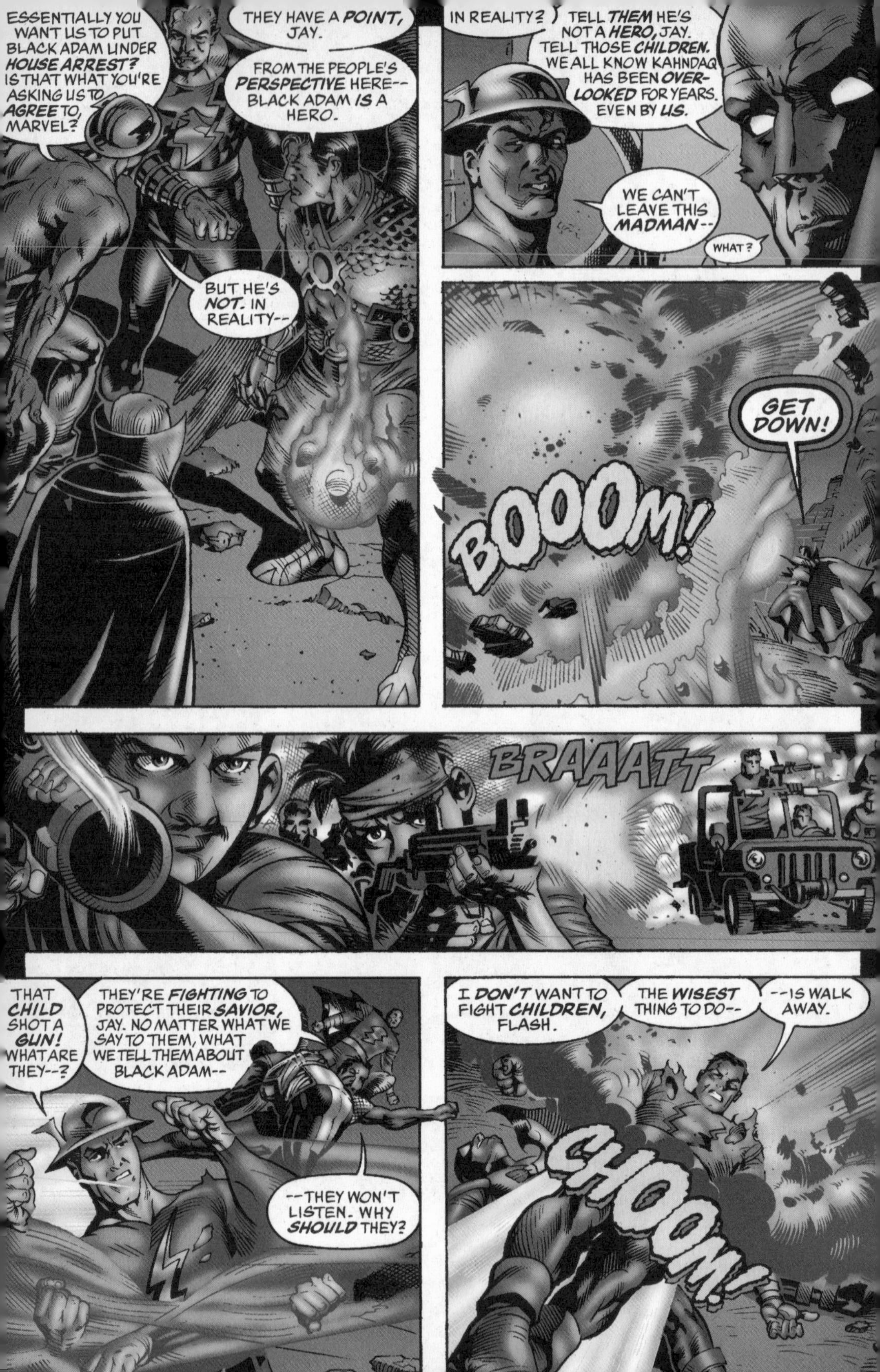
ESSENTIALLY YOU WANT US TO PUT BLACK ADAM UNDER HOUSE ARREST? IS THAT WHAT YOU'RE ASKING US TO AGREE TO, MARVEL?
THEY HAVE A POINT, JAY.
FROM THE PEOPLE'S PERSPECTIVE HERE-- BLACK ADAM IS A HERO.
BUT HE'S NOT. IN REALITY--
IN REALITY?
TELL THEM HE'S NOT A HERO, JAY. TELL THOSE CHILDREN. WE ALL KNOW KAHNDAQ HAS BEEN OVER-LOOKED FOR YEARS. EVEN BY US.
WE CAN'T LEAVE THIS MADMAN--
WHAT?
GET DOWN!
BOOOM!
BRAAATT
THAT CHILD SHOT A GUN! WHAT ARE THEY--?
THEY'RE FIGHTING TO PROTECT THEIR SAVIOR, JAY. NO MATTER WHAT WE SAY TO THEM, WHAT WE TELL THEM ABOUT BLACK ADAM--
--THEY WON'T LISTEN. WHY SHOULD THEY?
I DON'T WANT TO FIGHT CHILDREN, FLASH.
THE WISEST THING TO DO--
--IS WALK AWAY.
CHOOOM!

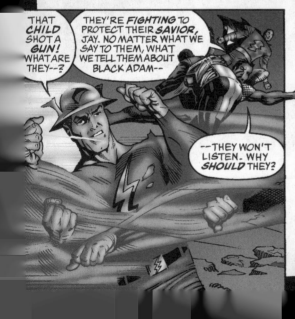

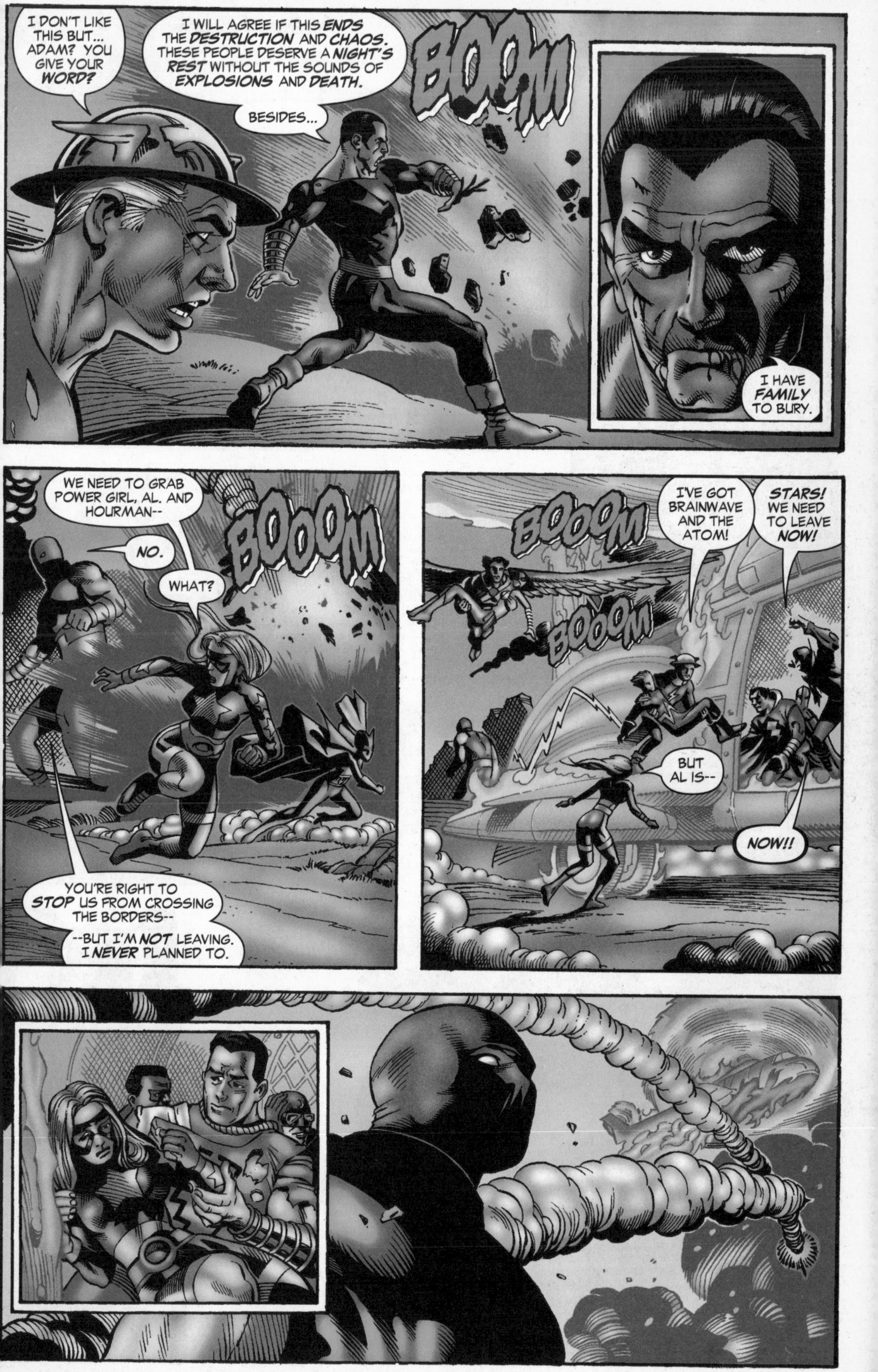
I DON'T LIKE THIS BUT... ADAM? YOU GIVE YOUR WORD?
I WILL AGREE IF THIS ENDS THE DESTRUCTION AND CHAOS. THESE PEOPLE DESERVE A NIGHT'S REST WITHOUT THE SOUNDS OF EXPLOSIONS AND DEATH.
BESIDES...
BOOOM
I HAVE FAMILY TO BURY.
WE NEED TO GRAB POWER GIRL, AL. AND HOURMAN--
NO.
WHAT?
BOOOM
YOU'RE RIGHT TO STOP US FROM CROSSING THE BORDERS--
--BUT I'M NOT LEAVING. I NEVER PLANNED TO.
BOOOM
I'VE GOT BRAINWAVE AND THE ATOM!
STARS! WE NEED TO LEAVE NOW!
BOOOM
BUT AL IS--
NOW!!

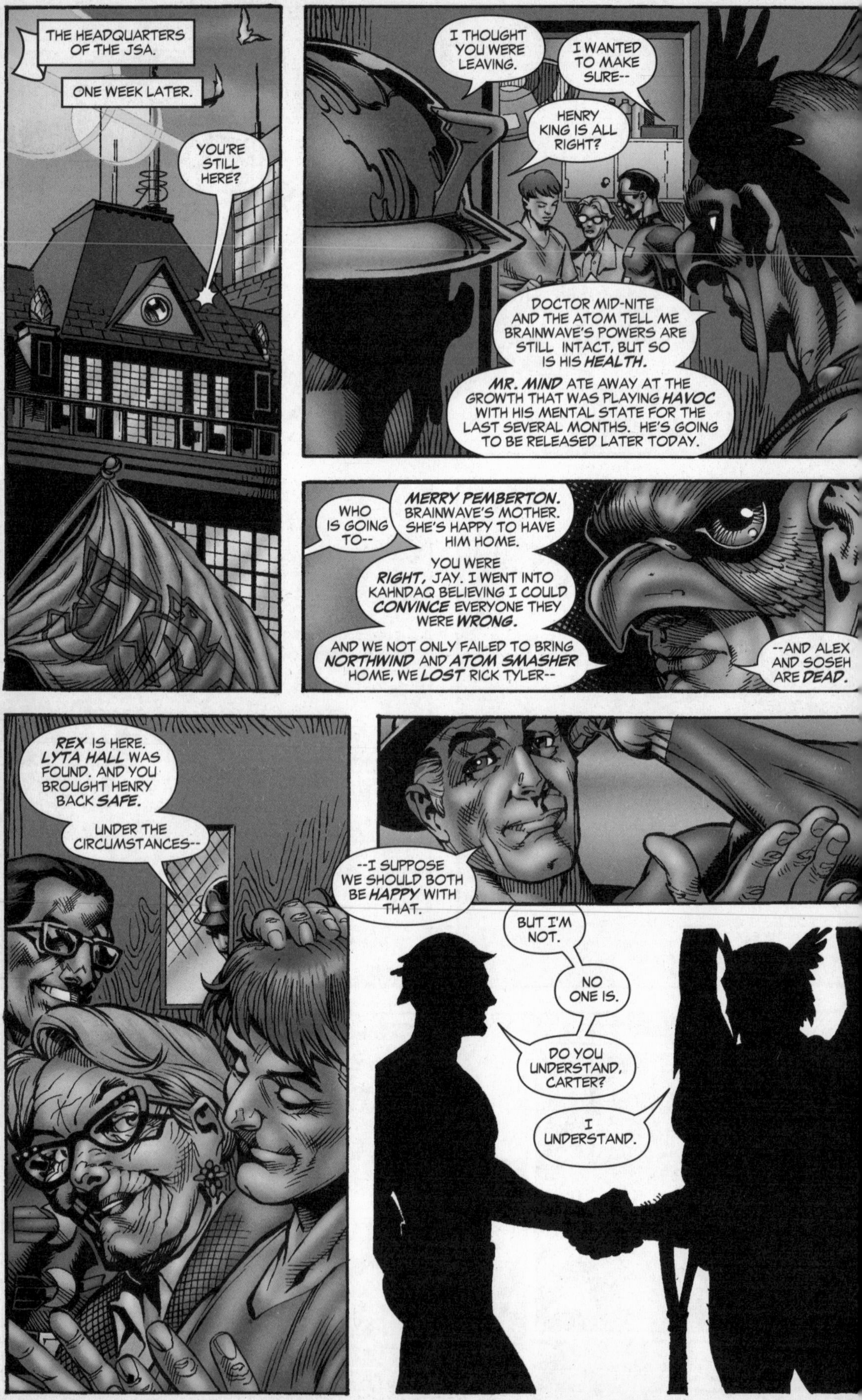

THE HEADQUARTERS OF THE JSA.
ONE WEEK LATER.
YOU'RE STILL HERE?
I THOUGHT YOU WERE LEAVING.
I WANTED TO MAKE SURE--
HENRY KING IS ALL RIGHT?
DOCTOR MID-NITE AND THE ATOM TELL ME BRAINWAVE'S POWERS ARE STILL INTACT, BUT SO IS HIS HEALTH.
MR. MIND ATE AWAY AT THE GROWTH THAT WAS PLAYING HAVOC WITH HIS MENTAL STATE FOR THE LAST SEVERAL MONTHS. HE'S GOING TO BE RELEASED LATER TODAY.
WHO IS GOING TO--
MERRY PEMBERTON. BRAINWAVE'S MOTHER. SHE'S HAPPY TO HAVE HIM HOME.
YOU WERE RIGHT, JAY. I WENT INTO KAHNDAQ BELIEVING I COULD CONVINCE EVERYONE THEY WERE WRONG.
AND WE NOT ONLY FAILED TO BRING NORTHWIND AND ATOM SMASHER HOME, WE LOST RICK TYLER--
--AND ALEX AND SOSEH ARE DEAD.
REX IS HERE. LYTA HALL WAS FOUND. AND YOU BROUGHT HENRY BACK SAFE.
UNDER THE CIRCUMSTANCES--
--I SUPPOSE WE SHOULD BOTH BE HAPPY WITH THAT.
BUT I'M NOT.
NO ONE IS.
DO YOU UNDERSTAND, CARTER?
I UNDERSTAND.

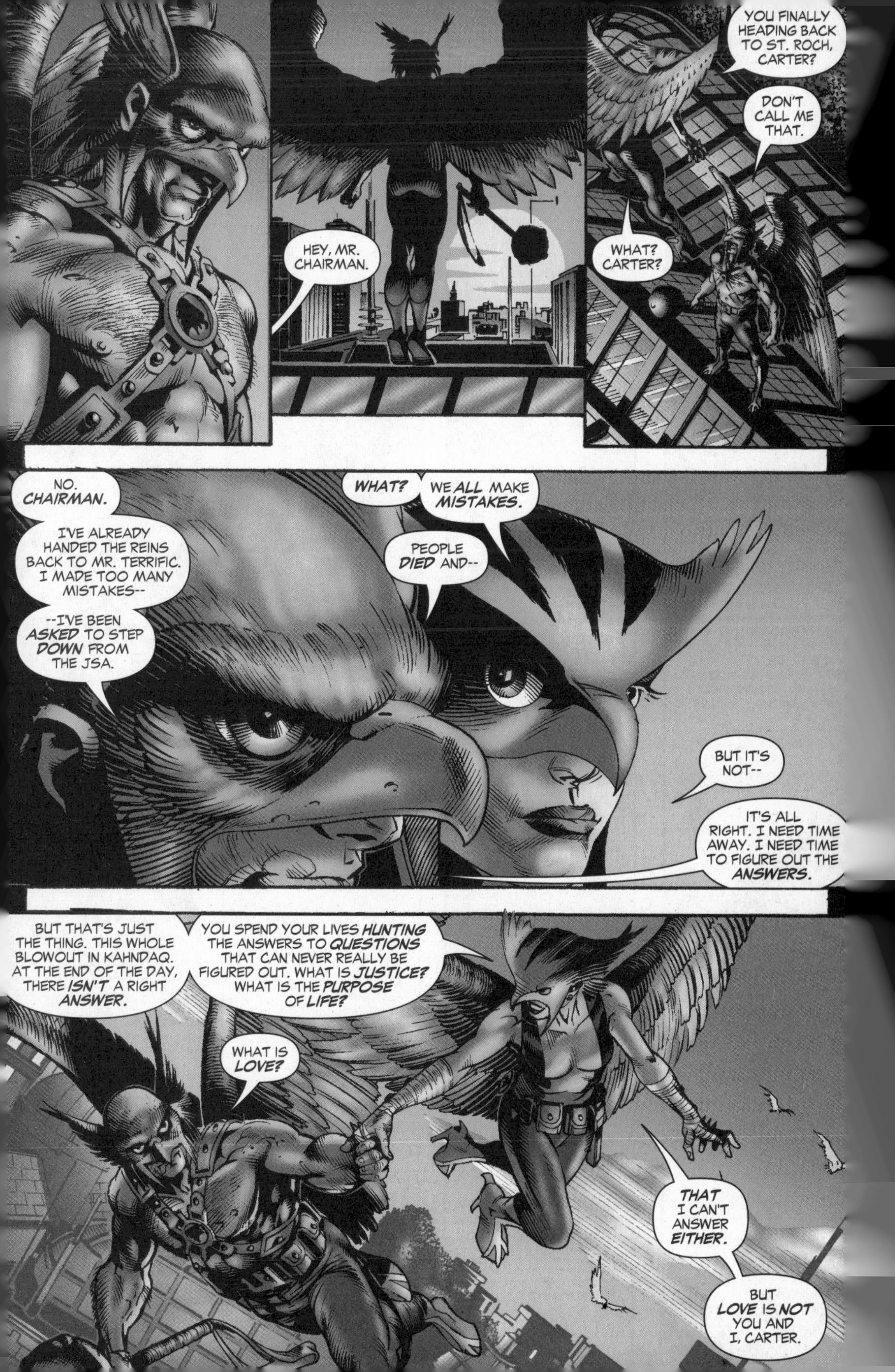
HEY, MR. CHAIRMAN.
YOU FINALLY HEADING BACK TO ST. ROCH, CARTER?
DON'T CALL ME THAT.
WHAT? CARTER?
NO. CHAIRMAN.
I'VE ALREADY HANDED THE REINS BACK TO MR. TERRIFIC. I MADE TOO MANY MISTAKES--
--I'VE BEEN ASKED TO STEP DOWN FROM THE JSA.
WHAT?
WE ALL MAKE MISTAKES.
PEOPLE DIED AND--
BUT IT'S NOT--
IT'S ALL RIGHT. I NEED TIME AWAY. I NEED TIME TO FIGURE OUT THE ANSWERS.
BUT THAT'S JUST THE THING. THIS WHOLE BLOWOUT IN KAHNDAQ. AT THE END OF THE DAY, THERE ISN'T A RIGHT ANSWER.
YOU SPEND YOUR LIVES HUNTING THE ANSWERS TO QUESTIONS THAT CAN NEVER REALLY BE FIGURED OUT. WHAT IS JUSTICE? WHAT IS THE PURPOSE OF LIFE?
WHAT IS LOVE?
THAT I CAN'T ANSWER EITHER.
BUT LOVE IS NOT YOU AND I, CARTER.

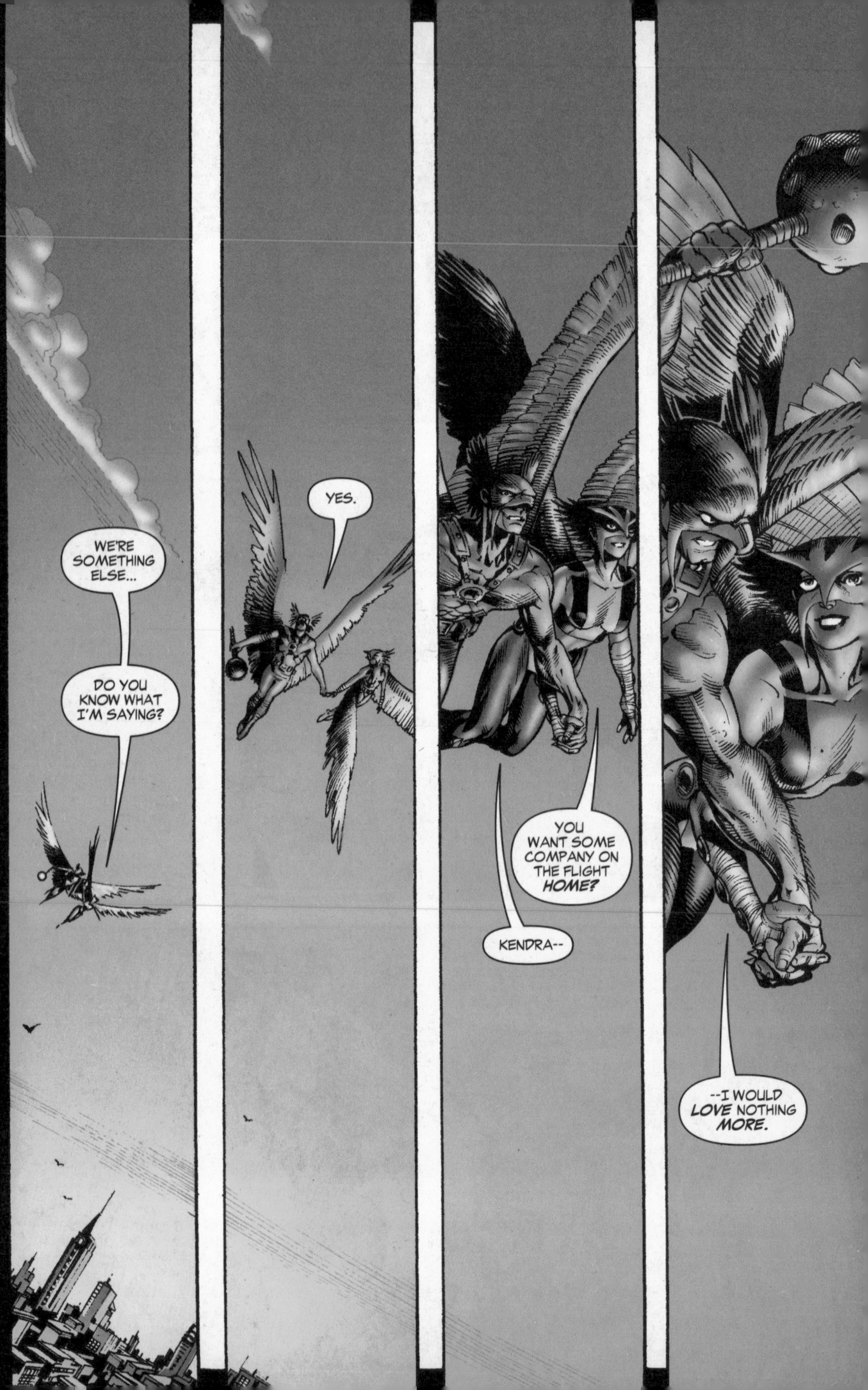
WE'RE SOMETHING ELSE...
DO YOU KNOW WHAT I'M SAYING?
YES.
KENDRA--
YOU WANT SOME COMPANY ON THE FLIGHT HOME?
--I WOULD LOVE NOTHING MORE.

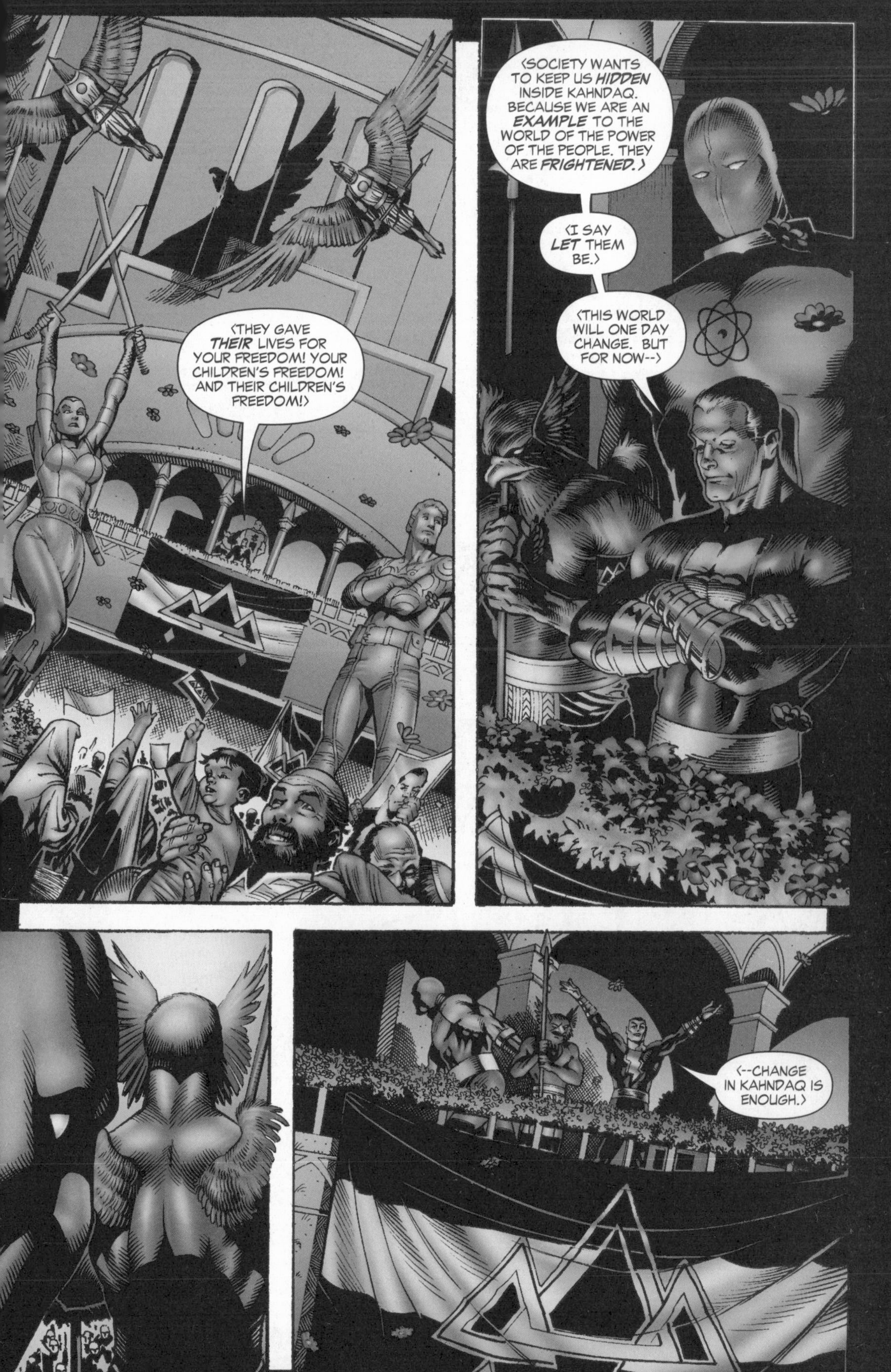

‹THEY GAVE THEIR LIVES FOR YOUR FREEDOM! YOUR CHILDREN'S FREEDOM! AND THEIR CHILDREN'S FREEDOM!›
‹SOCIETY WANTS TO KEEP US HIDDEN INSIDE KAHNDAQ. BECAUSE WE ARE AN EXAMPLE TO THE WORLD OF THE POWER OF THE PEOPLE. THEY ARE FRIGHTENED.›
‹I SAY LET THEM BE.›
‹THIS WORLD WILL ONE DAY CHANGE. BUT FOR NOW--›
‹--CHANGE IN KAHNDAQ IS ENOUGH.›

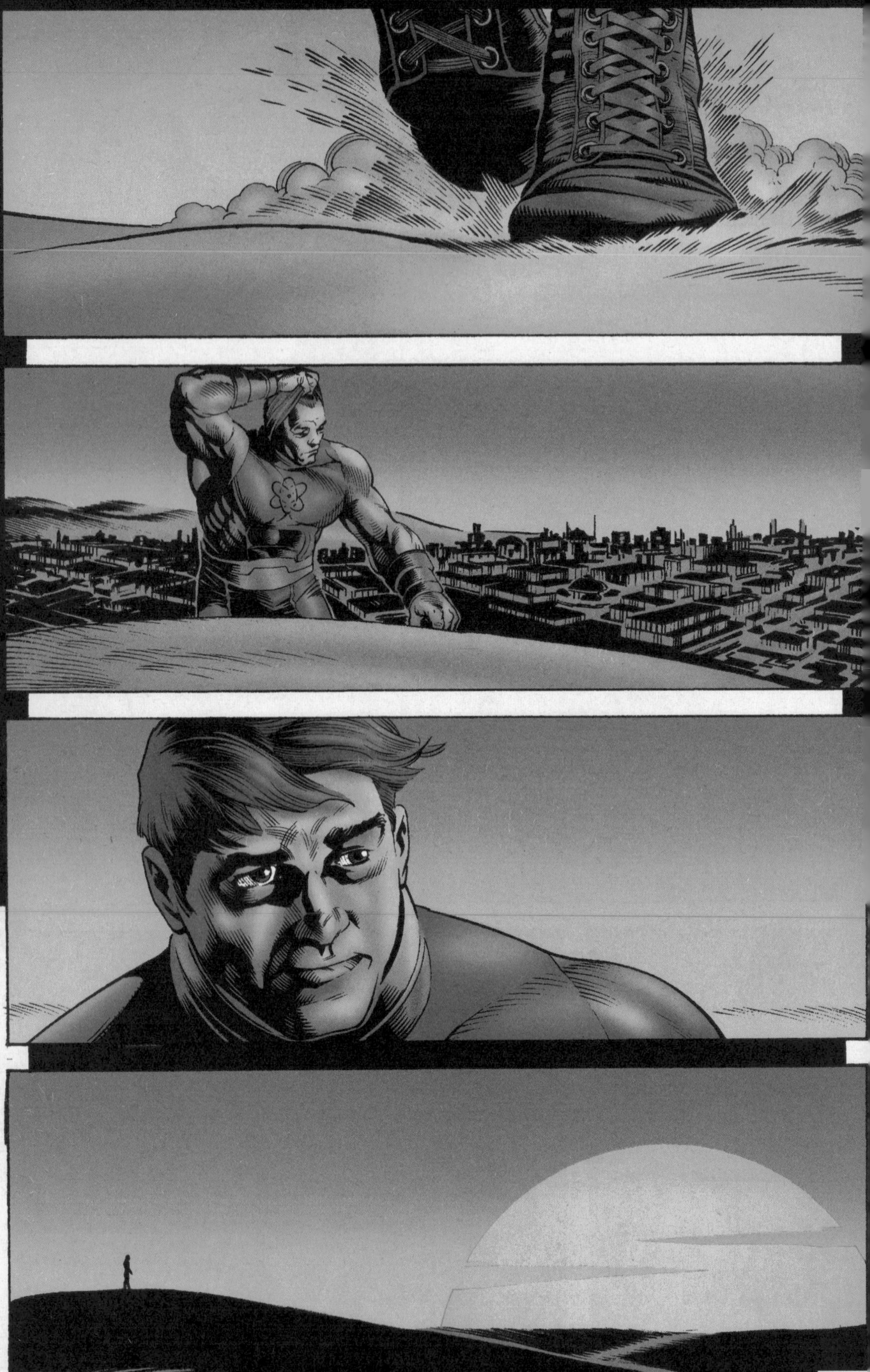
END

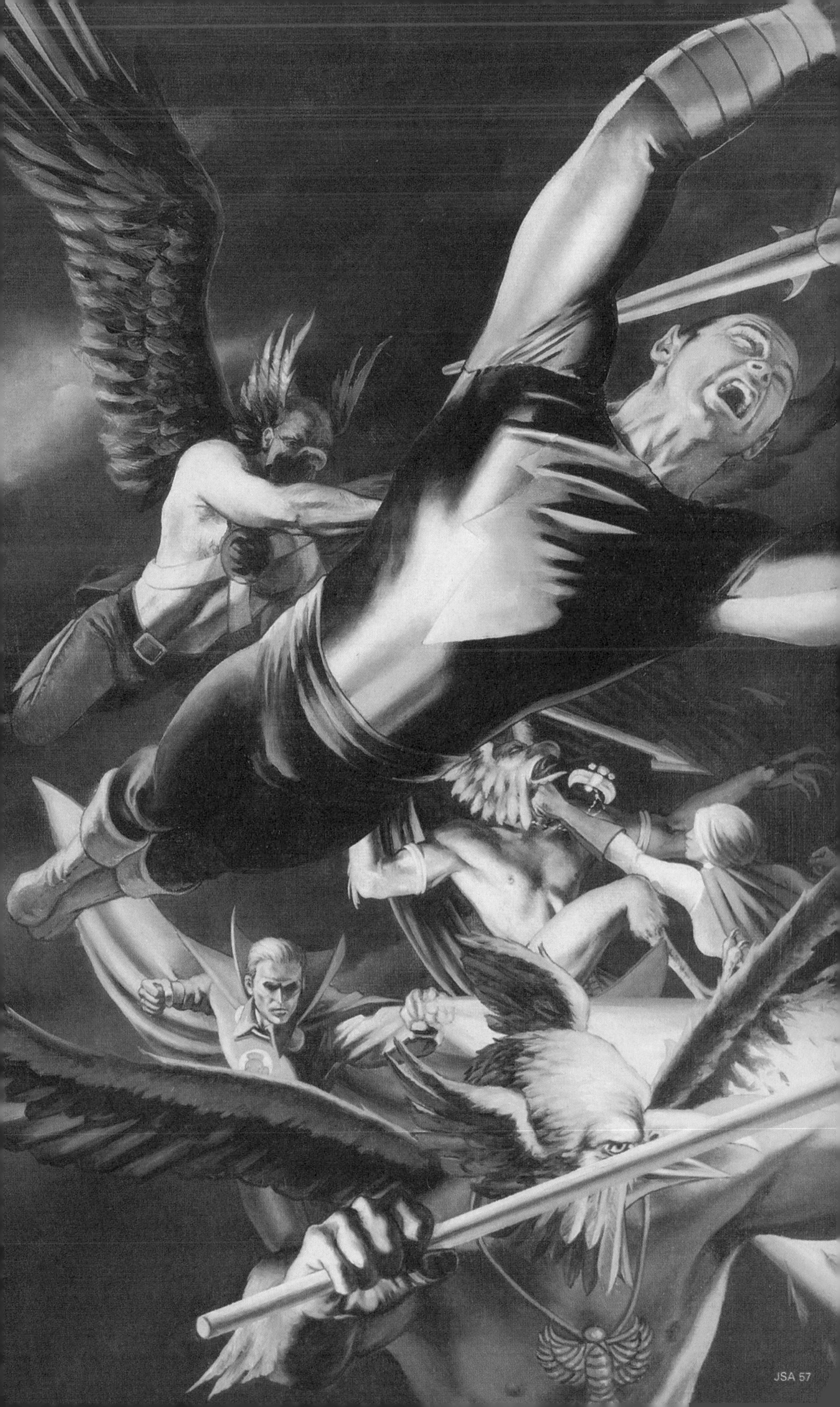

JSA 57

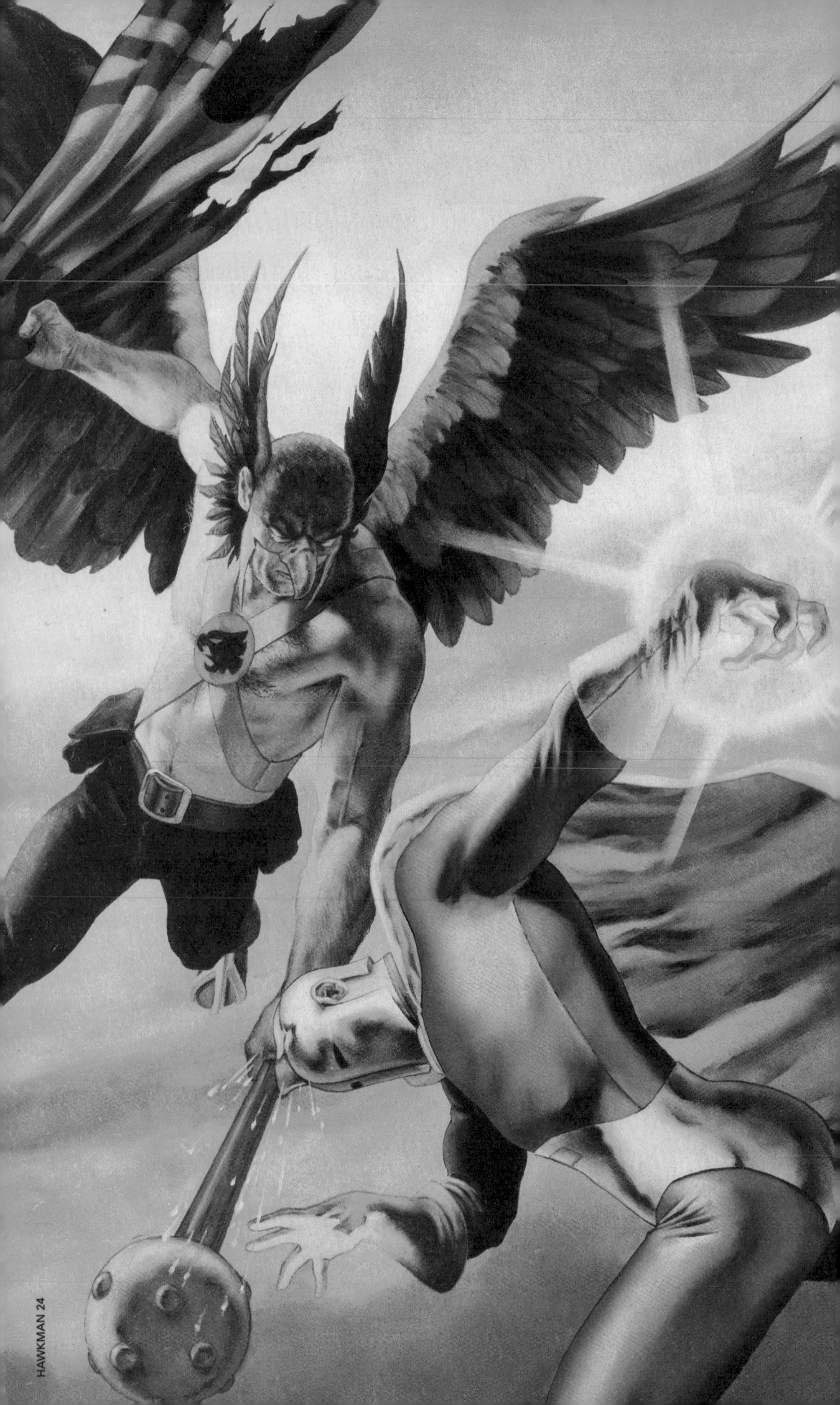
HAWKMAN 24